Trader Vic—Methods of a Wall Street Master

VICTOR SPERANDEO
with T. SULLIVAN BROWN

John Wiley & Sons, Inc.

New York • Chichester • Brisbane • Toronto • Singapore

Charts and data generously supplied by:

CQG, Inc.   Daily Graphs
PO Box 758   11915 La Grange Avenue
Glenwood Springs, CO 81602   Los Angeles, CA 90025
303-945-8686   213-820-2583

Library of Congress Cataloging in Publication Data:

Sperandeo, Victor.
    Trader Vic—Methods of a Wall Street Master / Victor Sperandeo
with T. Sullivan Brown.
        p.   cm.
    Includes bibliographical references and index.
    ISBN 0-471-53576-1 (cloth)   ISBN 0-471-30497-2 (paper)
1. Stocks.   2. Speculation.   3. Investment analysis.   I. Brown.
T. Sullivan.   II. Title.
HG4661.S68   1991
332.63'–dc20   90-25716

Printed in the United States of America

16 17 18 19 20

Foreword

When Victor Sperandeo sent me his manuscript, I wasn't surprised at its bulk. Nor was I surprised that, in some respects, it just scratches the surface of his wide-ranging knowledge of the markets.

I talk to Victor about three or four times per month. We share market perspectives, and he always generously offers his current view of the likely direction the market will take. It often strikes me how he never divorces his opinion on the markets from his broader view of the world. In any conversation he is likely to bring philosophy, psychology, politics, and economic theory into the conversation before he tells you what range he is looking for on the Dow or key commodities. His are not idle interests. His active mind is always trying to make connections between these subjects and their influences on the market.

His approach to the market, and in this book, is unique and integrated. Victor isn't a technical analyst; he's not simply a fundamentalist, and he's not a value player or an astute market timer. His approach is both eclectic and focused, and I'm glad he finally put it into writing.

Victor chooses the best elements of various approaches, and those gained through his independent research, that makes this book valuable to everyone, regardless of their level of interest or expertise in the stock or commodities markets. The chapters on economics and the business cycle, written in clear, understandable terms, offer an insightful view that will help anyone understand what often seems to be the incomprehensible workings of our economy. The entire second part of the book is a must read for anyone interested in the psychology of success and failure.

I don't always agree with Victor, or with any market expert. When it comes to books on the markets I've always believed that if you get even one good idea from reading one, then your money is well spent. Viewed in these terms, this book not only is a good buy, it is an exceptional bargain, as well as a generous contribution to market literature.

Leon G. Cooperman
Partner, Goldman, Sachs & Co.
Chairman and Chief Executive Officer
    Goldman Sachs Asset Management

Dedicated to:
Aristotle, for the laws of logic;
Dr. Karen Horney, for her insights on the Pride System;
Ayn Rand, for her method of Thinking in Principles;
Robert Rhea, for his method of Stock Market movement classification.

Contents

Preface

Books on the financial markets . . . I must have 1200 of them in my personal library alone. There are books about securities analysis, options strategies, futures strategies, technical analysis, and so forth. Most of these books have good ideas in them, and about 2% of them are truly superior. But most of them share a common problem: they try to sell you an approach that relies on one basic method to "beat the market," one that in many cases hasn't even been fully tested in the real world. Other books contain material so specific that you need a lot of previous knowledge and often years of experience before you can understand and use them.

Newcomers and established market professionals alike waste countless hours of valuable time learning about the markets through trial and error and by reinventing the wheel. I've looked for a book that could eliminate this tremendous waste, one that ties together all the basic ideas required to understand the markets and make money with the knowledge. I couldn't find it, so I decided to write one. In addition, I decided to divulge some proprietary observations and discoveries that helped me achieve an average annual nominal rate of return of 70.7% during a 10-year period without a losing year, as shown in Table P.1.

During my career on Wall Street, I have developed a unique approach that integrates knowledge of odds, the markets and their instruments, technical analysis, statistical probability, economics, politics, and human psychology. Most market players rely on one, two, or three of these areas, but I combine all of them, assessing risk/reward from every possible dimension to keep the odds in my favor. This may sound complex and cumbersome, but it's really not. Reducing all these elements to fundamentals that can be applied in a direct, straightforward manner makes the complex relatively simple and manageable. This book is an exposition of those fundamental ideas and is designed for market players who, like myself, rely on books as their main source of information.

The first books I ever read were about baseball players. I really loved baseball as a kid and dreamed about being a top professional. So I read about proven athletes—Hall of Famers such as Ty Cobb. I emulated them, copying their batting and fielding styles, and practiced continually until one day I realized I was no longer emulating, but playing my own game. I have followed this pattern of learning throughout my life: choosing a goal, observing and reading the teachings of

Table P.1 Victor Sperandeo's Annualized Rate of Return

Year	Nominal Annualized Rate of Return[a]	S&P 500[b]
1978 (10 mos.)	115.26%	15.18%
1979	74.48	18.65
1980	98.49	32.42
1981	49.99	(4.97)
1982	127.44	21.56
1983	30.79	22.55
1984	12.99	6.29
1985	9.58	31.75
1986	10.72	18.67
1987	165.36	5.20

[a] 10-year nominal annual rate of return for V. H. Sperandeo— 70.71% (does not include interest on cash balances).

[b] 10-year nominal annual rate of return for S&P 500— 11.5% (including dividends).

skilled professionals, and learning through practice and observation until eventually I developed my own unique style of achievement.

One thing, however, has changed. As a child, part of my motivation was the desire to be a hero—to be another Ty Cobb, to win a gold medal at the Olympics when I was in gymnastics, and so on. But at some point, I recognized that there comes a time when you have to let the quest for glory go.

There is a pervasive idea, especially in the United States, that if you are not number one in your field, then you are lacking something. But only one person can be number one, and I think that people who make being number one their primary goal are asking for a life of frustration, even if they do reach the top. Like the gunslingers in the Wild West, once you're recognized as the best you become a target to be shot down, and when that eventually happens, what are you left with? Glory is nice while it lasts (if it ever comes at all), but it usually never lasts very long. For example, in watching the U.S. Open recently, one of the commentators quoted Steffi Graf as saying she was happy with only 1 out of every 30 games she played. This phenomenal tennis player, who has won 97% (!) of her professional matches in the last three years, is generally unhappy with her game. It is unfortunate that someone so great at what she does is probably basically unhappy.

The essence of success and happiness results from actualizing your potential, which requires a constant process of learning and growing, as well as the recognition that making mistakes is an inevitable, even essential, part of life. Realizing this, I write this book for those who seek from their participation in the financial markets the greatest reward life has to offer: self-satisfaction.

Heroes like Ty Cobb, Babe Ruth, Willie Mays, Mickey Mantle, and their modern counterparts provide role models for child athletes and give sports a glorious image to kids and adults alike. But every pro ballplayer who makes a career out of the game is exceptional. Out of an enormous pool of talent, the unsung career pro emerges and proves himself through consistent performance year in and year out. Within this group are men of solid character, and perhaps our children could learn as much or more from them than from the stars, especially since so many of the modern day, top-performing athletes lose control of their lives and abilities by succumbing to drugs or other problems that are often the offspring of fame and glory.

I'm a market professional—a major league player, if you will—and I am very good at what I do. But if there were a Trader's Hall of Fame, I probably wouldn't be inducted. There are plenty of market players who have made more money than I in any given time period. There are guys who have won trading competitions and guys who have taken huge gambles and won. There are also those who have seen their glory days come and go. I've never entered a trading competition, and I never gamble more than I can afford to lose. I think my unique strength is in my consistency. Like the baseball players who never achieve heights of glory, I pride myself in my ability to successfully stay in the game and keep after it, constantly striving to improve my skills or adapt them to changing conditions.

Whenever I pick out a book to learn about any subject, I always choose those written by or about men with proven records of success or achievement. So if I claim to be consistent, then I'd better prove it.

When I started my career on Wall Street as a quote boy in 1966, I had one major goal: to make money consistently month after month, year after year. From the start of my independent trading career in 1971 until I stopped regular intraday trading in January 1988, I never had a losing year on my own account. For the period starting July 1, 1972, and ending December 31, 1987, I generated more than $10,000,000 in gross trading income for my own and other accounts where I had sole discretionary authority.[1] In these accounts, I always had at least 50% of the responsibility for losses.

Shown in Table P.2 is an indication of my performance from 1972 to 1987. These figures show my track record while trading on my own business's account from 1972 through 1987, and for others as indicated by the notes. What is not shown is that while at Interstate Securities, I was also trading for myself and others through my own company, Hugo Securities. My production at Interstate was matched by my own at Hugo and in one other private account, so the total income generated from 1978 to 1987 is almost triple what is shown in Table P.2. To avoid confusion, I didn't include the production numbers from Hugo during that period because they include not only my performance, but the performance of other traders that I hired. But even if you ignore that income, I think the numbers in the table are more than just a respectable batting average; they are definitely good enough to indicate that I can teach a few people the basics of hitting.

There is a lot more involved, however, than just learning the basics. Even the best hitters have slumps, and some sparkling college players can't cut it in the

Table P.2 Net Performance Record: Monthly Gross Trading Profit and Loss[a]

	1972	1973	1974	1975	1976	1977	1978	1979
January	*	$ 17,016	$ 37,913	$ <146,983>	>$25,613	***	$ 29,482	$ <44,926>
February	*	<4,088>	13,261	90,634	37,498	***	****	122,894
March	*		15,730	16,187	113,225	33,900	***	<7,567>	1,008
April	*		16,752	<27,539>	38,247	<59,548>	***	17,869	90,872
May	*		34,630	35,000	95,333	39,792	$ 5,464	78,507	<7,884>
June	*		8,090	6,551	<79,290>	46,777	16,843	50,974	56,421
July	$ 15,693	33,002	103,999	**	10,637	40,190	22,639	<13,625>
August	30,002	37,078	269,300	**	26,222	232,182	105,375	116,010
September	7,737	44,081	25,593	196,086	9,824	97,910	52,369	60,952
October	21,804	54,005	61,805	47,836	18,058	16,145	36,884	10,140
November	11,272	56,577	81,116	33,041	***	<14,817>	67,280	<2,222>
December	21,893	53,662	13,001	3,142	***	14,961	103,094	11,065
Rebate							48,854	64,812
transfer tax								
Total/Year	$108,401	$366,535	$636,187	$391,271	$188,773	$408,878	$605,60	$465,517

"Figures show net income and loss from trading before office expenses.

*Began trading Ragnar's firm account in July of 1972.

**No trading during this period—interim restructuring of Ragnar Options Corp.

***No trading—liquidating Ragnar Options in preparation of move to Weeden & Co.

****Time off in preparation of move to Interstate Securities.

major leagues. If I have learned anything in my career, it is that knowledge alone is no guarantee for success. In addition to knowledge, you must have a management plan to implement it and the emotional discipline to consistently execute according to your plan in a way that keeps you free of psychological turmoil. That's what this book is all about: defining the means to be a success in the markets, both personally and financially.

Unfortunately, for the sake of economy, I have to assume that the reader has a basic knowledge about the workings of the financial markets. I've written the book primarily for aspiring professionals seeking an off-campus PhD in speculation, but also for the amateur who isn't satisfied leaving market decisions solely in the hands of a broker or money manager and for the established professional who is looking for vital information on economic and market forecasting.

There are market players and value players, both in stocks and commodities. The market player relies on his knowledge of price movements in the market as a whole to make money. The value fundamentalist looks for buy-and-hold opportunities in specific stocks or commodities that are likely to appreciate in value over time. Most consistently successful pros are both, but more the former than the latter. The same is true for me—I'm primarily a market player. Consequently, my primary focus in this book is how to predict market price movements in general and how to manage risk in any market, equities or commodities. Of secondary importance is a method of selecting groups of stocks that merit further analysis

Table P.2 *(continued).*

1980	1981	1982	1983	1984	1985	1986	1987
$ 22,813	$78,221	$ 148,971	$201,650	$166,573	$ 6,816	$ 40,890	$ <27,634>
56,200	89,813	140,334	43,703	31,699	62,110	15,620	<30,045>
4,347	156,169	<14,856>	87,672	65,600	11,039	30,527	<38,935>
86,402	91,461	42,442	96,229	<1,718>	4,063	30,124	71,802
25,512	41,006	<29,870>	<5,497>	<26,188>	121,643	16,958	16,397
86,440	54,504	173,507	151,067	74,708	<27,247>	<1,219>	9,006
214,345	17,744	<93,951>	<73,841>	<34,668>	<20,558>	83,926	<5,755>
89,118	26,861	130,856	107,170	84,441	11,360	<9,490>	<40,270>
68,554	<3,194>	180,533	69,610	93,368	19,102	84,629	33,933
74,167	<29,924>	853,908	18,452	104,116	36,114	<12,050>	86,623
60,299	178,655	120,651	3,564	<349,722>	28,572	<9,471>	644
122,015	<3,659>	259,110	69,894	116,514	10,391	<5,125>	11,662
74,734	31,381	0	0	0	0		
$984,945	$729,038	$1,911,633	$769,672	$324,721	$263,405	$265,320	$87,488

Trading capital alloted to each period: 1972 through 1976, $250,000; 1977, $500,000; 1978 through 1986, $2 million; 1987, $100,000.

and an explanation of the essential measure of when specific stock prices are likely to go up. But for detailed analysis of specific stocks, I'll defer to any of the many good books on stock picking, and to the many bright and talented analysts who spend their lives evaluating companies. Thank goodness they exist, for they provide useful, albeit often contradictory, information.

My experience in the markets dates back to 1966. Thus far, it has been a very rewarding career. I have developed a way to make money in the financial markets without pouring over countless corporate financial statements or trying to balance the many divergent opinions of "the experts."[2] In the first part of this book, I'll explain the knowledge behind my approach to playing the markets—that's the easy side of it. In the second part, I'll explain what it takes to put all the knowledge together and make it happen—and that's the tough side of this business.

There has been an unusual, yet common, occurrence that has taken place since this book was originally published: the markets have remained the same because they always change. The stock market has become an institutionalized "bubble" type of investment instrument. The years I learned to trade were populated by volatile, up-and-down markets. During the years 1966 through 1974, there were four up years and five down years. Since 1974, the market has been up 15 years and down only 3. The extent of these three drops were minor, with only a 7.3% drop in 1977, 4.9% in 1981, and 3.1% in 1990 (based on the total return of the S&P 500). In the last 10 years, the total return for the S&P 500 has been 19.1% per year annualized. The stock market, like the real estate market from the 1940s to the mid-1980s, has become a "guaranteed" investment vehicle.

Because of this, CD investors have chosen the stock market over a 3% yield in CDs. The "no lose" psychology in the public and institutional mind will eventually cause the greatest losses in people's wealth since the 1930s. The reasons are not difficult to understand. In 1975, the Fed and President Carter chose inflation as the way to return "growth" to the U.S. economy. In the 1980s, inflation was replaced by debt to create "growth." In the 1990s, President Clinton is trying to return to inflation. The reasons the stock market did well between 1990 and 1993 are simple:

1. Lower tax rates for corporations from an average of 43% to 37%.

2. Lower interest rates, with the Fed Funds rate dropping from 10% in March 1989 to 3% in the last quarter of 1992. This caused a guaranteed increase in earnings to corporations. Take note that America is a leveraged instrument—for every one dollar of pre-tax profit, corporations (in 1990) had 70 cents in interest expense, which has since dropped to 50 cents.

3. Increased productivity (people were fired)!

This is not a growing U.S. economy, but rather a temporary increase in corporate earnings. This will result in a major blow to corporate earnings under Clinton, as interest rates and tax rates rise! I suggest you read carefully Chapter 9 and 10 for an understanding of what is going to occur fundamentally. Also, the technical chapters (6 and 7) fully apply to today's markets.

I sincerely hope that this book helps those who read it, and wish you the best of luck. In my opinion, for the remainder of the 1990s, you'll need it!

ACKNOWLEDGMENTS

I was stimulated to write this book when I saw the movie *Wall Street.* The media often present such a distorted view of what life is like in this business that I wanted to counter that view. With a lot of hard work, some good decisions, a couple of laughs, and a few good friends, it *is* possible to be both a happy and successful market professional without turning into the kind of villain presented in the movies.

What started as an idea after watching a movie turned into a much larger project than I expected. Without the help of my family, friends, and employees, I couldn't have done it. First of all, I want to thank T. Sullivan Brown, whose writing ability and similar philosophic beliefs made it possible to produce a book I am truly proud of. I am also grateful to my partners, Norman Tandy and Douglas Kent, whose help and recommendations are part of the book.

I can never thank my wife Teresa enough. Without the dedication, patience, and loyalty she has shown throughout my career, I couldn't have developed skills worth writing about. I also want to thank my two daughters for their love, understanding, and interest in the project.

Thanks, too, to all my employees, past and especially present, who have helped me in so many ways, too numerous to mention. And thanks to all those friends whose care and concern has been an integral part of my personal growth and achievement.

Part I

BUILDING YOUR KNOWLEDGE FROM THE GROUND UP

Introduction: The Secret of the Gamboni

The secret of the Gamboni is the secret of how to survive in the financial markets. Understand it . . . really understand it . . . and you are on your way to success as a trader, speculator, or investor. So, here it is:

Joe was a card player, a good one. He was so good, in fact, that he had to move from city to city and find games where he wasn't known in order play for high stakes. One afternoon, in a bar in the suburbs of Chicago, he's shooting the breeze with the bartender and asks, "Say, where can I find a good card game around here?"

"What kind of stakes are you talking about?"

"Big," Joe says, "the biggest game you know about."

"Well now, I hear there's a game out in the farm country. It's a bit of a drive, but these particular farmers play for big money. Let me make a call and see if it's OK."

So the bartender makes the call, and then gives Joe directions to the game.

That evening, after a long drive, Joe pulls up to this barn in the middle of nowhere. Tentatively, he walks inside, tiptoeing around the fetid piles on the floor. At the back of the barn, he spots a partially open door, with light and smoke pouring through the opening. The familiar rush of anticipation and energy sweeps through him as he enters the room and introduces himself.

Farmers in overalls sit around the table, chewing cigars and puffing their pipes. In a quick glance, Joe estimates the current pot to be about $40,000—perfect. So he sits down. "Ante up," says the farmer holding the deck of cards. And Joe begins to play.

About an hour later, Joe is holding his own. He is about even when he draws three aces and two queens—a full house. With a large pot already on the table,

1

he raises $15,000. The next two guys fold, but the leather-faced farmer across the table calls him and raises another $15,000, without so much as batting an eye. Joe, certain that the guy is bluffing, calls the bet and lays down his aces-high full house. The farmer lays down junk: three clubs and two diamonds of mixed numbered cards. Joe, suppressing a smile, starts to rake in the pot.

"Wait just a darn minute," says the farmer, a stern and reprimanding tone in his voice.

"Whattaya mean, wait a minute," says Joe, "you got nothin."

"Take a look at the sign over your right shoulder," smiles the farmer.

Joe looks:

THREE CLUBS AND TWO DIAMONDS CONSTITUTE A GAMBONI, THE TOP WINNING HAND IN THIS ESTABLISHMENT

Joe is really angry, but after all, rules are rules, so he continues to play with what is left of his holdings. About an hour later, he draws three clubs and two diamonds . . . a Gamboni! He bets everything, and on the final round of betting with the same leather-faced farmer he has to throw in his solid gold Rolex to make the call. The farmer turns over his cards a queen-high spade flush. Joe turns over his Gamboni and starts to rake in the pot.

"Hold it there, fella," says the farmer, his grin cutting deep lines in his cheeks.

"But I got a Gamboni!" cries an exasperated Joe.

"Sure 'nough, but look at the sign over there," and he points over Joe's left shoulder.

Joe looks:

ONLY ONE GAMBONI WILL BE PERMITTED PER NIGHT IN THIS ESTABLISHMENT

Joe, broke but thankful for the invention of credit cards, leaves the barn with dung on his shoes, and the leather-faced farmer drives his tractor home feeling the weight of a solid gold Rolex on his wrist.

So the secret of the Gamboni is this: if you want to win, you've got to know the rules; and also, you can't win if you're not at the table.

That's what this book is all about: defining the knowledge and rules necessary to stay at the table and make money consistently year after year. All the knowledge in the world is worthless without a plan to put it into practice and rules to give organization to the plan. In the financial world, this means acquiring the necessary knowledge, defining a business philosophy, instituting a method of money management, and sticking by well-defined rules to guide your day-to-day decisions. With the ideas set forth in this book, you can put your money to work, and if you are consistent in your execution, you will be profitable.

1

From Gambler to Market Master: The Making of a Professional Speculator

People call me a trader, yet here I am writing a book primarily for speculators and investors—an apparent contradiction to those of you familiar with the distinction. So let me begin by doing what politicians never do: defining my terms. There are three price trends that are simultaneously active in any market: the short-term trend, which lasts from days to weeks; the intermediate-term trend, which lasts from weeks to months; and the long-term trend, which lasts from months to years. Within each market there are three basic types of participant: traders, speculators, and investors.

Traders focus their activity on the intraday and/or short-term trend. They buy and sell stocks, bonds, commodities, or whatever within a time frame varying from minutes to weeks. Speculators focus on the intermediate trend, taking market positions and holding them for a period lasting from weeks to months. Investors, dealing mainly in the long term trend, hold their positions from months to years.

Before I go any further, I want to state for the record that I will not apologize for using the term *speculator*. When I use the term, I mean just what I said above: a market player who participates primarily in the intermediate trend. The term *speculation* has, in my opinion, gained an unearned negative connotation. People think of speculators as the people who drive prices up in shady stock transactions, real estate deals, and so forth. But in reality, all market speculators do is focus their attention on intermediate price movements, trying to profit by their buying and selling activity. Speculators provide crucial liquidity to the markets and in most cases facilitate the orderly transfer of assets to their best use. I will make other critical distinctions between speculators and other market participants as the book progresses.

For most of my career, I have primarily been a speculator. Primarily, but not solely; I play all three trends, and every transaction I make involves knowledge of each of them, so I guess that makes me a speculative trader who also invests. For lack of a better term, I'll take the title "trader."

In my approach to the financial markets, there is an overlap of knowledge that spreads both ways from the middle; that is, the principles of speculation apply, with some refinements, to trading and investment as well. If you understand speculation, then it is relatively easy to shift to either trading or investing. Even more importantly, I firmly believe that the dramatic volatility in the markets that has developed over the last decade or so makes it foolish to buy and hold without understanding the importance of moving in and out of the markets or making portfolio adjustments with changes in the intermediate trend. That is why I decided to focus the subject matter on speculation.

This book presents the essentials of my knowledge to date about the art of speculation, which has many elements. I use the term *art* here in the general sense, not in the sense of the fine arts. But just as each painter has a unique form of expression on canvas, each speculator has a unique style of playing the markets. Still, every consistently successful market player must employ a similar set of tools: essential ideas and knowledge that guide decision making with unchanging validity. From my knowledge, including that gained by observing other speculators, I have abstracted those essentials for presentation to you.

My approach to speculation integrates knowledge of odds, the markets and their instruments, technical analysis, statistical probability, economics, politics, human psychology, and philosophy. It took me 10 years (1966 to 1976) to acquire and organize my knowledge into a systematic form. Prior to 1974 I traded by common sense, technical methods, and prudent risk management. Since then, I've learned to look at the big picture. If there is one fatal flaw in this business, it is allowing isolated information to drive trading or investing decisions—committing money without understanding *all* the risks. And there is only one way to understand all the risks: through systematic knowledge.

Before I present the knowledge behind my methods, let me sum up my career history, touching on the key elements that led me to formalize my knowledge about speculating. The 11-year period from 1966 to 1977 was like an apprenticeship (a very long apprenticeship), training me to take advantage of a golden opportunity to work as an independent contractor via Interstate Securities from March 1978 through September 1986. During that period, trading stocks, bonds, futures (both commodity and index), and options of all kinds, I earned for myself an average of approximately $600,000 per year, trading on my own and on a 50-50 profit/loss basis with Interstate and a few selected financial partners. I felt I had found the freedom I always wanted.

A QUEST FOR FREEDOM

Freedom to me means a lot more than political liberty; it means the ability to make a living doing what I want and like to do, which requires maintaining a financial independence so secure that nothing short of outright robbery or my own foolishness can take it away. Even as a teenager, the thought of relying on a paper route or a job as a bag boy at the corner grocery was tantamount to slavery in my mind—too much of the control was out of my hands. Instead, I made money doing something I had a lot more control over: gambling.

I didn't really gamble; I speculated. Gambling is taking a risk when the odds are against you, like playing the lottery or pumping silver dollars into a slot machine. Speculating is taking a risk when the odds are in your favor. The art of speculation consists of being able to accurately decipher and play the odds, knowing how to place your bets so that you will be able to play in the next hand even if you lose, and having the emotional discipline to execute according to your knowledge, not your whims.

"Gambling" was never very risky for me. When I started playing poker, I read every book I could find on the game and learned that winning was a matter of managing odds; that if you play out your hand only when the odds are in your favor and fold when they are not, you will win more than you lose over time. So I memorized the odds of every card combination possible and played each hand accordingly. I didn't know it at the time, but I was learning what was to become the heart of my approach to risk management.

I read one particular book, by a man named John Scarne,[1] that indirectly changed my life. He talked a lot about cheating, and how it was done. I realized that if I was going to master poker, then I had to learn how to recognize a cheat. In my search for this new knowledge, I discovered Lou Tannen's Magic Shop, a specialty store for illusionists and card magicians (and cheats). There, I met a man who dramatically influenced my life, Harry Lorayne.

Harry is one of the foremost experts on card magic and is probably best known for his many books on memorization techniques. As a teenager, I really looked up to him, and I still do. Everything he accomplished he did on his own through sheer force of will, energy, intelligence, practice, and innovation. He is a totally self-made man, and, as a teenager, I emulated him in many ways. Harry was both a role model and friend to me, and I spent most of my free Saturdays at Lou Tannen's watching him and other card magicians performing their art.

I learned not only Harry's card-handling techniques, but more importantly, his memorization techniques, which I still use today. To learn the card handling, I carried a deck of cards with me everywhere. When I went to the movies with my girlfriend, I practiced one-handed shuffles and cuts in my left hand, while my right hand roamed about as a 16-year-old boy's hands are apt to do with girls in movie theaters. I made a good living from ages 16 to 20 playing poker and performing card magic for paying audiences.

In the latter part of 1965, however, I realized that smoky card games and operating on the edge of the law didn't appeal to me in terms of a lifelong career. So I made a complete survey of the *New York Times* employment section and found that biologists, physicists, and securities traders made the most money — $25,000 per year! Since I knew more about odds than analyzing cells or atoms, I went to work for Pershing & Co. as a quote boy, with my sights set on achieving my concept of freedom as a trader on Wall Street.

THE WISDOM OF THE TAPE

I approached my career by observing successful men in the field and reading everything I could find on the financial markets. At Pershing, I observed Milton Leeds, who appeared godlike to me as he sat on the platform overlooking the trading room in his tailored suits and immaculate, white, custom-made shirts. Over a microphone he would yell out "99!" which meant that a trade for the firm was forthcoming and would take priority over everything else. The clerks would look up at him in an electric silence until he would call out something like "Buy 3000 Telephone at the market!"

Leeds was known as a "tape reader," but what he generally did was trade on news. He would sit and watch the Dow Jones and Reuters tapes for news, and the moment any significant news broke he would make a decision and place an order. In seconds, his floor brokers were executing his order. His quickness of mind in judging the impact of news on the market plus the physical setup of his organization gave him a jump on the market, and that's how he made so much money. He was a very shrewd man, and his trading record was excellent, especially in its consistency. Although I never emulated his particular methods, his very image became a symbol of success for me. I thought that I wanted nothing more than to become a successful tape reader.

In those days, tape reading was *the* way most well-known traders and speculators made their money, and I intended some day to join their ranks. I read the few books that were out on the subject, and practiced watching the tape and memorizing the latest print on many different stocks. Through consistent practice, I began to get a sense of the market.

For those of you who don't know about tape reading, it was the infant that grew into modern technical analysis. As technical analysis does today, tape reading relied on pattern recognition. The biggest difference was that the pattern recognition was as much or more subconscious than conscious. Like being "on" in sports, if you stopped to ask yourself what you were doing right, you could lose your concentration. All kinds of factors came into play, too many for your mind to be explicitly aware of. You watched a group of 10 to 40 stocks, constantly memorizing prices, previous high and low points, and volume levels. Simultaneously, you were subconsciously aware of the speed and rhythm of the tape movement, the sound of the ticker, the frequency of new prints on a specific stock, the rate of change of prices of the market averages and on any given stock, and repeating price and volume patterns. The subconscious conclusions drawn from all this contributed to what was often called an "intuitive feel" for the market.

Advances in knowledge, particularly in computer and communications technology, have made tape reading a dead art. Today, all the formerly "intuitive" knowledge is available at the fingertips of anyone who can afford to pay for any of the fine computerized information systems available. You can track the movement of any stock, stock group, index, or futures market with charts that are updated automatically tick by tick. With some software, you can draw trendlines, alarm-buy and -sell points, and much more. I believe tape reading required a special kind of aptitude that just isn't practical or necessary anymore, except maybe on the floor of the exchanges. Consequently, trading is open to a wider field of competition.

There is at least one thing, however, that all good tape readers knew that still holds true today. When you make a trading decision, you should feel absolutely confident that you are right, *but* you must also recognize that the market can prove you wrong. In other words, you are absolutely right until you are proven wrong. Consequently, you have to trade by rules and principles that take precedence over your feelings or wishes. Whenever you buy or sell any market, you have to ask yourself, "At what point will the market prove that I'm wrong?" Once you establish that point, *nothing* should stop you from closing out when the market hits it. This is the basis for the rule: cut your losses short. Violating this rule is the single biggest reason that people lose large sums of money in the financial markets. It is a curiosity of human nature that no matter how many books talk about this, saying the same thing in different ways, people still keep making the same mistake. It is my investigation of this problem, and my pursuit of an explanation that led to my interest in the emotional and psychological part of trading discussed in the second part of this book.

Back to ancient history. Along with working at Pershing, I enrolled in night school at Queens College to study economics and finance. In addition, I began to read *The Wall Street Journal* and whatever books I could find on the markets. After six months making $65 a week at Pershing, I did some disastrous time on a statistics desk at Standard & Poor's. The pay was better, $90 per week, but I simply couldn't perform well in the hushed, library-like atmosphere, crunching and transferring numbers from one column to the next for hours on end. I used to be grateful when somebody sneezed; it gave me the opportunity to say "Bless you!" and break the oppressive silence. I made too many mistakes, and I got fired. It was my first failure in a job, and I was too devastated to have the sense to be thankful to the guy who gently encouraged me to pursue my trading career, but to take a different path within it.

Fortunately, my courses in accounting at college helped me to land a position maintaining the books, accounts, and records in the private tax department for 12 of the 32 partners at Lehman Brothers in late 1966. Lehman Brothers, a pioneering firm in investment banking, made a fortune on such deals as buying huge quantities of Litton Industries at four cents a share and holding it while it appreciated to $120 a share. Working at Lehman Brothers, I got an insider's look at the world of investment banking and a first-hand view of the stock and options portfolios of one of the world's largest market participants. I gained an understanding of how options worked and became somewhat of an expert in options tax accounting.

I learned a huge lesson at Lehman Brothers that I'll never forget. In keeping the books, I knew how much money these guys made. One day, in going through the paperwork, I saw that Lehman was building up a huge position in Superior Electric for its trust funds. In my youthful naïveté, I figured that the firm must know what it was doing, so I called Harry Lorayne and told him about it. On my say-so, Harry took a large position of his own in the stock, going long at $44 per share. Over the next few months, I watched in dismay as the stock price plunged to $30. Harry closed his position, losing $40,000 on the trade. I felt worse about it than any personal loss I had ever suffered. It was the last time I ever recommended a stock to a friend but, unfortunately, not the last time I would be suckered into taking a position because people who "knew what they were doing" were involved. But I did learn a lesson: don't do your friends a favor by offering them unsolicited advice on any market position. It's one thing to manage someone's money, even a friend's, on a professional basis; if you lose, it's just part of the professional agreement. It's another thing to offer market advice when you think you're doing people a favor—you usually hurt them more than you help them.

Anyway, while I continued my work at Lehman, I kept studying, including memorizing the symbols of all 1458 New York Stock Exchange–listed stocks using Harry's memorization techniques. In 1968 I demonstrated this skill during a job interview to Ricky Bergman, a partner at Filer Schmidt & Co. Impressed, Ricky hired me, and I began my trading career in earnest.

HORSETRADING OPTIONS

Relative to today, options were in their infancy in 1968. They were traded over-the-counter only and were tailormade. Let me explain what I mean. A stock option is a contract giving the holder the right to buy (a call) or sell (a put) a defined amount of a specific stock, at a stated price (the strike price), within a specified time period. In 1968 the standard number of shares per contract was 100 (as it is today); the strike price was virtually always the current market price of the stock; and the most popular time period was 6 months and 10 days (because you had to hold an investment for 6 months and 1 day for it to be declared a long-term capital gain for tax purposes). The biggest difference between then and now, however, was that the *price* (the premium) of options varied from moment to moment and dealer to dealer.

When Joe Optionsbuyer called Typical Options Company for the price of an OXY (Occidental Petroleum) 6 and 10 call, there was no guarantee that he could buy the contract at the quoted price. Further, he may have called another dealer or two and found a 20 to 30% price difference either way! The dealer would quote the buyer a "workout" price of, say, $225 per contract, and then try to find a seller bidding $150 to $175. Once found, he would turn the contract over to his buyer and "make the middle." If he couldn't find a seller at a reasonable price, then Joe was out of luck and received a "nothing done."

From 1968 to 1970 I horse-traded options first at Filer Schmidt, earning a flat rate per contract ($6.25), and then at U.S. Options for a percentage of "the middle." While at Filer, I also managed my first hedge fund for a man named Starret Stephens, whom I had been introduced to at Lehman Brothers. He had a $1 million portfolio that I suggested he hedge on the short side with puts instead of shorting stocks, and he allocated $50,000 to me for that purpose. This was a relatively new practice at the time. Puts used this way provide leveraged "insurance" and free up capital for use on the long side.

The fund served its purpose, catching the July–August correction just prior to the bull market top in December 1968. Tragically, Starret Stephens died too young in 1969, just before the first major down leg of the 1969–70 bear market. The fund was dissolved because of his death. This was my first direct experience with managing money and hedging, and it gave me the opportunity to apply my untested ability to gauge the market by reading the tape. It also taught me the value of playing the short side—something that is still a specialty of mine.

Shortly after the fund was dissolved, when the 1969 bear market was fully underway, I quit Filer Schmidt & Co. and moved to U.S. Options in search of greater autonomy in my trading decisions. Afraid to commit to giving me a salary in the middle of a bear market, the management offered me a percentage of the spread on each piece of paper I filled (we called options contracts "paper"). I accepted, explicitly telling them that I was going to make $100,000 in my first year. I said this as a warning, because I knew that the vice-president of the company was only drawing about $25,000 a year in salary, and that the other options traders on salary were making about $12,000 to $15,000 per year.

Sure enough, six months later I had made $50,000 in commissions, and my boss pulled me aside one day and said, "Victor, you're doing such a good job we want to put you on salary."

"Oh yeah?" I said, "How much?"

"$20,000 per year," he replied, as if he was doing me some kind of favor.

"But M_____," I said, "I'm on the track of making $100,000 this year, and I've already made $50,000!"

"Oh yes, well, we're setting up a point-allotted bonus system. For each piece of paper you write, you get a point. At the end of the year, we'll put 15% of the profits into a bonus pool to be divided up in proportion to points accrued by each trader."

"Mmmm," was about all I said, but obvious questions—such as what if the company didn't make a profit, and how were profits to be calculated—were buzzing around in my head. Needless to say, I started looking for greener pastures. Three weeks later, I was managing a stock/options portfolio on a 50% profit basis at Marsh Block. A good friend, who also quit U.S. Options eventually, later told me that my ex-boss had called him during the three-week interim and said, "It sure is a good thing we put Vic on salary; he's having a terrible month." Amazing. The man actually expected me to take an 80% cut in pay and work happily along! My desire for freedom was reinforced.

At Marsh Block, for the first time, I started actively trading stocks against options, relying on my accumulated knowledge of both tape reading and options strategies. Typically, I would buy a straddle of options and buy or sell the stock according to my reading of the market. A *straddle* is a pair of options: one put and one call with the same strike price and expiration date. Let's say the market price of XYZ was $25 per share, and I thought the price was going to $21. Paying wholesale rates, I would buy a 95-day straddle for about $400, looking to sell the stock short on a weak rally.

If the stock price hit $27, I would sell 100 shares of stock short for the sell-off. If the market went against me to $30, I would exercise the call at $25 and buy back the stock on the expiration date, taking a loss of $200 on the trade, while the put would expire worthless. If it went to $21, as I thought it would, then I would buy 200 shares, thus making a $600 profit while still having a 200-share play on the upside (100 shares plus the call) if the stock price rallied above $25, while having a 100-share hedge against the put with a guaranteed profit. Or I might simply buy back the 100 shares of stock, making $600, and essentially have a free straddle for use in another cycle. I always set it up so that the risk/reward was at least 1:3 in my favor. Employing various strategies, I made substantial gains when I was right and lost only a little bit when I was wrong—the essence of my approach to money management today.

Unfortunately, the management at Marsh Block turned out to be playing the same tune as at U.S. Options, with just slightly different arrangement. When I received my monthly profit/loss statements, I found that my "expenses" were enormous. I had one phone with one line and got charged up to $500 a month! To make a long story short, I wanted greater control of my overhead.

After six months, I decided that the only thing to do was to go into business for myself. Evidently, a lot of other traders on the street were thinking the same way; nearly every good trader I knew and respected was ready to take a risk and come to work with me. I found a partner to finance the operation, hired some of the best talent on Wall Street, and started Ragnar Options Corp. in mid 1971.

A TASTE OF INDEPENDENCE

At Ragnar, we took a radical new approach to the options business. To the best of my knowledge, we were the first broker/dealer that offered guaranteed contract delivery at the quoted price without an exceptionally high premium. We called it "offering reasonable firm quotes." If we couldn't find an existing option contract on the market and then sell it at a premium to fill an order, we wrote it ourselves. Our competitors thought that we had tremendous capital to take on that kind of risk. Actually, we only started with $500,000—$250,000 in working capital and $250,000 for the firm's trading account. Our concept was to secure high volume by offering firm quotes and guaranteed delivery, thus enabling us to absorb small losses. The strategy worked. Within six months, Ragnar was, to the best of my knowledge, trading more over-the-counter-options (OTC) than any other dealer in the world.

I managed Ragnar and horse-traded options along with the other traders in the firm until July 1972, when I took over "running the inventory" from my partner. "Running the inventory" was our term for managing Ragnar's portfolio of options and stocks. This is what I consider to be the beginning of my career as an independent trader. It was the first time I had *complete* discretionary control of an account, and as the record in Table P.2 on pp. xii–xiii shows, I was achieving my objective of consistent profitability.

In 1973 the CBOE (Chicago Board Options Exchange) standardized the options business, and we lost some of the competitive edge we had gained by standardizing the business in our own way. But we bought three seats on the exchange and did over 15% of the volume on the floor in the first year. We continued to compete effectively until July and August of 1975, when my major partner, without my knowledge or consent, traded on a huge scale and lost a tremendous amount of money. Although my trading account was in good shape, we were forced to reorganize the operation to meet our capital requirements after my partner's losing trade.

With some quick thinking, we managed to stay afloat. I remember the meeting we had with Jim Brucki, then the head of compliance on the CBOE (Jim later came to Interstate, and we became friends). Because of my partner's loss, we were in violation of some capital requirements established by the exchange. Jim was a big, gruff man, and he looked at me and said, "What are you going to do about this problem?"

I answered, "We'll talk about it, and come up with a way to make the margin requirements for the positions we have on."

Jim said, "Okay, you've got 20 minutes to find a way to stay in business."

I, the partner that lost all the money, and John Bello went into the next room and did some quick negotiating. I bought my major partner out, and put up some more capital to get back into compliance. I managed to keep Ragnar intact, and the rest of us continued operations for another 15 months, until Weeden & Company offered to take on the whole staff, myself included, under very favorable conditions. At Weeden, I became a block trader of the "glamour stocks"—market leaders such as IBM, National Cash Register, and Eastman Kodak. I maintained the existence of Ragnar as a business entity, and I still use it as a trading vehicle today.

Prior to the reorganization, something happened that proved to be the major turning point in my career. I missed the sharp rally in early October 1974 and the subsequent sell-off to a 12-year low on the Dow in December. I managed to make money in those months, but it shook me—I had missed a great opportunity to make money. What was I missing? What did I need to learn so that it wouldn't happen again? I asked myself, "What exactly is a trend? What is its nature? How long does it normally last? How high or low does it normally go? What is the nature of a correction? How long does it normally last?" I began to study as I never had before.

DISCOVERING THE NATURE OF TRENDS

To answer these questions, I first had to define, measure, and classify all trends and corrections and identify a standard by which to define "normal." From 1974 until 1976, I spent almost every spare moment studying market history via Dow Theory, which gave the best definitions of market movements that I could find. Building on the work that Robert Rhea carried out until his death in 1939, I classified every trend within the Dow Industrial and Transportation averages from 1896 to the present (I keep the study current to this day) as short-term, intermediate-term, and long-term, logging their extent (how big) and duration (how long) in actuarial tables. Then, using statistical analysis, I reduced the data to terms that I can apply to my trading, specifically in risk assessment. I will discuss how I apply the data later in the book.

It was this period of study that established an essential new element of my approach to forecasting market behavior, an approach that I would learn to apply to the futures markets as well. Without a doubt, the knowledge I gained in those two years of study contributed more than any other single factor to my record at Interstate. My best month, and the best month on record for any trader at Interstate at the time, was September 1982, when I grossed $880,000 with trading capital of $1 million on my Interstate account, and did proportionally well on my two other accounts. The bulk of that month's profit came from one market call arising directly from applying the knowledge and statistical methods I had worked out between 1974 and 1976.

As an aside, I want to point out that although this period of intensive study helped me immeasurably in my ability to call the markets, it cost me substantially in my personal life. My daughter, Jennifer, was at a crucial formative age (three to five), and I spent almost no time with her. I would get home from the office, eat, and go straight back to work in my study. When she came into my office, I would shoo her away impatiently, totally ignoring the fact that she needed her father's attention and love. It was a bad mistake that both of us are paying for today. If I had it to do again, I would draw out the study period and give Jennifer more time.

I point this out not for the sake of catharsis, but to make a very important point. As I note in the Preface, this book is about attaining and maintaining both financial and personal success. I failed to integrate both at that point in my life, and it was a mistake. I relate this story with the hope that it will help you avoid making similar mistakes. There is a balance in life, and the bottom line is not measured in the dollars you make, but rather in your overall happiness.

After 1974 everything wasn't completely roses on the business end either. In 1983 I agreed to manage a $4 million fund called Victory Partners. Maybe I was a little cocky, or maybe I did it for the challenge, but I agreed to set it up so that I had to achieve a 25% cumulative return after commissions in order to receive any compensation at all. The first year, I made 13.3% when the market was down 15%. That meant in the next year I had to achieve a minimum return of almost 40% on the fund!

Intermediate-term trading was terrible in 1984–85. There was very little volatility—the market was flat—and I was forced to move in and out of the market in the short term. While I was making money on my three trading accounts, I lost about 13% for Victory Partners, most of it in commissions. At Interstate I was paying floor brokerage, which was comparable to institutional rates today. With Victory Partners, I paid *retail* commission rates—about five times higher—which made high turnover trading in a flat market impractical. In addition, program trading began to dramatically affect the nature of the short-term trend, invalidating rules that I had used for years. I recommended that we dissolve the fund, and we did in 1986 . . . ouch.

I don't want to give the impression that I use only one particularized method of analysis when making market calls. I always combine technical, statistical, and fundamental economic factors to assess the risk of any speculative position. Only when all three factors point in the same direction do I get involved in any significant way. Moreover, through experience, I have learned how crucial it is to be aware of existing or potential government intervention in the marketplace. In particular, it is crucial to be aware of the effects of monetary and fiscal policy as established by Congress, the President, the Federal Reserve Board, foreign governments, and foreign central banks. You must not only understand the *effects* of government policy, but you must also be able to *anticipate* it by understanding the character and intent of the men and women in crucial positions of power. I will cover some aspects of these areas in coming chapters, and in detail in a second book.

FINDING MY FREEDOM

When Howard Shapiro, a truly great trader, recruited me to work at Interstate Securities in 1978, it was the best thing that had ever happened to me. Initially, I was put on the payroll and given a $500,000 account with the freedom to trade it with complete autonomy. In 1979 Interstate changed my status to independent contractor, and I founded Hugo Securities, a private trading partnership still in existence. Under this organization I traded Interstate's capital, my own, and that of a few smaller partners. The only condition was that in the Interstate account everything was a 50-50 split—profits, losses, expenses—as it was with all the trading accounts I managed for others. The performance numbers in Table P.1 from 1978 to 1986 represent my gross trading income before expenses on the Interstate account alone. I also had my own account, which was relatively small, plus one other, which was nearly as large as the Interstate account; so actually my production was almost double what is presented in Table P.1.

The environment at Interstate could not have been better. I had the benefits of trading large size, but I didn't have to put up my own money unless I lost. The organization had an excellent information network, which was available at a cost minimized through the economies of scale. I was free to come and go as I pleased. I was able to save and secure my profits, while living the life-style that pleased me. I had found my freedom.

I was privileged to work among some of the best traders on Wall Street, including Frankie Joe, Howard Shapiro, and others. We all had different styles, and all but a few made considerable amounts of money. In observing many different traders, however, I began to see a different aspect of the business: the personal cost paid by those who worked at odds with their emotions. I saw some men at the top of their field who were fundamentally unhappy, and I wanted to know why. I wanted to understand what it took to attain success in the broadest sense of the term. The results of what I have learned are contained in Part II.

The golden days at Interstate came to an end when the company went public and dissolved the trading department in September 1986. The reasoning was that trading profits were erratic on a quarterly basis, and Interstate was afraid that its stock would react negatively to erratic changes in earnings. I think it was a mistake. To my knowledge, the trading department made money every year. In one single year that I remember, just 10 of us grossed over $30 million, meaning that Interstate netted somewhere in the neighborhood of $15 million off 10 traders! Nevertheless, the decision was made, and it was time to move on.

I set up my own offices in October 1986 and traded actively until January 1988, when I decided to start a money management firm: Rand Management Corp., for which I am now trading again.

2

The Alligator Principle: Proof of the Need to Think in Essentials

When men abandon principles... two of the major results are: individually, the inability to project the future; socially, the impossibility of communication. [1]

—*Ayn Rand*

BEING EATEN ALIVE

I have a trading rule I call the "Alligator Principle." It's based on the way an alligator eats; the more the victim tries to struggle, the more the alligator gets. Imagine an alligator has you by the leg; it clamps your leg in its mouth and waits while you struggle. If you put one of your arms in the vicinity of its mouth while fighting to get your leg free, it lunges and then has your arm and leg in its clutches. The more you struggle, the more the alligator takes you in.

So if an alligator ever gets you by the leg, remember that your only chance is to sacrifice the leg and drag yourself away. Translated to market terms, the principle is *when you know you are wrong, close your position!* Don't rationalize, hope, pray, or anything else, just get out... don't change your position, hedge it, or anything else; just take the loss and get out!

Like a lot of things I know, I learned this principle the hard way. In the mid 1970s, I had a small options position in INA Insurance. I bought 20 December $25 calls for 1¼ ($125 per call). Shortly after buying them, the stock started to go down, and the options dropped first ⅛ ($12.50 per call), then ¼ ($25 per call). My rule for options at the time was that if you lose a quarter, close out. But instead of taking my $500 loss, I attempted to cover my loss by selling 60 of the December

15

$30 calls for ⅜. Of course, then the stock started to go back up on merger rumors. The December $30 calls I sold at ⅜ went to 1⅝, and the December $25 calls were at 2½. So then what did I do? Why naturally, I sold 25 puts at 1⅛ on the merger rumors! Then the merger rumors were denied and the puts went from 1⅛ to 1⅜! Every step I took made the matter worse. That alligator had a full meal—I turned a $500 dollar loss into a $6000 loss, all because I didn't maintain the discipline to apply principles I knew to be correct.

You see, at the time INA was a lackluster stock; it wasn't traded heavily and didn't move much. When the price did move, it was pretty predictable. I felt that admitting that I had made a mistake on INA was like saying I didn't know the alphabet. I violated rule after rule and principle after principle, all out of "false pride"[2] and vanity. Thinking back on it now, my behavior was nuts, but it nevertheless taught me a hard-earned lesson: always think in essentials.

THINKING IN ESSENTIALS

Let me provide a little motivation by showing what thinking in essentials can do for you. On the morning of Friday, October 13, 1989, I awoke to a market that was ripe for correction. Before the market opened, I began calling my clients and the people I advise, telling them, in essence, the following:

> I'm looking for the market to go down in a major secondary correction. Since March 23, the market has been in a sustained primary upswing. Only 29% of primary swings in all bull markets in history have lasted longer. Moreover, the Transports have appreciated 52% in the same period. By comparison, in the 92-year history of the Industrials average, of 174 upward movements in both bull and bear markets, only eight have appreciated more than 52% before failing. The junk bond market is falling apart— there are no buyers. Further, the averages are down four days in a row from the new highs established in the Industrials on October 9, which were not confirmed by the Transports or by breadth—a definite bearish indication.

> The continual upward movement in the averages and the general bullish atmosphere have been fueled by takeover and glamour stocks, while a large percentage of individual stocks have topped and are in an intermediate downtrend. The Japanese and Germans have raised interest rates; U.S. inflation is running at an annual rate of about 5.5% and the Fed has reduced Free Reserves over the last two reporting periods relative to the previous periods. I don't see any signs of the Fed easing in this atmosphere.

> Consequently, I'm building a short position in the market by buying index puts; relatively small now, but if the market sells off on high volume (around 170 million shares), breaking the 2752 level on the Dow (the August high), then it is time to go short aggressively.

In the early afternoon, the market was on the way down, but on moderate volume. I was buying puts at a moderate rate to build up my short position, expecting the market to continue to sell off into a correction the following week. I was keeping a close eye on volume. The news broke that financing for the United Airlines takeover had fallen through, and at about 2:45 P.M., volume swelled, the S&P 500 Index futures started to plunge, and I began to buy puts as fast as I could. By a little after 3:00 P.M., I couldn't get any more orders executed—all hell had broken loose. The Industrials average closed down 191 points.

Monday morning I expected the market to open down about 50 points or so, and I had prepared a list of stocks and options to go long if this occurred. I put in orders to sell back my puts on the opening, and waited. The market opened down and sold off over 60 points in the first two hours. I cashed in my short position and went long stocks and options. The short position cost approximately $73,605, and produced income of about $831,212, for a net profit of $757,607. I remained long for several weeks, and cashed in another nice profit.

I had no way of knowing that the market would close down 191 points (Figure 2.1)—the second largest drop in history—on Friday the Thirteenth or that the catalyst would be the collapse of financing for the takeover of United Airlines. I was fortunate that the move was so large, but I wouldn't say that I was lucky to catch it. Every single analytical criterion that I use, including several that I haven't mentioned, pointed to being postured for a correction; all the odds were in my favor.

I will explain, as the book goes on, each component of making this kind of market call. But if I had to reduce all the components of my methods to a single phrase, it would be *thinking in essentials*.

It's not necessarily how much you know, but the truth and quality of what you know that counts. Every week in *Barron's* there are dozens of pages of fine print summarizing the week's activities in stocks, bonds, commodities, options, and so forth. There is so much information that to process all of it, and *make sense* out of it, is a task beyond any genius's mental capacity.

One way to narrow down the data is to specialize in one or two areas. Another way is to use computers to do a lot of the sorting out for you. But no matter how you reduce the data, the key to processing information is the ability to abstract the *essential* information from the bounty of data produced each day.

To do this, you have to relate the information to principles—to fundamental concepts that define the *nature* of the financial markets. A principle is a broad generalization that describes an unlimited number of specific events and correlates vast amounts of data. It is with principles that you can take complex market data and make it relatively simple and manageable.

Take, for example, the simple statement "Savings is required for growth."[3] Is this true? Is it a principle? On a common sense level, it seems self-evident that it *is* a principle. To buy a house, you need the money for the down payment; and to get the money for the down payment, you have to save for it. On the other hand, Keynesian economists have been telling us for years that we can deficit-finance ourselves into prosperity; that saving actually discourages growth, and spending is the key to continued prosperity. Who is right? What is the principle involved?

Data for chart courtesy: Daily Graphs

Figure 2.1 The stock market mini-crash of October 13, 1989. In a single day, the Dow Industrial dropped 191 points, the second largest drop in history. On the same day, the Transportation index finished over 78 points, sparked by the UAL financing problem.

Assume for the moment that savings *is* required for growth, and that this is true not just in a specific case such as buying a house, but for all individuals and groups engaged in economic activity—that it is a principle. What does this tell you in terms of the markets? The answer is "Plenty!" It tells you, for example, that leveraged buyouts can't go on forever, especially when the stock market is at peak levels. A corporation with debt far exceeding the value of its cash reserves and liquid assets is especially jeopardized in a general economic decline (a recession or depression). Such a company is totally dependent on future income or additional credit availability for its economic survival. In an economic downturn, a highly leveraged company would be hit with both decreased sales and increased credit costs. Its survival, its potential for future profitability, and therefore its value as a potential investment would be questionable if you consider the risk as well as the potential reward.

Similarly, the principle can be applied to evaluating the economy as a whole. If growth requires savings, then the producers of a nation must create more wealth than is aggregately consumed and invest the balance to produce goods and services in the future. When the federal government continually operates at a deficit, it is financing today's programs at the expense of tomorrow's products. Only one of two possibilities exists. Either (1) Americans will produce so much more in the future that the government will be able to confiscate a portion of what would have been their savings to pay for the debt and still leave enough for investment; or (2) there will be a decrease in growth, or rate of growth, as the government taxes or inflates away the existing wealth of producers. More importantly, if the government attempts to continue operating at a deficit, the attempt to spend what does not exist will eventually lead to financial disaster—a severe bear market.

Whether you agree at this point with the truth or falsehood of the principle in this example isn't the point. The example illustrates how one sentence, one bit of knowledge, leads to a whole chain of reasoning and conclusions. What initially seems enormously complex is made relatively simple by understanding the underlying principle.

In any endeavor, making good decisions requires the development of essential knowledge such that every observation can be related to the fundamental ideas governing the cause-and-effect relationships involved. In the financial markets, this means discovering the principles of price movements and price trends. It means understanding the *nature* of markets in general and defining the distinguishing characteristics that separate one market from the next.

To develop this knowledge requires a constant process of relating concrete events to abstract ideas and vice versa, projecting the long term based on an analysis of today's events, and understanding today's events according to the same ideas applied in the context of both recent and past history. I call this process *thinking in principles,* or *thinking in essentials.*

It is one thing to say that you should think in principles; it is quite another to identify those principles. In reading books and magazines about the financial world, you can find almost as many opinions as you can find "experts," and many of them will be diametrically opposite. Part of the reason for this is a problem of definitions. Consider some of the terms that we hear every day: bull market, bear market, trend, depression, recession, recovery, inflation, value, price, risk/reward, relative strength, and asset allocation, just to name a few. Most people in the financial world would recognize these terms, but few would actually be able to *define* them precisely. But defining them isn't just an abstract exercise; it is an essential step to understanding the markets and identifying the principles that govern them.

For the remainder of this book, I'm going to present the *essentials* necessary to understand the markets and profit from the knowledge—the *principles* of speculation that you'll need to be a successful market player.

3

A Business Philosophy for Consistent Success

If you read about many of the great traders in history, you'll find that a very large percentage of them blew out (lost all their money) at least once, and some of them blew out two or three times in their career. Add to this the fact that only about 5% of commodity traders make money, and you have to wonder, "What's going on here?"

There are many reasons why people lose money in the markets, but one huge and easily avoided mistake is putting too much capital at risk in a single position—betting it all. The mistake arises because people don't set forth a business philosophy for themselves before making a trade in the markets.

My objective as a trader has always been to obtain and maintain the freedom secured by financial independence; consequently, my goal has been to make money consistently, month in and month out, year after year. I have always approached my career as a *business,* and a prudent businessman wants to first cover his overhead each month and then concentrate on achieving a steady growth in earnings. Rather than striving for the big hit, I protect capital first and work for consistent returns, and take more aggressive risk with a portion of profits. Not accidentally, the big hits still come along; but they come along without excessive risk.

Translated into more businesslike terms, I base my business philosophy on three principles, listed here in order of importance: preservation of capital, consistent profitability, and the pursuit of superior returns. These principals are basic in the sense that they underlie and guide all of my market decisions. Each principle carries a different weight in my speculative strategy, and they evolve from one to the other. That is, preservation of capital leads to consistent profits, which makes pursuit of superior returns possible.

PRESERVATION OF CAPITAL

Preservation of capital is the cornerstone of my business philosophy. This means that, in considering any potential market involvement, risk is my *prime* concern.

Before asking "What potential profit can I realize?", I first ask, "What potential loss can I suffer?" In terms of risk/reward, the maximum acceptable ratio is 1:3, the measurement of which I will discuss in this chapter and in Chapter 11. When the risk/reward of remaining in any market is poor, I go into cash, regardless of the contemporary wisdom. Consequently, I don't concern myself with "outperforming the averages." I work for *absolute* not *relative* returns.

In my terms, money isn't green . . . it's either black or white. Black and white have come to be associated with false or true, wrong or right, bad or good. In ethical terms, most of society has been taught that "there are no blacks and whites—there is only gray": gray—the mixed and contradictory—the lack of absolutes. But on a ledger sheet, there are nothing but absolutes: $2 + 2$ is always 4, and $2 - 6$ is always -4! Yet, in a subtle way, the modern investor has been taught to accept gray by the money management community. He is encouraged to rejoice if his account goes down only 10% when the averages are down 20%—after all, he has outperformed the averages by 10%! This is B.S., plain and simple.

There is one, and only one, valid question for an investor to ask: "Have I made money?" The best insurance that the answer will always be "Yes!" is to consistently speculate or invest only when the odds are decidedly in your favor, which means keeping risk at a minimum. For example, if all your indicators lead you to conclude that the long-term trend in the stock market (or soybeans, or crude oil, and so on) is approaching a top, at least for the intermediate term, then why put your portfolio at risk by being 100% invested on the long side? Why attempt to gain a few more percentage points over the T-bill yield when you risk the possibility of losing 50% or more of your portfolio value?

Referring to Figure 3.1, you can see that an investor who bought the Value Line at the lows in December 1984 and held until August 25, 1987 (my indicators gave sell signals on August 25) was up 67.9% before dividends. If the same investor held through October 5, when again there were signs of a top, then he was still up 65.9%. But if he continued to hold, then by October 19 he had lost all of his accumulated return—he was back down to a 0% return before dividends—two years and ten months' worth of profits down the tubes in just 14 days! Clearly, the risk/reward wasn't there. You might say that "hindsight is always 20-20," but I was almost completely flat—most of my money was in T-Bills—from August through October, and I was short through the crash. As the book progresses, you'll see why this wasn't luck.

Another case where I consider the risk too great to participate is to invest heavily in takeover stocks and junk bonds in the latter part of bull markets. Some people will tell you, "There is always a good deal out there, no matter what the condition of the stock market." Well, maybe so. But I have lived through and seen what bear markets are like. Stock prices drop day after day with no end in sight. Previously strong businesses are forced to liquidate assets to service their debt, and many weak and/or highly leveraged businesses go bankrupt. Leveraged buyouts (LBOs) are just that—leveraged—and the speculative bubble that made them popular in the eighties was bound to burst, as was indicated by the United Airlines fiasco in October 1989.

Value Line Monthly Bar Chart

TQ 20/20 © 1991 CQG Inc.

Figure 3.1 Value Line monthly bar chart. An investor who bought the Value Line at the December 1984 low and held it until the August 1987 high was up 67.9% before dividends. If the investor continued to hold until October 2, 1987, he or she was still up 65.9%. But a mere two weeks later, at the close of October 19, all the gains were wiped out.

By my philosophy, the only reasonable way to be involved in an LBO near market tops is to get involved early, buy calls with a risk/reward ratio of 1:10 or better, and participate in a small way. Then before the stock price reaches the target takeover values . . . take your profit and run!

On the other hand, the ideal time to get involved in a takeover is at bear market bottoms or in the early stages of a bull market. This is where the real value is. As Robert Rhea put it, the last stage of a bear market "is caused by distress selling of sound securities, regardless of their value, by those who must find a cash market for at least a portion of their assets." The market player who avoids being invested near the top of bull markets—where he can really get hurt in a panic crash—and plays the short side in bear markets can be in the position to take advantage of such distress selling. You *might* miss the last 10 or even 20% of the gains to be made near bull market tops (while making T-bill yields), but you'll *definitely* still have your capital when the time comes to buy value with tremendous upside potential and almost no downside risk. In my view, the way to build wealth is to preserve capital, make consistent profits, and *wait patiently* for the right opportunity to make extraordinary gains.

CONSISTENT PROFITABILITY

Obviously, the markets aren't always at or near tops or bottoms. Generally speaking, a good speculator or investor should be able to capture between 60 and 80% of the long-term price trend (whether up or down) between bull market tops and bear market bottoms in any market. This is the period when the focus should be on making consistent profits with low risk.

Consistent profitability is a corollary of the preservation of capital. Now what do I mean by a *corollary?* A corollary is an idea or a principle which is a direct consequence of another more fundamental principle. In this case, consistent profitability is a corollary of the preservation of capital because capital isn't a static quantity—it is either gained or lost. To gain capital, you have to be consistently profitable; but to be consistently profitable, you have to preserve gains and minimize losses. Therefore, you must constantly balance the risks and rewards of each decision, scaling your risk according to accumulated profits or losses, thereby increasing the odds of consistent success.

Suppose, for example, that you operate on a quarterly accounting basis. When entering a new quarter, any new positions should be small relative to the risk capital available because there are no profits accumulated for the period. In addition, predefined exit points should be established at which you admit being wrong, close out your position, and take the loss. If your first positions go against you, the size of any new position should be scaled back in proportion to your loss. That way, you never end a quarter losing all of your risk capital—you always have some left to build with. Conversely, if you make profits, you should apply a portion of the profits to your new positions while banking the balance, thus increasing your upside potential while preserving a portion of gains.

If I were a young speculator with $50,000 to trade in the commodities futures markets, I would take an initial position of no more than 10% of the total—$5000— and set exit points to limit potential losses to 10 to 20% of that—a $500 to $1000 loss. In other words, I would set it up so that my losses were no more than 1 to 2% of the total risk capital. Upon losing $1000 in the first trade, I would scale back my next opening position to $4000 and limit my losses to somewhere in the $400 to $800 range. And so forth.

On the upside, if I made $2000 on my first trade, I would bank $1000 and increase the opening size of my next position to $6000, in effect reducing my *initial* capital at risk ($5000) by 20%, while increasing my *actual* risk capital by the same amount. That way, even if I lost on my next trade, I would still be up money for the period. Assuming that I was right in my market calls 50% of the time, I would make a lot of money by employing this strategy. And I would make a respectable living being right on only one out of three trades, *provided I maintained a risk/reward ratio of, at most, 1:3.* In other words, if you pick opportunities so that the *probable* reward is at least three times greater than the *objectively measurable* potential loss, you will make profits consistently over time.

Anyone who enters the financial markets expecting to be right on most of their trades is in for a rude awakening. If you think about it, it's a lot like hitting a baseball—the best players only get hits 30 to 40% of the time. But a good player knows that the hits usually help a lot more than the strikeouts hurt. The reward is greater than the risk.

This concept of constantly balancing risk/reward to keep the odds in your favor applies no matter what trend you are involved in. For example, when I day trade the S&P futures, the smallest movement I am interested in is one where I can select spots to limit losses (usually by setting stops when I place the order) to between three and five ticks (a tick is equal to $25 per contract), while the nearest resistance or support levels on the profitable side are a minimum of 15 to 20 ticks away. If I were looking for an intermediate movement, I would apply the same principles but with different dimensions, such as one to three points of risk versus three to ten or more points of profit.

For example, although I took my short position with options to increase my leverage in October 1989, I considered shorting the S&P Index futures as well. Basing my decision on reasons described earlier, I would have gone short (refer to Figure 3.2) the S&P Index on Thursday, October 12 when prices failed through the August 5 high of 359.85; and I would have been looking for a sell-off of several days to at least 346.50—the previous minor sell-off low. The market would prove me wrong if it went above 364.50—the high set on October 10. What was my *objective* risk? It was 4.65 points or $2325 per contract. What was my *probable* reward? It was 13 points or $6500 per contract—for a risk/reward ratio of 1:2.8. Although this doesn't strictly meet my criterion, my other risk assessment factors would have overridden the small discrepancy.

Once the market moved through the probable reward point (point 2), I would have lowered my exit points to ensure a profit. I would have watched further minor support points (points 3, 5, and 6) to see how the market reacted to them, while lowering my stops on the way down. There is a trading rule that says, "Let your profits run, and cut your losses short." My interpretation of this rule is, "Never give back more than 50% of any gain." In this case, once prices broke 346.85 (point 2), I would have set my stop at 347.10, then moved it down when they broke through points 6 and 7. The most likely result is that I would have been stopped out at 342.15 (four ticks above point 7), for a profit of 17.7 points, or $8850 per contract. Because of all the factors pointing to a correction, I would have considered this a low-risk trade; but I was so confident that the market was going to turn down that I bought out of the money puts to maximize leverage instead of playing it this way.

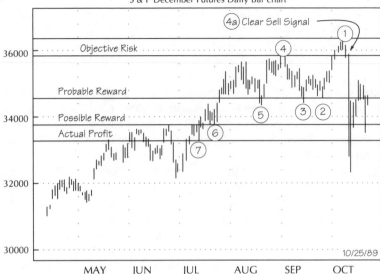

S & P December Futures Daily Bar chart

TQ 20/20 © 1991 CQG Inc.

Figure 3.2 Trading the S&P Futures through the October 13, 1989 crash. Important trading levels.

1. October 9 high—364.50
2. Immediately preceding sell-off low—349.85; the probable reward point.
3. Potential support on the way down; resistance on the way back up.
4. August 27 high—359.85; the level to watch for a break.
5. Support established in the sell-off prior to August 27; a potentially good place to set stops when prices broke through it.
6. Another tangible support point.
7. The likely reward point if trading October 13 through the 16th. Once prices broke through this level, it would become a good place to set stops.

PURSUIT OF SUPERIOR RETURNS

As profits accrue, I apply the same reasoning but take the process a step further to the pursuit of superior returns. If, and only if, a level of profits exists to justify aggressive risk, then I will take on a higher risk to produce greater percentage returns on capital. This *does not* mean that I change my risk/reward criteria; it means that I increase the *size* of my positions.

A good example occurred in July and August 1974 when I was running the inventory at Ragnar Options Corporation. Our fiscal year ended in June, and I began every fiscal year with $250,000 of risk capital allotted for trading. In July, I made about $104,000, bringing me to over a 40% return for the quarter. I was a strong bear at the time, so I decided to take half of my profits and go short big the next month. No puts were traded on the CBOE (Chicago Board of Exchange) back then, so I went short by taking a position in what is called *synthetic puts*. Risking about $50,000, I shorted 3500 shares each of Texas Instruments, Kodak, McDonalds, and IBM and bought 35 calls of each. In net effect, the only money at risk was what I paid for the calls; each 100 shares of stock sold short was perfectly hedged with a call—thus, a synthetic put.

I took the position when the Dow Industrials average broke 750—the previous low established in July—and the market began to sell off as I expected. Then on August 8, Nixon resigned and the market crashed, accelerating the down move. I closed out the month up over $269,000 in my account, more than doubling the initial capital for the fiscal year in a single month. That is what I mean by *aggressive* risk taking; the odds are in my favor, but I put more money on the line. Even if I had been totally wrong, I would have lost only about half of my previous profits, with plenty of money left to take lower risk positions.

CONCLUSION

Preservation of capital, consistent profitability, and the pursuit of superior returns are three simple principles that, if properly understood, will guide you toward making profits in the markets. But to put these ideas into practice, much more information is needed. The best starting point is to understand the nature of market movements. And I know of no better way to discuss these ideas than to introduce a body of knowledge that I consider indispensable if one is to truly understand market behavior: Dow Theory.

4

Finding Order in Market Chaos: An Introduction to Dow Theory

There is a new theory in science—the theory of chaos—that postulates that certain types of natural activity are chaotic and unpredictable except in terms of probabilities. For example, doctors can monitor and chart a heartbeat on highly sensitive equipment, but given certain conditions, a heart will go into *random fibrillation* (random chaotic beating that can be deadly) during which the heartbeat cannot be predicted or modeled mathematically. This kind of chaos is life-threatening, but ironically, researchers have found that the brain waves of a healthy mind in a state of intense concentration are chaotic, whereas those of an epileptic during seizure or a drug addict on a "high" are regular and predictable.

Weather forecasting is another area where many scientists think that chaos theory applies. The unpredictability of weather comes from what is called *sensitivity to initial conditions*. Mathematical models fail in weather forecasting because the slightest divergence between simulated and actual conditions multiplies in a complex chain of cause and effect relationships, giving rise to results in the model totally different than in nature. The best, chaos theory says, that meteorologists can ever do is forecast the weather within the limits of probability.

If this seems like a hopeless and futile theory, it is only because I don't do it justice. By studying what gives rise to chaotic behavior, scientists believe they will find the means to prevent it in some instances and to induce it in others. The potential applications are unlimited: medical, biochemical, psychiatric, meteorological, computer, and many more. So, while admitting that certain events in nature don't follow a perfect mathematical and predictable order, chaos theory says that they can still be understood and in some cases predicted and controlled.

So it is with the financial markets. People are not machines ordered and structured by mathematics; they are beings of choice. And people *are* the markets.

Literally millions of market decisions are made each day, and the results of each one has its effect on price movements. The idea that such a complex set of components, which includes free will, can be modeled and predicted with mathematical exactness is laughable. You can never predict with *absolute certainty* how the collection of individuals that make up the markets will react to events nor what new conditions will arise. But there is order to the chaos, and it is the speculator's job to find it.

Market forecasting is a matter of probabilities; the risk of being wrong is always present. The best you can do is minimize risk by maximizing knowledge — by understanding the original conditions that give rise to probable future events. That way, it is possible to keep the odds in your favor and to be right more often than not in making market decisions. The first step in obtaining this knowledge is to find a way to monitor the pulse of market behavior.

Dow Theory, if properly understood, is like the physician's highly sensitive heart monitor or the weather forecaster's barometer; it is one tool to be used as an aid in forecasting future events within the bounds of probability. It won't tell you the causes of change, but it will indicate the symptoms that lead to change. It won't tell you exactly what is going to happen, but it will give you a general overview of what is *likely* to happen. As William Peter Hamilton[1] put it, "Dow theory is a commonsense method of drawing useful inferences as to future market movements from the recorded daily price fluctuations of the . . . [market] averages."

Properly considered, Dow Theory provides the key starting point with which to analyze stock market behavior. Many of its definitions and principles apply not only to the stock market but to all financial markets as well.

GOOD IDEAS OFTEN MISUNDERSTOOD

The body of ideas known as Dow Theory is a composite of the work of Charles Dow, William Peter Hamilton, and Robert Rhea. Charles Dow was the founder of Dow Jones & Company and co-founder and editor of the *Wall Street Journal* until his death in 1902. He originated the idea of an index of stock averages with the Dow Jones Industrial average in 1895. In 1897, he created an average index for railroad stocks on the premise that the industrial and rails indexes would be indicators for the two basic economic sectors, production and distribution.

Dow intended the indexes to be an indicator of business activity and never himself employed them to forecast stock price movements. Although he had only five years of data to work with until his death, his observations were nevertheless remarkable in both scope and accuracy.

Dow himself never organized and formalized his ideas into a theory of economic forecasting, but a friend of his named A. J. Nelson attempted such a formalization in *The ABC of Stock Speculation,* published in 1902. It was Nelson who dubbed Dow's methods Dow Theory.

William Peter Hamilton, who worked under Dow, was the most articulate Dow Theory advocate of his day. After Dow's death in 1902, Hamilton continued to expound upon and refine Dow's ideas primarily through editorials in the *Wall Street Journal* from 1903 until his death in 1929. In addition, he wrote a book called *The Stock Market Barometer* in 1922 in which he gave Dow Theory a somewhat more detailed and formal structure beyond the scope of what was permissible in an editorial format.

Robert Rhea, forced through injury to work from his bed from 1922 until his death in 1939, was an admirer of both Hamilton and Dow and profited handsomely by applying their principles to stock price forecasting. Through detailed study, Rhea better defined the principles and methodology of the theory and developed the first set of publicly available charts of the daily closings of the Dow Jones Industrial and Railroad averages with volume included.

Among the many contributions Rhea made to the theory were his observations characterizing volume relationships as a further indication of the future of price movements. In addition, although he didn't coin the name, he discovered the concept of relative strength, which will be discussed in Chapter 8. His book, *The Dow Theory,* published by *Barron's* in 1932 and now out of print, synopsizes Hamilton's work and provides an excellent reference for understanding the principles of Dow Theory. In a later book, *Dow Theory Applied to Business and Banking,* Rhea demonstrated the consistency with which Dow Theory accurately predicted the future course of business activity.

In all his writings, Rhea emphasized that Dow Theory was designed as an *aid* or tool to enhance the speculator's or investor's knowledge, *not* as an all-encompassing, rigorous, technical theory that could be divorced from knowledge of fundamental market and economic conditions. Dow Theory is, by definition, a technical theory; that is, it is a method of forecasting which relies on the study of patterns of price movements to infer future price behavior. In this sense, it is the father of modern technical analysis.

After Rhea's death, Dow Theory fell into less competent hands. Men who failed to grasp the essential principles of the theory misapplied and misinterpreted it, to the point that it is now generally considered dated and of little use as a technical tool in the modern markets. This is simply not true. I performed a study applying Dow Theory's principles to the Industrial and Railroad (later Transportation) averages from 1896 to 1985 and found that Dow Theory tactics accurately captured an average of 74.5% of business expansion price movements and 62% of recession price declines from confirmation date to market peaks or bottoms, respectively.

In addition, the study shows that, except for periods of World War, the stock market accurately predicted changes in the business trend with a median lead time of six months and anticipated the peaks and troughs of business cycles with a median lead time of one month. The average theoretical rate of return attained by buying and selling the Industrial and Transportation indexes according to a strict interpretation of Dow Theory from 1949 to 1985 is a 20.1% uncompounded average annual return.[1] To this it should be added that Dow Theory would have had an investor short through the 1987 crash (as I was). No other forecasting method can boast such a consistent and enduring record of success. Dow Theory therefore warrants significant investigation by any serious speculator or investor.

THE "HYPOTHESES" OF DOW THEORY

In his book, *The Dow Theory,* Rhea listed what he called the "hypotheses" and "theorems" of Dow Theory. Actually, they should be termed principles and definitions, because Dow Theory isn't a strict system like mathematics or the physical sciences. That aside, since so many interpretations of Dow Theory are wrong, I'm going to go right to the source. I'll present Rhea's observations in the order he gave them and in his own words.[2] For the most part, these ideas stand firm today but warrant some clarification and minor revision, which follows after each quote.

According to Rhea, Dow Theory rests on three basic hypothesis that must be accepted "without any reservation whatsoever."

Hypothesis number 1:
Manipulation: Manipulation is possible in the day to day movement of the averages, and secondary reactions are subject to such an influence to a more limited degree, but the primary trend can never be manipulated.

The essence of this observation is that the stock market is too diverse and too complex for one person or group to affect prices in the market as a whole for a sustained period of time. It is a crucial tenet of Dow Theory because if the movement of market prices as a whole *could* be artfully changed according to the will of one person, looking at an average index would lose any meaning beyond deciphering what the manipulator was up to. The critical importance of Hypothesis 1 will become even more evident when we examine Hypothesis 2.

Dow, Hamilton, and Rhea all thought that the degree of manipulation in their time, both by individuals and through pools, was highly overestimated. They all thought that cries of manipulation were, predominantly, desperate attempts by individuals who made mistakes in speculation to explain away their errors without claiming self-responsibility.

I believe the same is true today. In the context of our modern, highly regulated markets, manipulation by individuals is practically impossible, even in the short term. Program trading, however, can be an important form of manipulation, as will be described in Chapter 6. It is still true that the primary trend cannot be manipulated in a fundamental, long-term sense, but the character of the trend can be changed, as we learned during and since the crash in October, 1987. Institutional trading, because of the billions of dollars involved, can accelerate the primary trend in either direction.

Hypothesis number 2:
The Averages Discount Everything: The fluctuations of the daily closing prices of the Dow-Jones rail and industrial averages afford a composite index of all hopes, disappointments, and knowledge of everyone who knows anything of financial matters, and for that reason the effects of coming events (excluding acts of God) are always properly anticipated in their movement. The averages quickly appraise such calamities as fires and earthquakes.

[Note: To Rhea's parenthetical observation "(excluding acts of God)," should be added "and excluding acts of government, especially acts of the Federal Reserve Board."]

In Charles Dow's terms, the same basic idea was stated as follows:

The market is not like a balloon plunging hither and thither in the wind. As a whole, it represents a serious, well-considered effort on the part of farsighted and well-informed men to adjust prices to such values as exist or which are expected to exist in the not too remote future.[3]

The major refinement necessary to bring these observations up to date is that they apply not just to the Dow Jones Industrial and Transportation averages, but to all well-formulated market indices, including bond, currency, commodity, and options indices.

There is nothing mystical about either the discounting effect or the business forecasting value reflected in the market averages. Investors (those who hold securities and other instruments long-term) use the stock and other market exchanges to allocate their capital toward companies, commodities, or other financial instruments which they think are most likely to be profitable. They place their economic resources according to their evaluations of past performance, future prospects, individual preferences, and future expectations. Ultimately, the companies and investors who best anticipate the future demand of consumers (consumers in the broadest sense, including those in the capital, wholesale, and retail markets) survive and are the most profitable. Correct investments are rewarded with profits, and incorrect investments suffer losses.

The result of the actions of speculators and investors through the financial markets is a tendency to expand profitable ventures and restrict the unprofitable. Their actions can do nothing about the past and cannot solve the problem of the limited convertibility of capital goods already in existence, but they generally do stop good money from being thrown after bad. The movement of the market averages is simply a manifestation of this process.

If, on average, market participants failed to correctly anticipate future business activity, we would experience a continuing decline in wealth, and there would be no such thing as a sustained bull market. The fact that, on average, stock traders do properly predict the future of business activity causes the cycle of stock price movements to lead changes in the business cycle. The time lag results from the fact that stock transactions are liquid, whereas business adjustments, because of the limited convertibility of inventories and capital goods, are not.

When Rhea stated "the effects of coming events (excluding acts of God) are always *properly* anticipated" (emphasis added), he really meant it. But implicit in his statement is a recognition that "properly" discounting includes a divergence of opinion on the effects that present events will have on future business activity. The market averages represent optimists, pessimists, and "realists"—a full spectrum of individuals and institutions with specialized knowledge that no one person can duplicate.

Rhea didn't intend to imply that market participants are *always* predominantly right in their interpretation of coming events, but he did mean to imply that the averages always reflect the predominance of opinion. To the practiced observer, the averages will indicate the direction and strength of the long-term trend, they will show when the markets are *overbought* or *oversold,* they will tell when the tide of opinion is changing and when the risk of involvement in the markets is too great to participate in any significant way.

I added the note "excluding acts of government" to Rhea's hypothesis because government legislation, monetary and fiscal policy, and trade policy, like natural disasters, can have an immediate and dramatic impact on market price movements because they have enormous long-term economic impact. And because government policy makers are human beings, it is impossible to always correctly anticipate what they will do. An excellent example of this occurred on July 24, 1984, when Fed Chairman Paul Volcker announced that the Fed's restrictive policy was "inappropriate." In anticipation of easier credit policies, the stock market averages made their low that day, and the new bull market began.

Hypothesis number 3:

The Theory Is Not Infallible: The Dow Theory is not an infallible system for beating the market. Its successful use as an aid in speculation requires serious study, and the summing up of evidence must be impartial. The wish must never be allowed to father the thought.

The stock market is a collection of individual human beings, and human beings are fallible. With almost every stock trade, one person is right and another is wrong. While the averages do in fact represent the net effect, or "collective wisdom" of market participants' judgements about the future, history shows time and again that millions of people can be as wrong as one, and the stock market is no exception. The nature of the market simply allows participants to *adjust and correct their errors rapidly.* Any method of analysis that claims the markets are infallible is flawed at its roots.

The theory of "efficient markets" is a case in point. The main premise is that with the advent of computers, information is disseminated so fast and efficiently that it is impossible to "beat the market." This is nothing more than an extrapolation into absurdity of Dow Theory's tenet that "the averages discount everything." It is also ridiculous. The idea that everyone receives all significant information simultaneously is absurd because everyone doesn't agree on what is "significant." Even if everyone did receive exactly the same information simultaneously, they would respond to it according to their own particular circumstances and preferences. If everyone knew exactly the same things and responded the same way, then *there would be no market!* You must always remember that markets exist to facilitate exchange, and exchange is the result of differences in value preferences and differences in judgments.[4]

The predictive value of the market indices lies in the fact that they are statistically representative of a consensus of opinion expressed with money invested in the markets. Ultimately, it is people's judgements and preferences that determine prices. If you ask floor traders what is behind a price rise in their market, many will half-jokingly respond, "More buying than selling." What that answer really means is, "I don't know the reasons, but the predominance of opinion, as expressed by money changing hands on the exchange floor, is that prices are going up."

The primary task of the speculator is to identify the major active factors which drive or will change the predominant trend of market participants' opinions, and the market indices provide the best tool with which to correlate events with public opinion on financial matters. The events considered can include everything from political and economic developments, to technological innovations, to fashion trends, to the earnings prospects of a particular company. Since this can only be done in the context of history, the best you can do is identify the predominant factors of the past and project them on to the future. Some factors remain constant throughout history; and in general, the fundamentals which guide opinion change slowly over time. With effort, you can abstract those fundamentals and forecast the future with a high probability of accuracy.

In Hamilton's terms, the averages are a *barometer* for economic forecasting. In weather forecasting, the barometer is a tool for measuring changes in atmospheric pressure. Since changing atmospheric pressure always precedes changes in weather conditions, the barometer is an invaluable tool in predicting weather changes. But the barometer in itself tells the forecaster nothing about the type or quantity of precipitation to expect, nor will it accurately correlate to exact temperature changes. Similarly, the market averages are an essential tool in economic forecasting, but a great deal of supplemental information is required to piece together the entire puzzle.

THE "THEOREMS" OF DOW THEORY

After Rhea stated the hypotheses or assumptions of Dow Theory, he went on to deduce a set of what he called "theorems" from the writings of Dow and Hamilton. Rhea published these formulations in 1932, and they are essentially accurate to this day. But they cannot be taken out of context. To better understand these formulations, I recommend obtaining a complete set of the Dow Industrial and Transport averages, including volume figures, and relating the movements of the averages to the editorials of Hamilton and Rhea, which can be found in the archives of *The Wall Street Journal* and *Barron's*. Unfortunately, there is no substitute for doing this on your own. Once you grasp the nature of Hamilton's and Rhea's thinking, you can more easily apply it to our modern context, especially if you bear in mind a few refinements which will be included in the following discussion as they apply. (Refer to Figure 4.1 throughout the discussion.)

Theorem number 1:
Dow's Three Movements: There are three movements of the averages, all of which may be in progress at one and the same time. The first, and most important, is the

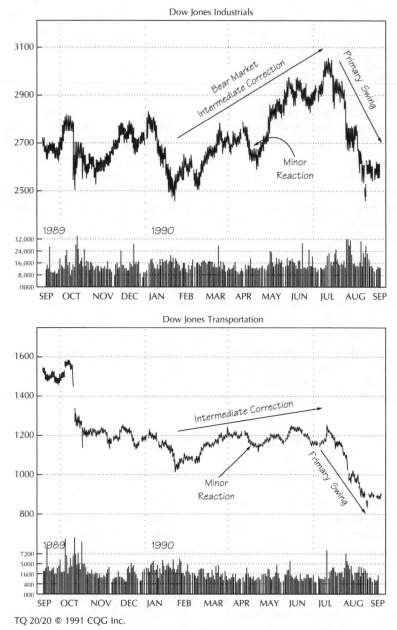

TQ 20/20 © 1991 CQG Inc.

Figure 4.1 The Daily Bar Chart of the Dow Industrial and Transportation Average, with volume included.

primary trend: the broad upward or downward movements know as bull or bear markets, which may be of several years duration. The second, and most deceptive movement, is the secondary reaction: an important decline in a primary bull market or a rally in a primary bear market. These reactions usually last from three weeks to as many months. The third, and usually unimportant, movement is the daily fluctuation.[4]

While basically accurate in Rhea's terms, Dow's three movements apply not only to the averages, but to any market. An easy to remember reformulation of Rhea's first theorem is:

There are three trends in the stock averages and in any market: the short-term trend, lasting from days to weeks; the intermediate-term trend, lasting from weeks to months; and the long-term trend, lasting from months to years. All three trends are active all the time and may be moving in opposing directions.

The long-term trend is by far the most important trend and the easiest to identify, classify, and understand. It is of primary concern to the investor and, to a lesser extent, the speculator. The intermediate- and short-term trends are subsidiary components of the long-term trend and can only be understood and fully taken advantage of through a recognition of their status within the long-term.

The intermediate-term trend is of secondary importance to the investor and of primary importance to the speculator. It can move with the long-term trend or against it. If the intermediate-term trend significantly retraces the long-term trend, it is characterized as a secondary reaction or a correction. The characteristics of a secondary reaction must be closely evaluated to avoid confusing it with a change in the long-term trend.

The short-term trend is the least predictable and is of primary concern only to the trader. The speculator's and investor's interest in the short-term trend should consist almost solely in optimizing profits and minimizing losses by timing of buys and sells within the short-term movement.

Classifying price movements in terms of the three trends isn't just a mental exercise. The investor who is aware of the three trends focuses on the long-term trend, but depending on how hard he wants to work, he can use intermediate- and short-term movements that run contrary to the primary trend to optimize profits in several ways. First, if the long-term trend is up, he may choose to profit from a secondary reaction by selling stock short throughout the correction and then using the profits to pyramid his long position somewhere near the turning point of the correction. Second, he may do the same thing by buying puts or selling calls. Third, he may ride through the contra-move with confidence, knowing that it is an intermediate-, not a long-term, move. And finally, he may use short-term movements to time buys and sells for optimum profitability.

For the speculator, the same kind of thinking applies, except that he is not interested in holding positions through secondary reactions that move against him; his object is to move with the intermediate-term trend in either direction. The speculator can use the short-term trend to look for signs that the intermediate-term trend is changing. The mind set is different from that of the investor, but the basic principles used to identify change are very similar.

Since the early eighties, program trading and improvements in the dissemination of information have dramatically increased the volatility of intermediate market movements. Since 1987, daily fluctuations of 50 or more points in a day have become commonplace. Because of this, I think the wisdom of the long-term "buy and hold" approach to investment is now questionable at best. To me, it seems self-evident that it is a waste to hold long positions through corrections, watching as years of gains are whittled down to almost nothing. True enough, in most cases those gains will come back over a period of months to years. But if you focus on the intermediate-term trend, the bulk of these large losses are avoidable. I therefore think the main focus of the prudent investor should be on the intermediate-term trend.

But to accurately focus on the intermediate-term trend, you have to understand it in relation to the long-term, or primary trend.

Theorem number 2:

Primary Movements: The primary movement is the broad basic trend generally known as a bull or bear market[5] extending over periods which have varied from less than a year to several years. The correct determination of the direction of this movement is the most important factor in successful speculation. *There is no known method of forecasting the extent or duration of a primary movement.* [Emphasis added]

Knowing the long-term trend, or primary movement, is the essential minimum requirement for successful speculation and investment. The speculator who knows and is confident of the long-term trend has enough knowledge to make a decent living, given at least minimum prudence in timing specific market selections. Although there is in fact no way to predict with certainty the extent (how big) or duration (how long) of a primary movement, it is possible to characterize primary movements and secondary reactions statistically using historical price movements as a data base.

Rhea characterized all price movements in Dow history as to type, extent, and duration but had only about three decades of data to work with. Remarkably, there is little difference between the characterizations he made then, and those made now with 92 years of data.[6] For example, the bell curve distributions of both the extents and durations of secondary reactions in both bull and bear markets, classified jointly or separately, is virtually the same now as it was when Rhea published his data in 1932; there are just more data points now.

This is truly remarkable because it tells us that, with all the sophistication and knowledge gained in the last half century, it is obvious that the *psychology* which drives market price movements is very similar over time. What this means to the professional speculator is that it is *highly probable* that market movements will fall within a limited range of their historical extent and duration medians. If a price movement extends beyond its median levels, then the statistical risk of being involved in that trend grows each day. If carefully weighed and applied, this dimension of risk assessment can add significantly to the probability of accurately forecasting the future of price movements.[7]

Theorem number 3:

Primary Bear Markets: A primary bear market is the long downward movement interrupted by important rallies. It is caused by various economic ills and does not terminate until stock prices have thoroughly discounted the worst that is apt to occur. There are three principal phases of a bear market: the first represents the abandonment of hopes upon which stocks were purchased at inflated prices; the second reflects selling due to decreased business and earnings, and the third is caused by distress selling of sound securities, regardless of their value, by those who must find a cash market for a least a portion of their assets.

Several aspects of this definition need to be clarified. The distinguishing characteristic of the bear market movement is that the "important rallies," or secondary corrections, in both the Industrials and the Transports never penetrate the previous bull market top or previous intermediate highs jointly. The "economic ills" referred to are, almost without fail, the result of government action: interventionist legislation, grossly restrictive tax and trade policies, irresponsible monetary and/or fiscal policy, and major wars.[8]

Based on my own Dow Theory classification of the market averages from 1896 to the present, some of the key characteristics of bear markets are as follows:

1. The median extent of bear markets is a 29.4% decline from the previous bull market high, with 75% of all bear markets declining between 20.4% and 47.1%.

2. The median duration of bear markets is 1.1 years, with 75% of all bear markets lasting between 0.8 and 2.8 years.

3. The beginnings of bear markets *usually* follow a "test" of the previous bull market high on low volume followed by sharp declines on high volume. A "test" is when price levels closely approach but never reach the previous high point jointly. The low volume during this "test" is a key indication that confidence is at a low ebb and can easily turn into an "abandonment of hopes upon which stocks were purchased at inflated prices" (see Figure 4.2).

4. After an extended bear swing, secondary reactions are *usually* marked by sudden and rapid advances followed by decreasing activity and the formation of a "line," which ultimately leads to slower declines to new lows (see Figure 4.3).

5. The confirmation date of a bear market is the date when prices on both the averages break below the low point of the last bull market correction and continue to move downward. It is not atypical for one average to lag the other in time (see Figure 4.4).

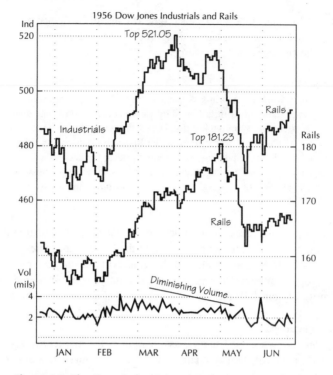

Figure 4.2 The Dow Industrial and Rails Averages—the be-gining of the 1956 bear market. An example from history of the typical beginnings of a bear market. The highs made on low volume indicate the "abondonment of hopes on which stocks were purchased at inflated prices."

6. Intermediate bear market rallies are usually inverted "V" patterns where the low is made on high volume and the high is made on low volume (see Figure 4.5).

Rhea made another observation about bear markets that deserves critical at-tention:

At the end of the bear period the market seems to be immune to further bad news and pessimism. It also appears to have lost its ability to bounce back after severe declines and has every appearance of having reached a state of equilibrium where speculative activities are at low ebb, where offerings do little to depress prices, but where there ap-pears to be no demand sufficient to lift quotations. . . . Pessimism is rampant, dividends are being passed, some important companies are usually in financial difficulty. Because of all these things, stocks make a "line." [W]hen this "line" is definitely broken on the upside, the daily fluctuations of the . . . averages show a tendency to work to slightly higher ground on each rally, with the ensuing declines failing to pass through the last

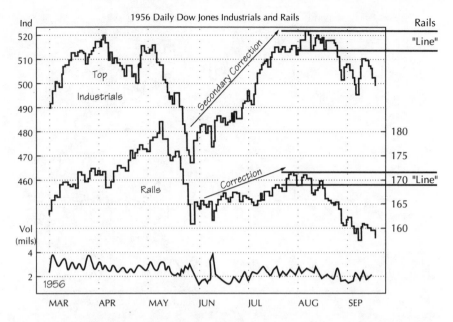

Figure 4.3 The Dow Industrial (top) and Rails Averages (lower)—the first secondary correction of the 1956 bear market. In bear markets, secondary reactions are *usually* marked by sudden and rapid advances followed by decreasing activity and the formation of a "line," which ultimately leads to slower declines to new lows.

immediate low. It is then . . . that a speculative position on the long side is clearly indicated. [See Figure 4.6.]

This observation applies equally to the commodities markets minus, of course, the statement made about dividends.

Theorem number 4:

Primary Bull Markets: A primary bull market is a broad upward movement, interrupted by secondary reactions, and averaging longer than two years. During this time, stock prices advance because of a demand created by both investment and speculative buying caused by improving business conditions and increased speculative activity. There are three phases of a bull period: the first is represented by reviving confidence in the future of business; the second is the response of stock prices to the known improvement in corporations earnings; and the third is the period when speculation is rampant and inflation [of stock prices] apparent—a period when stocks are advanced on hopes and expectations. [See Figure 4.7.]

This definition also needs clarification. The distinguishing characteristic of a bull market is that price movements in all major averages continue jointly to establish new high points, react in declines to low points somewhere above the lows

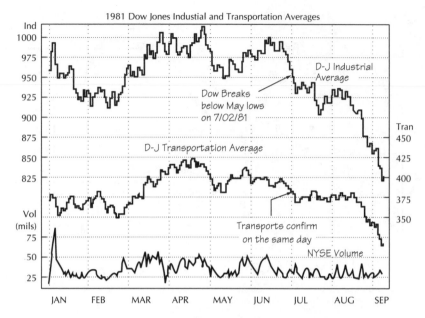

Figure 4.4 The 1981 Dow Jones Industrials and Transportation Averages—the bear market confirmation. In order for a bear market to be confirmed, both averages have to pass below previous important intermediate lows. In this case, the Dow breaks below the May lows on July 2. The Transports confirm the bear market on the same day. The confirmation date should not be confused with a sell signal, which occurred on July 2.

in previous secondary reactions, and then proceed to new high points. Declines in secondary reactions do not jointly fall below the previous important market lows. Some of the major characteristics of primary bull markets are:

1. The median extent of primary bull markets is a 77.5% increase in prices from the previous bear market low point.

2. The median duration of primary bull markets is two years and four months or 2.33 years. 75% of all bull markets in history have lasted more than 657 days (1.8 years), and 67% have lasted between 1.8 and 4.1 years.

3. The beginnings of bull markets are virtually indistinguishable from the last secondary reaction in the bear market until the passage of some time. (See Rhea's quote above and replace "the endings of bear markets" with "the beginnings of bull markets".) (See again Figure 4.6.)

4. Secondary reactions in bull markets are *usually* marked by sharp rates of price decline relative to the preceding and ensuing price increases. In addition, the beginning of the reaction is usually marked by high volume, with the lows made on low volume (see Figure 4.8).

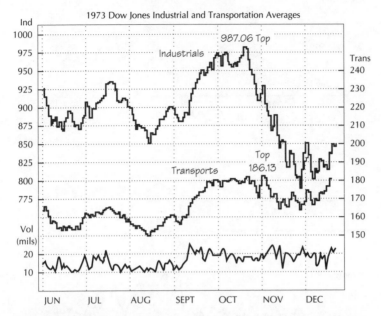

Figure 4.5 The 1973 Dow Jones Industrials and Transportation Averages—a typical "V" pattern for secondary corrections in bear markets. The bear market correction that began in August and topped in November shows the typical inverted "V" pattern of bear market corrections. Note how the highs (987.06 on the Dow, 186.13 on the Transports) were made on relatively low volume, whereas the subsequent sell-off occurred on accelarating volume.

5. The confirmation date of a bull market is the date when prices in both the averages break above the high point of the last bear market correction and continue to move upward.

Theorem number 5:

Secondary Reactions: For the purpose of this discussion, a secondary reaction is considered to be an important decline in a bull market or advance in a bear market, usually lasting from three weeks to as many months, during which intervals the price movement generally retraces from 33% to 66% of the primary price change *since the termination of the last preceding secondary reaction* [emphasis added]. These reactions are frequently erroneously assumed to represent a change of primary trend, because obviously the first stage of a bull market must always coincide with a movement which might have proved to have been merely a secondary reaction in a bear market, the contra being true after the peak has been attained in a bull market.

A secondary reaction, or a correction, is an *important* intermediate-term price movement that significantly retraces the movement of the primary trend. Determining when an intermediate movement that opposes the primary trend is "important"

Figure 4.6 The Dow Industrial and Transportation Averages—the formation of a "Line" at the end of the 1976-78 bear market. When a line is
clearly broken on the upside, it is often a good time to go long. Note:
this breaking of a line on the upside is characteristic of *both* the beginnings of a secondary correction in a bear market and the beginnings of
bull markets.

is the most subtle and difficult aspect of Dow Theory, and misreading such a move
can be very damaging financially to the highly leveraged speculator.

Judging when an intermediate move is a correction requires looking at volume
relationships, statistical data on the historical probabilities of it being a correction,
the general attitude of market participants, the financial conditions of different
companies, the state of the economy, the policies of the Federal Reserve Board,
and many other factors. The classification is somewhat subjective, but it is very
important to be accurate. Quite often, it is difficult or impossible to tell the difference between a secondary reaction and the ending of a primary movement. There
are, however, some helpful indications which will become clear in this discussion
and in later chapters.

My own research bears out Rhea's observation that most secondary corrections
retrace from ⅓ to ⅔ of the previous primary swing (a primary swing is the leg
of the primary movement between secondary reactions) and last from three weeks
to three months. Of all the corrections in history, 61% retraced between 30 and 70%

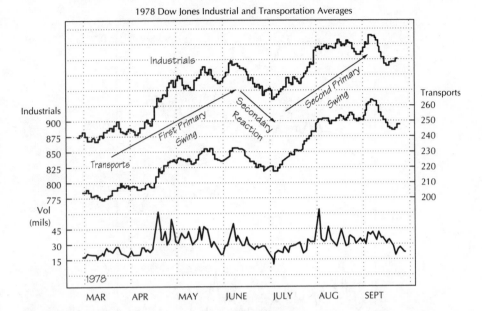

Figure 4.7 The Dow Industrial and Transportation Averages—the early stages of the 1978-81 bull market. The typical early stages of a bull market—in this case, the first and second primary swings interrupted by the first secondary reaction. The first primary swing illustrates what Rhea described as, "...reviving confidence in the future of business.

of the previous primary swing, 65% last between three weeks and three months, and 98% last from two weeks to eight months. Another distinguishing characteristic is that the rate of change of price movements in secondary reactions are typically swifter and sharper than the movement of the primary trend.

Secondary reactions should not be confused with *minor* reactions that occur frequently within primary and secondary price movements. Minor reactions move in opposition to the intermediate trend and last less than two weeks (14 calendar days) 98.7% of the time. They have virtually no impact on the intermediate or long-term trends. Only nine movements lasting less than two weeks of the 694 intermediate movements (both up and down) in the history of the Transports and Industrial averages to date (October 1989) warrant classification as secondary corrections.

The key term in Rhea's definition of a secondary reaction is *important*. As a general rule, any movement retracing more than ⅓ of the previous primary swing is *important* if it occurs as a result of fundamental changes in the economy, not just technical factors. For example, if the Fed raised margin requirements from 50 to 70% in the stock market, there would be a substantial liquidation that had nothing to do with the health of the economy or of the companies whose stocks were affected. Such a movement would be minor. If on the other hand, half of California fell into the sea in a major earthquake and the market sold off 600 points in three days, the sell-off would be major because the earnings of companies would be affected.

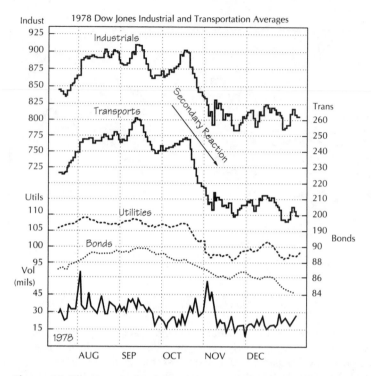

Figure 4.8 The Dow Indusrtial and Transportation Averages—a secondary reaction in the 1978 bull market. Secondary reactions in bull markets are *usually* marked by sharp rates of price decline relative to the preceding and ensuing price increases. The beginnings of secondary reactions are usually marked by high volume, with the lows made on low volume.

Making the distinction between minor reactions and secondary corrections isn't always this clear-cut, however, and is the only somewhat subjective element of Dow Theory.

Rhea likened secondary reactions to the pressure control system on a boiler system. In a bull market, the secondary correction is the safety valve which relieves the pressure of an overbought market. In a bear market, the secondary reaction is additional fire in the furnace to build up pressure that is lacking from an oversold condition.

CONCLUSION

Dow Theory alone is by no means *the comprehensive* way to forecast market behavior,[9] but it is an invaluable component of knowledge that no prudent speculator should ignore. Many of the principles of Dow Theory are implicit in the language of Wall Street and the vocabulary of market participants without their even knowing it. For example, most market professionals have a general impression of what a correction is, but no one that I know of has defined a correction in the objective terms that Dow Theory does.

By reviewing the basic tenets of Dow Theory, we have learned a general method of gauging the future of market price movements by studying both current and historical price movements of the market averages. We now have a general idea of what a trend is. We know that there are three trends that are simultaneously active in any market and the relative importance of each to the trader, speculator, and investor.

Bearing these ideas in mind, it is now time to gain a deeper understanding of price trends. After all, if you know what the trend is, and if you know when it is most likely to change, then you really have all the knowledge you need to make money in the markets.

5

A True Understanding
of Trends

UPTREND, DOWNTREND,
MOVE ALL AROUND TREND

One of the most amazing things to me is how few people, even market professionals, understand what a trend is. For example, if someone threw Figure 5.1 at me
and asked me what the trend was in gold, what do you think I would answer? The
best answer would be, "Which trend are you talking about?"

When I look at this chart, I see three separate and distinct trends: the long-term
trend, which is down; the intermediate trend, which is up; and the short-term trend
(or the minor trend), which is down (see Figure 5.2). When identifying a price
trend, you have to be very specific and very consistent.

When I was training traders, virtually every one of them would come up to
me with a chart with the trendline drawn incorrectly, and say something like, "Vic,
look at this, the trendline has been broken. Isn't this a terrific buy?" If you don't
truly understand what a trend is, you can draw a trendline on a chart virtually
any way you want to, and the conclusions you draw from looking at this so-called
"trendline" will be useless.

I'll demonstrate in detail how to correctly and consistently draw a trendline in
Chapter 7. For now, let's gain some broader insights into what a trend is exactly,
and how it changes.

LET'S REDUCE IT TO BASICS

Probably the single most important piece of information you can get from Dow
Theory is the definition of a trend, which is implied but never clearly stated, and
the distinction between the long-term, intermediate-term, and short-term trends. It
is only by understanding what a trend is that you can determine when a change of
trend occurs. And it is only by accurately identifying a change of trend that you

TQ 20/20 © 1991 CQG Inc.

Figure 5.1 Daily bar charts of December 1990 Gold Futures—what is the trend in gold? There are three trends which are marked and clarified in Figure 5.2.

TQ 20/20 © 1991 CQG Inc.

Figure 5.2 Daily (top) and weekly (bottom) bar charts of December 1990 Gold Futures—the three trends. The long-term trend (months to years), indicated by line A on the lower chart, is down. The intermediate-term trend (weeks to months), indicated by line B, is up. And the short-term trend (days to weeks), indicated by line C, is down.

can accurately time your buys and sells to maximize profits and minimize losses in any market. From Dow Theory, I have abstracted the following definitions:

Upward Trend—An upward trend is a series of successive rallies that penetrate previous high points, interrupted by sell-offs or declines which terminate above the low points of the preceding sell-off. In other words, an uptrend is a price movement consisting of a series of higher highs and higher lows[1] (see Figure 5.3).

Downward Trend—A downward trend is a series of successive declines which penetrate previous low points, interrupted by rallies or increases which terminate below the high points of the preceding rally. In other words, a downtrend is a price movement consisting of a series of lower lows and lower highs (see Figure 5.4).

If you learn anything from this book, learn these definitions. They are very, very simple but also of *crucial* importance. These definitions are completely general in that they apply to any market and to any time period. I think it is simple to see from the hypothetical figures that following the trend is the way to make money in the financial markets. What is not quite clear in the definitions is how you determine

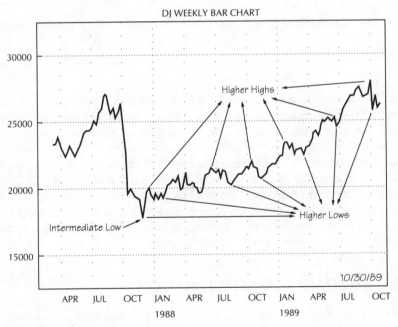

TQ 20/20 © 1991 CQG Inc.

Figure 5.3 The Dow Jones Industrials Weekly Bar Chart—the Dow in an uptrend (bull market). An uptrend is a price movement consisting of a series of higher highs and higher lows.

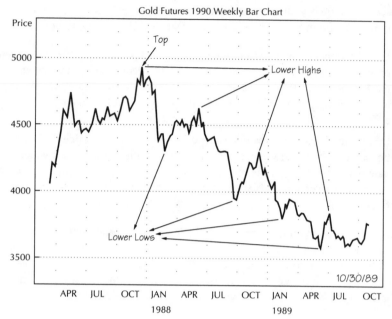

Figure 5.4 The 1989 Gold Futures Weekly Bar Chart—gold in a downtrend. A downtrend is a price movement consisting of a series of lower lows and lower highs.

where the previous high and low points are. This depends totally on whether you're focusing your trading activities in the short-term, intermediate-term, or long-term trend—that is, whether you are trading, speculating, or investing.

No matter what market or what time period you participate in, you won't make money (except by luck) unless you know the direction of the trend and how to identify a change of trend. While Dow Theory is still fresh on your mind, there are some additional observations from it that can be extremely useful. A few of these observations apply only to the equities markets, but most of them apply to any market. Understanding them is of tremendous help in identifying when a change of trend *is likely to occur* or *has already occurred.*

THE IMPORTANCE OF CONFIRMATION

In trading the equities markets, one of the biggest mistakes anyone can make is to draw conclusions based on the movement of just one market average. It is not infrequent for one average to reverse direction for a period of weeks or even months, while another average keeps moving in the opposite direction. This is called a divergence and is useful only in a negative sense. As Rhea put it:

Both Averages Must Confirm: — The movements of both the railroad and industrial stock averages should always be considered together. The movement of one price average must be confirmed by the other before reliable inferences my be drawn. Conclusions based upon the movement of one average, unconfirmed by the other, are almost certain to prove misleading.

Rhea made this observation in 1932. In addition to the Industrial and Railroad (Transportation) indexes, we now have the S&P 500, the Value Line, the Major Market Index, bond indexes, dollar indexes, commodity indexes, and so on. Therefore, bringing this principle up to date implies that instead of "both averages must confirm," the principle should now be "all related averages must confirm." A good example of how this principle must be applied occurred in the period following the October 1987 crash.

First of all, you will recall that one of the "theorems" of Dow Theory is "The theory is not infallible." This was borne out through the crash. Based on Dow Theory, I thought that the crash of October 1987 was the second downleg of a bear market. All related averages went to new lows that broke below previous important lows — a Dow Theory indication of a bear market. But we never entered one. Even so, by a strict Dow Theory reading after the fact, the period following October 19th, 1987, was a secondary correction in a primary bull market, the only one in 91 years that broke below previous secondary lows jointly without leading to a bear market.

It has to be classified as a correction because it did not meet the criterion as defined by Rhea in the definition of a primary bear market. My contention is that if the Fed had not eased in October, and if the Germans and Japanese had not stimulated their economies in December with an infusion of easy credit, a needed bear market would have ensued to correct the malinvestments of previous years. But they did intervene, the S&P bottomed in December, and eventually the market went to new highs. This is where the principle that "all related averages must confirm" came into play.

First, on April 18, 1989, the Transports broke highs established in August 1987. The Value Line followed on July 10th, followed by the S&P 500 index on July 24 (but only 29% of the group indices within the S&P's went to new highs in 1989). But by a strict Dow Theory reading, the confirmation date didn't occur until April 18, when the Industrials average broke through the August 1987 highs and continued to climb (Figure 5.5). Now, I classify the period from August 25, 1987, through to December 4, 1987, as a secondary correction in a primary bull market for the Transports, whereas August 25, 1987, to October 19, 1987, is the correction for the Industrials. It was a confusing time, and without the objectivity of Dow Theory to guide me, it would have been even more confusing.

I should point out that, despite the freak nature (in the context of history) of the 1987 market, a rigorous Dow Theory reading gave a clear intermediate sell signal on October 14 when the Dow Industrials broke below the September 21 lows on accelerating volume (the Transports had already made a new low). It didn't matter whether you classified the long-term trend as a bull or a bear. But if you considered

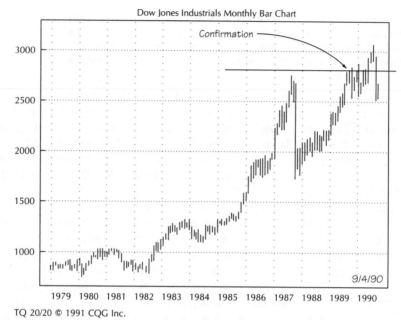

Dow Jones Industrials Monthly Bar Chart

TQ 20/20 © 1991 CQG Inc.

Figure 5.5 The Dow Industrials Weekly Bar Chart—confirmation of a continuing bull market. The confirmation that the bull market was still in progress occurred on April 18, 1989, when the Industrials average broke through the August 1987 highs and continued to climb.

the crash the second leg of a bear move, there were no clear long-term buy signals after that.

Assuming a bear market, I went long on October 24, 1987, looking for a secondary correction. After closing my long position in March 1988, I wasn't significantly involved until early October 1989, at which point I did as described in Chapter 2. Dow Theory was a major contributor to my October 13, 1989, call.

THE FOUR PHASES OF A MARKET

Two of the key indicators I'm referring to as "signals" are the formation of lines and volume relationships. A market is always in one of four technical phases: (1) It is being accumulated (bought by long-term investors), (2) It is being distributed (sold by long-term investors), (3) It is trending up or down, or (4) It is consolidating (adjusting after profit taking in a confirmed trend). Another way to put this is that if a market isn't in a trend, then it is drawing a line. Rhea defined a line as follows:

Lines:—A "line" is a price movement extending two to three weeks or longer, during which period the price variation of both averages moves within a range of approximately 5%. Such a movement indicates either accumulation or distribution. Simultaneous advances above the limits of the "line" indicate accumulation and predict higher prices; conversely, simultaneous declines below the "line" imply distribution, and lower prices are sure to follow. Conclusions drawn from the movement of one average, not confirmed by the other, generally prove to be incorrect.

When lines occur, it is usually at intermediate market tops and bottoms, in which case Rhea's definition applies well. At major market tops, prudent long-term investors with superior information try to sell off their (very large) portfolios over a period of time without creating significant downward pressure on prices. Because there is still enough speculative bullish interest, they manage to *distribute* their stocks in relatively small lots to traders and speculators. As a result, prices fluctuate up and down without trending up or down over a period of several weeks or more forming a "line." This may also happen on any particular stock and in the commodity markets.

When there is finally a predominance of opinion that prices are going to go down, the line is broken on the downside. In trading terms, this is called "a break"— an excellent opportunity to sell short in stocks or commodities (See Figure 5.6).

At major market bottoms, the same thing often happens, but in reverse. Prudent long-term investors see value after price declines and build up large positions for their portfolios to hold over the long-term. Whether to test the market, or to avoid putting upward pressure on prices, they build their positions quietly over a period of several weeks to months. The result again is the formation of a line. When there

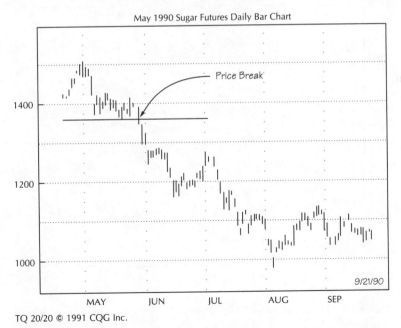

TQ 20/20 © 1991 CQG Inc.

Figure 5.6 May Sugar Futures—a price break, usually a good sell signal.

is finally a predominance of opinion that prices are going up, the line is broken on the up side. In trading terms, this is known as a "breakout"—an excellent buying opportunity in stocks or commodities (see Figure 5.7).

An interesting aspect of looking for breaks or breakouts is that it is the only time when watching the day to day trend of prices is important to every market participant, whether trader, speculator, or investor. As Rhea put it:

> Daily Fluctuations:—Inferences drawn from one day's movement of the averages are almost certain to be misleading and are of but little value except when "lines" are being formed. The day to day movement must be recorded and studied, however, because a series of charted daily movements always eventually develops into a pattern easily recognized as having a forecasting value.

Sometimes, tops and bottoms are reached, and the trend changes without lines being formed. In addition, lines sometimes form in the middle of a confirmed primary trend. This can happen for one of two reasons: either the market has been driven up (or down) rapidly and many traders and speculators take profits, thus temporarily halting the movement of prices; or the market is uncertain of the future and the mixture of opinion holds prices at a relatively constant level. In the first case, I call this process *consolidation*. In the second case, I call it a *waiting market*.

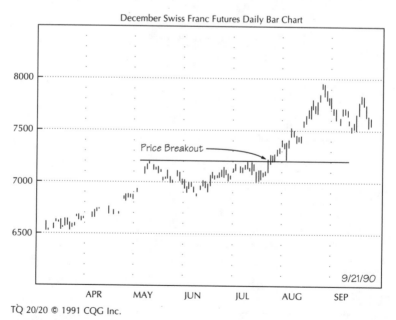

TQ 20/20 © 1991 CQG Inc.

Figure 5.7 December Swiss Franc Futures—a price breakout, usually a good buy signal.

IMPORTANT VOLUME RELATIONSHIPS

For trending markets, the volume relationship is very important. As Rhea put it:

> The Relation of Volume to Price Movements:—A market which has been overbought becomes dull on rallies and develops activity on declines; conversely, when a market is oversold, the tendency is to become dull on declines and active on rallies. Bull markets terminate in a period of excessive activity and begin with comparatively light transactions.

An "overbought" market is, by definition, one in which prices have been driven up by feelings, hopes, and expectations based on factors other than sound business judgement and value considerations. It occurs at a point after people with superior information have largely left the market, and general participants are beginning to abandon their former enthusiasm. The market is ripe for a minipanic wherein the slightest sign of a downward move in prices is enough to start a flurry of selling, putting downward pressure on prices. This is why you see relatively high volume on declines and low volume on advances in an overbought market.

Converse reasoning applies to an oversold market. It occurs after a point where shrewd investors have begun to buy securities whose prices have been driven down in a prior sell-off. A resurgence of hopes and expectations builds in the market which, with slight provocation, will build into a mini-boom in prices on high volume. Although volume relationships apply in any financial market, the stock market is unfortunately the only one where volume figures are immediately available. In the commodities markets, estimated volume figures are released on the following trading day and the actual numbers two days later. It is important to remember that volume relationships *usually,* but not always, apply. They should only be used as subsidiary, not primary, considerations.

CONCLUSION

Now you know what a trend is, what lines are, and some of the key factors which cause or indicate that a trend is changing. You've seen the importance of volume relationships and how they reflect the psychological status of the market. If you learn to think about market behavior in the terms described in this and the last chapter, you will already be a major step ahead of the crowd.

The next step is to reduce this knowledge, especially knowledge of a trend and the change of trend, into a simple and manageable system. What I'm going to present is a charting system that is truly unique and remarkably simple. The system is based on pattern recognition, which is, by definition, a technical method. But before I show it to you, I need to describe both the benefits and the dangers of any technical method.

6

The Merits and Hazards
of Technical Analysis

Wall Street is full of market technicians. Floor traders, upstairs traders, speculators, and even some long-term investors take advantage of the potential to anticipate market movements by identifying patterns that tend to recur over time. There is no mystery in the reason that these patterns develop. All things being equal, people tend, from a psychological standpoint, to respond to a similar set of conditions in a consistent way. But human psychology is enormously complex, and no two sets of market conditions are ever identical; so technical analysis must be applied cautiously to be used successfully in forecasting market behavior.

According to Robert Edwards and John Magee, "Technical Analysis is the science of recording, usually in graphic form, the actual history of trading (price changes, volume of transactions, and so on) in a certain stock or in 'the averages' and then deducing from that pictured history the probable future trend."[1] Their basic premise is very similar to that of Dow Theory—that all of the knowledge available in the marketplace is already factored into prices. But unlike Dow Theory, market technicians think prices and patterns of prices are the *only* considerations that matter.

I am *not* a pure technical analyst, but I have made too much money from technical observations to dismiss technical analysis as some "fundamentalists" do. It is an important auxiliary tool which is largely unrecognized by many market players, especially long-term investors, to help make market decisions in which *all* the odds are in your favor. But standing alone, as the primary means of evaluating investment or speculative alternatives, technical analysis can not only be ineffective but misleading.

A simple survey of professional traders, speculators, and investors would bear out the degree of efficacy of technical analysis. Those who rely totally on charting methods seldom have consistent records. For example, in 1974, I was approached by a technical analyst named Leo who told me that he thought I would profit from his knowledge. I hired him on a trial basis for $125 a week and planned to pay him a percentage on his recommendations that paid out well. Anyway, Leo was in the office at 6:30 A.M. every day, doing over 120 charts in living color, using methods I still don't understand. He worked 16-hour days, and he obviously knew a lot about the markets, maybe too much for his own good.

When I asked him for recommendations, he would show me the charts and say things like, "This stock *might* be forming a bottom," or, "This stock looks like it *may* fill in the gap." But whatever he said, it was always indefinite and always offset by a confusing array of other possibilities. I would ask, "Okay, but what should I do, *buy or sell?*" Leo just couldn't give me a simple, straight answer. And what I remember most about him is that the ends of his shirt sleeves were frayed, and that he ate homemade tuna sandwiches for lunch.

I'm not saying that this is the case for all technical analysts, but the point is that technical analysis, as such, does not lend itself to thinking in essentials. If you watch FNN (The Financial News Network), and you should, you'll see what I'm talking about. Different technical analysts interpret patterns differently, and they all have their own story. In my view, the best thing to do is identify just a few essential technical principles and use them as auxiliary tools. Those who encompass these kinds of technical methods into a broader system which includes rigorous and sound analysis of economic fundamentals and detailed evaluation of specific securities and commodities do quite well by them.

For purposes of this discussion, it is important to understand the activities of three major groups of technicians: tide watchers, manipulators, and purists.

TIDE WATCHERS

Tide watchers is what I call those who attempt to buy and sell in the direction of the intraday ebbs and surges of price trends. This group is relatively unconcerned with the state of the economy, the price-earnings ratio or earnings growth of a given stock, or any other underlying market fundamentals. Rather, their focus is almost entirely on the direction of price movements from moment to moment and day to day. The market moves up or down or sideways, and their goal is to be buyers or sellers or flat (no money in the market) accordingly.

Tide watchers are the locals in the pits of the futures exchanges, the market makers, and the floor traders on any of the major exchanges. They fit into the category of technicians because their sole interest is in the price trend—"The trend is your friend" is the essence of their thinking. Typically, in lieu of any significant news, they try to ride the trend while watching "resistance" and "support" points (see Figure 6.1)—previous highs or lows that make other tidal-type participants wary.

In an uptrend, a previous high point above the current price level is resistance; whereas a previous low is support. In a downtrend, a previous low point below the current price is resistance, whereas a previous high is support. In an uptrend, if a previous high is broken and prices continue to climb, then the tide watchers are buyers, and any significant succession of down ticks (a tick is the smallest

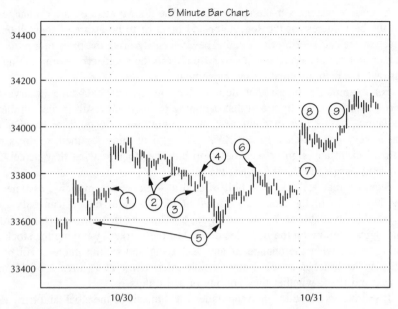

5 Minute Bar Chart

TQ 20/20 © 1991 CQG Inc.

Figure 6.1 December 1989 S&P Futures—intraday resistance and support levels.

1. Previous day's close is support if the market opens higher, and resistance if it opens lower.
2. In lieu of any other reference point, 00 ("evens") serve as resistance or support. In this case, support.
3. Prices test support of previous day's close.
4. "Evens" become resistance.
5. Prices test "evens" support, plus previous day's support level.
6. Prices test resistance established at point 4.
7. Market "gaps" open on positive news regarding leading economic indicators.
8. Initial high near opening becomes resistance.
9. Prices test resistance and then break out on high activity to new highs for the day.

possible price change in any market; ⅛ for stocks, ¹⁄₁₆ for options, and so on) is a possible sell signal. If a previous high is broken and prices fail to move further upward, they are sellers, and any significant upward movement is a possible buy signal. Converse reasoning applies to significant low points. Tide watchers always try to be attuned to what the ever-present "They" are thinking and what "They" will do next, and their method of measurement is the character of changing price movements.[2]

Since tide watchers make up the bulk of the floor traders on the exchanges, it is in the best interest of the speculator and investor to be aware of their potential impact on the short-term price trend. They can easily drive the price of a particular stock or commodity up or down several points in the short term, with nothing but their own interactions creating the movement.

For example, suppose that floor traders on a stock exchange observe that offerings for XYZ are light and that declining prices don't result in any significant liquidation. If this pattern continues, they might conclude quite reasonably that there is very little interest to sell XYZ. The logical thing for them to do is pick up the stock at any sign of weakness—to buy the stock at what they perceive as short-term bargain prices—and test the market.

Suppose that XYZ is 40¼ bid, offered at 40⅜.[3] For simplicity, assume that only 500 shares of the stock are offered at ⅜. The floor traders can only guess how much is available at ½, ⅝, and so on; but thinking that long interest is strong, some shrewd fellow on the floor decides to test the market by buying the stock and waiting to see what the change, if any, in buying and selling interest will be. In particular, he watches to see if any outside orders come in as a result of the price change, and if so, whether they are buy or sell orders.

If sell orders come in, then the trader rids himself of the stock and tries again another day. But if a few buy orders come in and are filled at perhaps ½ and ⅝, then a few more brokers join in. If the process continues, then very quickly a short-term bullish atmosphere is created for the stock.

Up to this point, the floor trader has no idea whether or not there was any change in the earnings prospects for XYZ company, although it is likely that there is some reason for the initial lack of interest to sell. But regardless of the company's prospects, if the movement gains a large enough following on the floor, a mini-boom in the price of the stock can occur. After all, the bullish floor traders involved all have an interest in the price going up.

On the other hand, large sell orders coming from outside can, at any point, squelch the rally. And like any pyramid scheme, to the extent that the mini-boom is purely speculative, those participants at the top stand to lose the most. Similar reasoning can be applied to a mini-bust, which quite commonly occurs shortly after the mini-boom. Program trading can initiate, accelerate, and/or amplify the whole process.

Speculators or investors who are aware of the effects of tide watcher-type activity can use their knowledge in several ways. First, practiced "upstairs"[4] observers can recognize this kind of activity on their monitors and optimize profits by careful timing of their intermediate-term and long-term buys and sells within the intraday cycle. Second, the "legitimacy" of price changes, in terms of their intermediate-term and long-term staying power, can be gauged according to the relationship of the price move to market fundamentals and the movement of the markets considered as a whole. And finally, the character of tide watcher's activity can be a key indicator of the consensus of opinion on the Street.

This last point is probably the most important for the speculator. Like geologists who attempt to predict volcanic activity or earthquakes by monitoring seismic activity, speculators can gauge the tremors of coming market events by monitoring intraday and day to day activity. Specifically, volume numbers, the ratio of advancing issues to declining issues, the short-term response to important economic or market news, and the rate of change of prices all can contribute to an estimate of the predominant driving psychology of market participants.

In the case of the October 13, 1989, sell-off in the stock market, the news that financing fell through on the United Airlines takeover sent the market into a selling panic. This was a clear indication that the tenor of the market was wary. Market opinion was clearly skeptical about the strength of the ongoing bull market—one more sign to indicate that a bear, or at least a secondary correction, might be near at hand.

THE MANIPULATORS

Manipulation is a dirty word on Wall Street. It carries a connotation of the kind of unfairness and dishonesty generally associated with a fixed horse race or dealing from the bottom of the deck in a card game. But in fact, it is an entirely different thing. According to the Random House Dictionary (1969 College Edition), to manipulate is to "manage or influence by artful skill." Webster's 1972 Collegiate Edition adds as a secondary meaning "to control or play upon by artful, unfair, or insidious means." But there is nothing manifestly "insidious" or "unfair" about attempting to profit by managing one's own buying and selling activity in an attempt to cause a change in a price and profit by the move—that is, unless the SEC (Securities and Exchange Commission) thinks there is. Then it becomes insidious because you can go to jail for it. Individuals go to jail, but institutions don't.

The large institutional houses use huge buy and sell programs to manipulate market prices in the short term. Their objective is to profit by playing the disparities in prices between related markets, disparities often induced or exaggerated by their own activity. They rely on the psychology of the tide watchers for their success.

Suppose for example that a $2 billion pension fund decides to liquidate $100 million of its stock portfolio. Knowing that the sale of such large blocks of stocks will probably send the market indexes lower, it decides to take advantage of the fact. During a typically quiet period, usually around 2 P.M., it begins to sell S&P Index futures to consolidate a $200 million short position. This is double the amount of the cash stock position and would take somewhere in the neighborhood of 1,000 to 1,500 contracts to attain—a number easily accommodated by the S&P futures market.

Then, at about 3:10 P.M., the institution begins scale selling of stocks to the tune of about $10 million worth of stocks every five minutes or so, finishing off with one large block sale at the close. Because of the huge amounts of money and stock traded, short interest is generated on floor of the stock exchange, and prices begin moving down. In response, the price of the futures moves down proportionally. Tide watchers ride the crest and accelerate the move in both the cash and the futures markets into a mini-bust.

The institution, while losing a little money by selling stocks on the way down, is more than compensated by the gain made in buying back a successful (and double-sized) short position in futures on the way down. Bear in mind that the margin requirement for the futures is 5%, whereas the margin requirement for stocks is 50%; so using leverage, the upside profit potential is 10 times greater in the futures market.

The next morning, the tide reverses, and buying interest builds, creating a mini-boom. By knowing in advance—with practical certainty—the results of its massive involvement, the institution is able to time its buys and sells and make a handsome profit for itself and for its clients in both markets and in both directions, plus generate some nice commission or fee business. In the end, the market is effectively unchanged, but a lot of money has changed hands. There are many different types of programs, some of them incredibly complex, and not all of them are manipulative. But all in all, it's a nice racket.

For the sake of justice, it should be noted that any "unfairness" inherent in program trading is due not to the practice itself, but to the government's arbitrary regulation of the markets. If "manipulation" is condemned when practiced by an individual, but tolerated if done on a camouflaged but massive scale by institutions, that is clearly unfair. As William J. O'Neil put it:

> They [the institutions] are allowed to hook up directly to the New York Stock Exchange's own computers and spit out massive market orders instantaneously. You and I must contact our brokers and have them transmit our orders by wire to New York, for execution several minutes later.[5]

In lieu of complete deregulation of the markets, which is the ideal alternative as far as I'm concerned, the least the regulators could do is define clearly what "manipulation" is, so that everyone understands the requirements of trading within the bounds of so-called "legality."

Beginning in the mid-1980s, programs completely changed the character of intraday price movements, introducing a degree of uncertainty that never existed before. Now, at any moment, the judgment of one program manager can start a buy or sell program that may create a swing in the market of from 5 to 30 or more points on a purely technical basis (that is, without any fundamental changes in the earnings prospects of the underlying stocks). (See Figure 6.2.)

I used to day-trade the S&P futures by the clock. Before programs, you *never* saw a sell-off last more than 1 ½ hours without some kind of rally. You also very rarely saw the kind of spikes in either direction as you see them now. Because the institutions deal in such huge size, and because the public has fled the markets, when you day-trade the S&Ps now, it feels like you are performing with a gun at your back. At any moment, a program manager can pull the trigger, and the market roars against you before you have time to get out with just a small loss, especially if you are trading large size.

Being caught on the wrong side of a program-induced swing in the short term can be deadly financially to the trader or speculator. But being on the right side

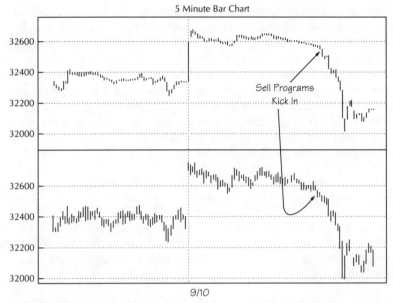

5 Minute Bar Chart

TQ 20/20 © 1991 CQG Inc.

Figure 6.2 Five-minute bar chart for December 1990 S&P Futures and S&P Cash Index—how program trading affects intraday price movements. Prior to program trading, the market never sold off this sharply for so long a period without being interrupted by at least a small rally. Programs move both the futures and the averages dramatically, often confusing one's perception of market price movements.

can be equally rewarding. The problem is that since one person's judgement causes the move, and since no one knows the plan but that person and perhaps a handful of others, being involved in short-term trading is much more difficult today and often can turn into something of a crapshoot. However, by watching the charts of the S&P 500 cash and S&P 500 futures index, prudent speculators or investors can learn to recognize the pattern of program price movements and time their buys and sells to optimize profits.[6] This kind of market timing can add significantly to portfolio profits. Conversely, to buy or sell large blocks of stocks or futures "at the market" in the presence of a program is simply foolish.

Over the intermediate-term and long-term, programs cannot fundamentally manipulate prices, but they can change the *character* of the price trend, accelerating intermediate price movements in one direction or the other. On the upside, their massive involvement can generate long speculative interest. On the short side, they can have a devastating impact on the speed of major market downturns, as happened in the October 1987 crash.

Coming into October, the market was in trouble from a fundamental point of view. Prices were at 21 times earnings, one of the highest PEs in history.

The average book value to price ratio was nominally higher than it was in 1929, and if adjusted for inflation, was *much* higher. These factors, especially when combined with record-breaking debt figures at all levels, made the market ripe for, at minimum, a major correction. The question at the time was not "if" but "when."

The billions of dollars of institutional money involved in the markets prior to October 19 was there purely to profit through various short-term hedge, arbitrage, and manipulative strategies. It was evident that if the Fed tightened substantially, or if the dollar fell significantly, this "hot" money would be withdrawn from the market, dramatically accelerating the downward move. As I said in a *Barron's* interview published in the September 21, 1987, issue:

> When the stock market does slip into a full-fledged downswing, program trading will *exaggerate* the move to such a degree that the sell-off may be the steepest on record . . .

This exaggeration of sell-offs, typically called "unwinding," induces such a degree of uncertainty and risk near the top of major bull movements that the risk/reward in being fully invested in the stock market is heavily weighted toward risk. When change is due, those that change first usually profit the most.

THE PURISTS

Some technical analysts believe, on a formal, theoretical basis, that price is everything, that everything known or knowable with respect to the future of the markets is already contained in market prices and their movements. These are the technical purists, notably R. N. Elliot, Krondodiov, and on a more limited scale, some unthinking followers of the teachings of Edwards and Magee, and some heretical Dow Theorists. In variant forms and to various extents, the technical purists presume that there is a metaphysical inevitability to price movements, that they are somehow *determined* by the dictates of fate, God, evolution, or some other nebulous universal force, and that economic analysis and forecasting consists in finding the right mathematical correlations or cycle times to characterize the movements.

Any attempt to forecast the future by rigorous cycle theory or by strictly mathematical means totally ignores the subjective nature of market activity. In addition, such attempts ignore the fact that government intervention and Federal Reserve policy can dramatically influence the long-term trend, as will be shown in Chapters 9 and 10. To the extent that individuals are successful in applying these types of theoretical systems to market forecasting and analysis, it is mostly because they depart from the rigor that consistency would require. Either their formulations temporarily characterize market behavior because of the consistent behavior of market participants, in which case it is simply a short-term technical observation, or the formulations themselves are so general and so loosely defined that they permit interpretation and individual reasoning to be imposed over them.

In the first case, basing speculative or investment decisions on technical models which predict in advance extent and duration points will be inconsistent—market conditions can change rapidly. In the second case, the formulations are little more than an obstacle to sound reasoning and analysis. In either case, inevitably, conditions will change, attitudes will change, and their market models fall flat.

Again, I want to emphasize that I am not speaking here of *all* methods and applications of technical analysis, just those that claim that the future is predetermined and therefore predictable with rigorous mathematical models.

SUMMARY

Technical analysis provides vital information as long as it is recognized for what it is: a method of characterizing recurring patterns of price movements. These patterns result from a predominantly similar psychological tendency of market participants in making decisions. The greatest value of technical analysis is that it provides a method of measuring the tendency of the market to react in a particular way under similar conditions throughout history.

Given this recognition, technical analysis adds a valuable dimension to market analysis and economic forecasting that is often overlooked by speculators and investors. If understood and concretely defined, technical observations add to the sum of one's knowledge about the nature of the markets and provide an opportunity to identify profitable opportunities that would otherwise go unseen.

7

Where Fortunes
Are Made:
Identifying a
Change of Trend

The fastest and most risk-free way to make money in the markets is to identify a change of trend in a market as early as possible, take your position (long or short), ride the trend, and close your position before or shortly after the trend reverses again. Any market professional will tell you that it is impossible to buy at the lows and sell at the highs (or sell at the highs and buy at the lows) consistently; but with practice, it is very possible to catch 60 to 80% of many intermediate-term and long-term market movements.

To be able to do this, you first have to know what the different markets are, what market instruments are available, where and how they are traded, what the margin requirements are, and so forth.[1] Given this information, the next step is to identify a way to find specific markets that may be good investment opportunities.

To do this, you *could* go to the library and do three or four years of research on all the markets in the world, but by the time you finished your research, you would have forgotten half of what you learned and still have been broke. The other alternative is to learn to look at charts.

To a practiced observer, using bar charts is the simplest and most effective way to pick *potential* buys and sells in any of the various markets. By learning a few simple techniques, you can look through as many as two or three hundred charts in an hour and pull out the roses from the slop. Then, with a more careful examination, you can pick the best of the best, and be left with a choice of five or ten markets that are worth doing some research on. When you go through these charts, what you are looking for is evidence of whether a specific stock, an index, or a commodity is likely to encounter a change of trend.

In the last chapter, I lambasted aspects of technical analysis, but I also said that I thought it was too useful to pass up as an aide in speculation. Now, I want to present my favorite technical methods for identifying a change of trend. They're my favorites for one reason: they have consistently made me money year after year. They are also very simple, easy to remember, and after you apply them for a while, you don't even have to put pencil to paper to "see" what's on the charts.

Interpreting data from charts—recognizing price patterns and inferring future price movements from them—is the province of technical analysis. If you read books on technical methods, you will find countless patterns that have been identified: triangles, head-and-shoulders formations, lines, wedges, bear flags, bull flags, 7-mountains, and many more. I employ very few of these, and attempt to keep my technical methods to certain minimum essentials that stand the test of time and change.

I divide my technical observations into two groups. The first group, which is included in this chapter, deals with the principles of a trend and the change of trend, and I weigh them quite heavily before taking any position in the markets. The second group, presented in the next chapter, deals with auxiliary factors which often accompany a change in trend; and I use them to add or subtract support for my decisions, as the case may be.

The methods I present in this chapter are derived from both my knowledge of Dow Theory and years of experience in evaluating market trends and turning points. Like Dow Theory, they are not infallible and are intended for use as supplemental tools in a broader market forecasting picture. A nice thing about them is that they apply to every market, without exception: stocks, indexes, commodities, bonds—everything. They give results that are right more often than not, and if applied carefully, they will always allow you to retreat from an incorrect decision without suffering heavy losses.

There are two important, and often overlooked, advantages in using charts for making speculative and investment decisions. First, it is easier for most people to think in terms of visual images. Second, by setting concrete points of entry and exit according to the charts, you can more easily remain aloof from the emotional pressures which are so often confusing when money is at stake.

Bear in mind that the technical consistency of charts is best in the long term, slightly worse in the intermediate term, and the most variable in the short term. Patterns on charts exist because market participants respond to similar conditions in similar ways. The mind of the investor works differently than the mind of the speculator, but they do have much in common; and those similarities are reflected in patterns on the charts. But the minds of those that trade on the intraday markets operate by a substantially different set of rules, and the patterns they create must therefore be characterized separately. It is fortunate that intraday traders exist, for they provide invaluable liquidity to the market which is essential for successful speculation and investment; but other than providing liquidity, their involvement does little to affect the intermediate-term and long-term trends.

Although these chart reading methods are "technical" observations, they are technical in the broadest sense; that is, they capture visually a character of human action that has been recurrent throughout the recorded history of market price movements.

DETERMINING THE TREND—DRAWING THE TRENDLINE

From preceding chapters, we already know what a trend is. But to review, a trend is the prevailing direction of price movements within a given time period. In an upward trend, prices rise consistently over time interrupted only by temporary sell-offs, which do not make lower lows than the previous sell-off. A downward trend is the converse of the upward trend—prices move consistently downwards interrupted by temporary rallies that do not make higher highs than the previous rallies. On the chart, trends appear as a sort of saw blade pattern, where prices make higher highs interrupted by higher lows on sell-offs during an uptrend, and lower lows interrupted by lower highs on rallies in a downtrend.

In analyzing a trend on the charts, the most useful tool is the trendline. One of the biggest mistakes made by amateurs and professionals alike is inconsistently defining and drawing the trendline. To be useful, the trendline must accurately reflect the definition of the trend. The method I have devised is very simple and very consistent. It fits both the definition of a trend and the inferences drawn from Dow Theory pertaining to the elements of a change in trend:

1. Select the period of consideration: the long term (months to years), the intermediate term (weeks to months), or short term (days to weeks). It can also be a smaller segment of any of these where a change of slope of the trendline is apparent.

2. For an uptrend within the period of consideration, draw a line from the lowest low, up and to the highest minor low point preceding the highest high so that the line *does not pass through prices in between the two low points* (Figures 7.1 and 7.2). Extend the line upwards past the highest high point. It is possible that the line will go through prices past the highest minor high point. In fact, this is one indication of a change in trend, as will be demonstrated shortly.

3. For a downtrend within the period of consideration, draw a line from the highest high point to the lowest minor high point preceding the lowest low so that the line does not pass through prices in between the two high points. Extend the line past the lowest high point downward (Figures 7.3 and 7.4).

While this method is quite simple, it is extremely consistent and very accurate. The slope of this trendline is a close approximation to the slope you would get by doing a linear regression analysis on the price data over the same time period. Unlike other methods, it prevents you from drawing a trendline to suit your purposes—it prevents you from imposing your wish onto the trendline. It also provides the basis to graphically determine when a change of trend has occurred.

Figure 7.1 December 1989 Live Cattle Futures—drawing the uptrend. For an uptrend, draw the trendline from the lowest low to the lowest low preceding the highest high. without passing through prices between the two points.

Figure 7.2 December 1989 Live Cattle Futures—drawing the uptrend incorrectly. This trendline is wrong because, while it passes from the lowest low to the low preceding the highest high, it passes through prices between the two points. This mistake will result in a false indication of a possible change of trend.

Figure 7.3 December 1989 Bean Oil Futures—drawing the downtrend correctly. For a downtrend, draw the line from the highest high to the highest high preceding the lowest low without passing through prices between the two points.

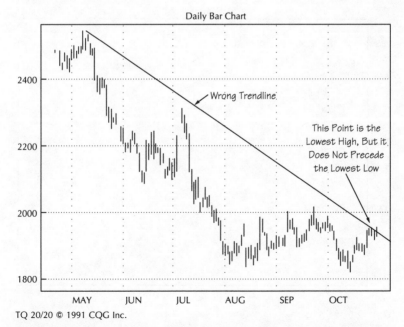

Figure 7.4 December 1989 Oil Futures—drawing the downtrend incorrectly. this trendline is wrong because it is drawn to a point which does not precede the lowest low. Note that while the trendline in the previous figure indicates a possible change of trend, this line doesn't give nearly as strong an indication. This demonstrates the importance of being consistent in drawing trendlines.

73

IDENTIFYING A CHANGE OF TREND: IT'S EASY AS 1-2-3

The ideal way to speculate is to buy at the bottom and sell at the top. Obviously, this is impossible to do with absolute consistency; the markets are too uncertain. But there is a way to determine technically when changes of trend have occurred so that you can catch 60 to 80% of most equities and commodity long-term price moves.

There are three basic changes in price movements that, when they occur in conjunction, *define* a change of trend in any market: stocks, commodities, bonds—everything. The changes are:

1. A trendline is broken. The prices cross the trendline drawn on the chart (Figure 7.5).

2. The trend stops making higher highs in an uptrend or lower lows in a downtrend. For example, in an uptrend after a minor sell-off, prices will rise again but fail to carry above the preceding high point or barely break the high and then fail. The converse would happen in a downtrend. This is often described as a "test" of the high or low point. This condition usually, but not always, occurs when a trend is in the process of changing. When it doesn't occur, price movements are almost always driven by important

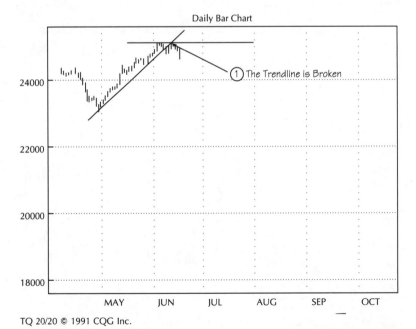

TQ 20/20 © 1991 CQG Inc.

Figure 7.5 The 1990 Value Line Cash Index—breaking the intermediate trendline. The first indication of a change in trend is when prices break a properly drawn intermediate trendline. Condition 1 of the 1-2-3 change of trend criterion.

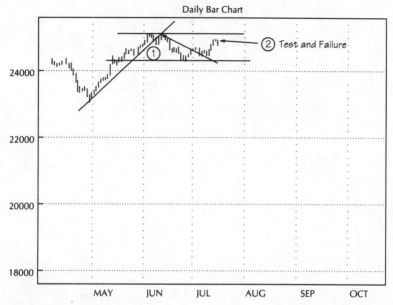

Daily Bar Chart

TQ 20/20 © 1991 CQG Inc.

Figure 7.6 The 1990 Value Line Cash Index—a test and failure of the previous intermediate high. The second indication of a change in trend occurs when prices approach but don't reach a previous high and then fail. Condition 2 of the 1-2-3 change of trend criterion.

news, which causes prices to gap up or down and move erratically with relation to the "normal" price movement (see Figure 7.6).

3. Prices go above a previous short-term minor rally high in a downtrend, or below a previous short-term minor sell-off low in an uptrend (Figure 7.7).

At the point where all three of these events have occurred graphically, there exists the equivalent of a Dow Theory confirmation of a change of trend.[2] Either of the first two conditions alone is evidence of a *probable* change in trend. Two out of three *increases* the probability of a change of trend. And three out of three *defines* a change of trend.

To watch for a change of trend on the charts, all you have to do is translate these principles to graphical terms as follows (refer back to Figures 7.5–7.7):

1. Draw the trendline as described above.

2. For a downtrend, draw a horizontal line through the currently established low point. Draw a second horizontal line through the immediately succeeding minor rally high.

3. For an uptrend, draw a horizontal line through the currently established high point. Draw a second horizontal line through the immediately preceding minor sell-off low.

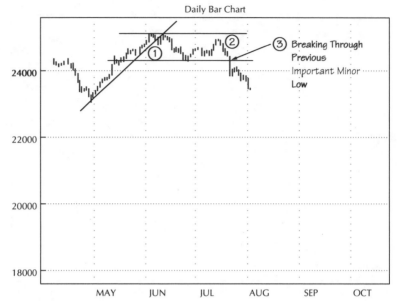

Daily Bar Chart

TQ 20/20 © 1991 CQG Inc.

Figure 7.7 The 1990 Value Line Cash Index—prices breaking below a previous intermediate low. The third and final indication of a change in trend occurs when prices break below a previous important minor low. Condition 3 of the 1-2-3 change of trend criterion.

Consider the case of an uptrend. If prices cross the trendline, mark the chart with a circled 1 at the point of crossing. If prices approach, touch, or slightly break the horizontal line corresponding to the current high and then fail to carry through, mark the chart with a circled 2 at that point. If prices carry through the line corresponding to the immediately preceding sell-off low, mark the chart with a circled 3 at that point. If two out of the three conditions are met, the chances are good that a change of trend will occur. If all three conditions are met, the trend change *has* occurred and is most likely to continue in its new direction.

After a little practice, you can learn to associate the three criteria of a change of trend visually and think of them in terms of 1-2-3: (1) a break in the trend line; (2) a test of the preceding high or low; (3) the breaking of a preceding minor rally high or minor sell-off low. It is as easy as 1-2-3—the trend has changed!

Naturally, trading on these rules alone isn't 100% effective—no method is. Illiquid, news-sensitive, and highly speculative markets and stocks are especially subject to sudden reversals (see Figure 7.9). If you trade on the 1-2-3 criterion, or any other change of trend criteria for that matter, and the market reverses, it is called "getting whipped" or "getting whipsawed." The best way to avoid being whipped, or to minimize your loss if you are whipped, is to follow these rules:

1. Trade only in highly liquid markets that historically aren't subject to sudden and large reversals. On the charts, illiquid markets are characterized by large price movements with sparse activity (Figure 7.8).

2. Avoid, if possible, highly news-sensitive markets or markets that are heavily subject to radical change from government monetary and fiscal intervention. The charts of such markets will be filled with "gaps"—large and sudden changes in prices with no prices printing[3] in between the changes (Figure 7.9).

3. Take positions only when exit points can be set at previous resistance or support levels, which allow you to minimize losses if the market proves you wrong. These exit points are called "stop losses" if they accompany your order, or they can be set and executed yourself, which I call a mental stop (Figure 7.10).

Trading by the 1-2-3 criterion is a simple and effective method that, if applied carefully, works more often than not. One negative when trading by it is that by the time all three conditions are met, you sometimes miss a large portion of a price movement. There are other observations, however, that can aid you in deciding to take a position much earlier. One of them, and my personal favorite, is what I call the "2B" criterion.

TQ 20/20 © 1991 CQG Inc.

Figure 7.8 December 1989 Commodity Index Futures—an example of an illiquid market. This intraday (15 minute) bar chart of the commodity index futures shows very light trading, characterized by large price swings, gaps, and dead periods in which no new prints appear.

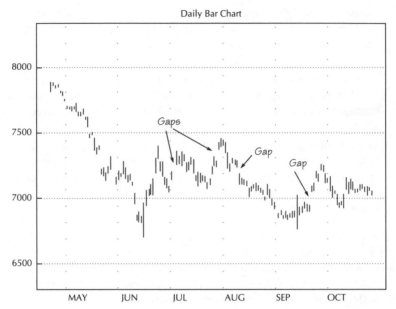

Daily Bar Chart

TQ 20/20 © 1991 CQG Inc.

Figure 7.9 December 1989 Japanese Yen Futures—a news-sensitive market. The currency markets, here the Japenese yen, are highly news-sensitive because supply is manipulated by government central banks. Note the "gaps" from day to day and the swiftness with which the trend can change. Except under exactly the right conditions, taking speculative positions in the currencies is very risky.

2B, OR NOT 2B? THAT'S WORTH SOME MONEY!

As mentioned in number 2 of the principles of a change of trend, sometimes the test of the previous high (or low) may actually break the previous high (or low) and then fail. Although this is really a special case of a test, when it occurs it *usually* signals a change of trend. In other words, this one observation, considered alone, has the greatest potential for catching the exact highs or lows; it carries more weight in terms of probability than any single one of the other three criteria for a change of trend. It has so much weight that it almost merits being called a rule:

The 2B Rule

In an uptrend, if a higher high is made but fails to carry through, and then prices drop below the previous high, then the trend is apt to reverse. The converse is true for downtrends. This observation applies in any of the three trends; short-term, intermediate-term, or long-term (see Figures 7.11, 7.12, and 7.13).

A 2B on a *minor* high or low will usually occur within one day or less of the time the high or low is made. For 2B's on intermediate highs or lows pre-

TQ 20/20 © 1991 CQG Inc.

Figure 7.10 December 1990 Daily Corn Futures Prices—a good market for setting stops. When condition 2 was met it presented a good, low-risk entry point for speculating on December corn. The market is liquid, and good points exist to set stops first at the low, and if prices break the minor high shown by the upper line, then you could raise your stop to that point.

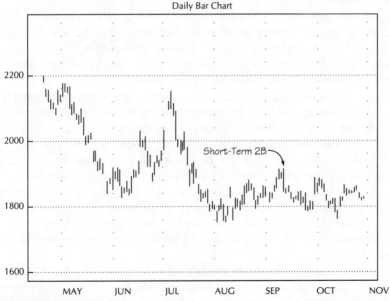

TQ 20/20 © 1991 CQG Inc.

Figure 7.11 December 1989 Soy Meal Futures—a short-term 2B. This daily bar chart of soy meal futures shows a 2B on a short-term basis. A day trader would have profited handsomely if he were to have sold after the new highs were made and prices then broke below the previous highs.

Daily Bar Chart

TQ 20/20 © 1991 CQG Inc.

Figure 7.12 December 1989 Cocoa Futures—an intermediate-term 2B. This daily bar chart of cocoa futures shows an intermediate-term 2B. The previous intermediate high at A is first broken at B, then fails three days later.

ceding a correction, the new high or low point will usually break within three to five days. At major market turning points, long-term 2B's, the new high or low will usually break within seven to ten days. In the stock market, after the new high is made, the failure to carry forward *usually* occurs on low to normal volume, and the confirmation of reversal occurs on higher volume.

When trading on the 2B criterion, it is essential that you admit defeat quickly if the trade moves against you. For example, if you are day-trading and you short the market on a 2B and then the market rallies to new highs again, you should immediately close your position when prices break past the new 2B high.

If they fail again, then you can short again, but you *must* limit your losses and let yourself get whipped out. As long as you take only small losses, you'll "stay at the table" and be able to keep trying. When day-trading, the 2B criterion may be right only 50% of the time, but if you limit losses when you're wrong and let your profits run when you're right, you'll make a lot of money trading on this basis. The probabilities of success using the 2B in the intermediate term are much higher.

A perfect example of an intermediate 2B occurred on October 13, 1989 on the Dow Industrial averages (Figure 7.14). On October 9, the Industrials set a new high of 2791.40 on low volume, and the new high was not confirmed by the Transports—a definite intermediate bearish indication. On the following days the market continued to sell off, and on October 12 closed at 2759.80, just 7.3 points

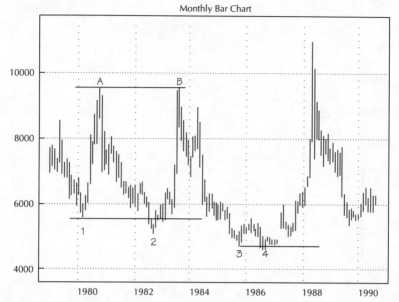

Monthly Bar Chart

TQ 20/20 © 1991 CQG Inc.

Figure 7.13 Monthly Bar Chart of Soy Bean Futures—trading on the long-term 2B. This *monthly* bar chart (each bar on the chart represents 1 month) of soy bean futures shows several long-term 2B's. At point B, the 2B presents an excellent selling opportunity when prices failed through the highs established in A. Point 2 is a long-term 2B which is an excellent buying opportunity when prices break out above the lows established in 1. At point 4, trading by the 2B criterion would have caused a long-term investor to be "whipped out" at least once. But the losses taken would have been very small relative to the ensuing long-term movement which finally followed where you should have re-established your long position.

off the high previous high of 2752.10 set on September 1. All related averages were also selling off. The chances for a 2B failure were high going into October 13. The rest is history. With a little push from the news, the market plunged 191 points on panic levels of volume.

THE CAUSE OF TESTS AND THE 2B PATTERN

To identify the roots of these patterns, you must understand what happens on the floors of the exchanges. The floors of the commodities exchanges, for example, are made of locals and brokers—professionals trading on their own account, and those who execute trades for others for a commission, respectively. Many of the brokers also trade on their own account. While the brokers execute orders for their clients, the locals always attempt to follow the daily trend, to move with daily tides of price movements.

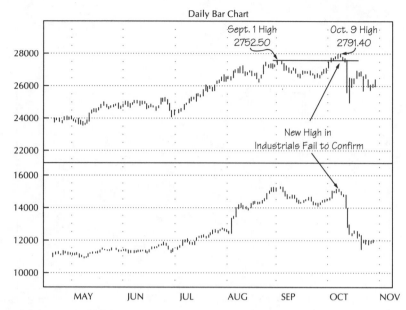

TQ 20/20 © 1991 CQG Inc.

Figure 7.14 The Dow Industrial and Transportation Averages, showing an intermediate 2B on the Dow Industrials. The Transports fail to confirm, further supporting the shorting opportunity.

People who trade the commodities markets from the outside through brokers frequently use stop orders. A stop order is an order to buy or sell "at the market" (the current market price) once a stated price in that order is reached or passed through. For example, when making an S&P 500 futures trade you might say to your broker, "Buy me five March S&P futures at 356.20 stop." If the market was trading at 356.10 and then shot up to 356.40, the floor broker holding your order would buy you five contracts at whatever the current market price was because your stop had been "hit."

Traders often use stops to limit their losses. A trader might, for example, buy five contracts at the market, and then put an order to sell five at a stop at some level where the market proves him wrong. Because locals are in "the pit" every day, the good ones develop a sense for how the world trades—in particular, where people set stops on their trades. In the absence of significant news, the only concrete points of reference for setting stops are previously set highs or lows, whether of a major or minor nature.

Aware of these stop points, the locals as well as the brokers who trade on their own account have a vested interest in driving prices slightly above or below these "resistance" or "support" points to force execution of the stop loss orders. This is called, "taking out the stops." After the stops are executed, the market will readjust. This is exactly what happens in the case of most 2B's and is typical action in all markets. Taking out stops is most prevalent on a short-term basis, but it also applies to the intermediate and long term. In the stock market, there is another subtlety which comes into play.

The floor of the stock exchange also has locals and brokers, but the locals are called "specialists"—men and women who specialize in trading specific stocks allocated only to them. They operate from a "book"—a list of orders to buy and sell specific quantities of stock at certain prices. It is the specialists' job to "make the market," to put together buyers and sellers for the stock(s) that they handle in an orderly fashion.

Often, the quantities of stock in the book are in the tens of thousands of shares, and the specialists are paid a flat fee per hundred shares traded upon execution, in effect, as a broker. It is obviously in their interest that prices move so that they can execute their larger orders, and they have the advantage of knowing ahead of time what the long and short interest of their stocks are, at least with respect to their books.

The talented traders, the big players that trade in size, know the identity of the specialists and can develop a feel for the levels at which large orders exist in their book by observing specialists' behavior. If so, then they, too, have an interest in driving the price movement to the point at which the large orders exist.

For example, suppose that, in the middle of a bull market, 5000 shares of IBM are bid at 110 $\frac{1}{8}$, 5000 offered at $\frac{1}{4}$. The specialist has buy orders for 10,000 shares at $\frac{3}{8}$, 20,000 shares at $\frac{1}{2}$, and another 20,000 at $\frac{5}{8}$.

A smart trader, a big player that the pack may follow, has a feel for the specialist's book and buys 5000 shares on his own account at $\frac{1}{8}$. The other traders who are aware of his activity follow suit, assuming accurately that the specialist has buy orders to execute on the way up. A long interest is generated on the floor for IBM. Volume swells, the price ticks up, and the specialist executes his orders, makes his commissions, and also makes profits by buying and selling for himself on the way up, knowing that he has nothing to lose. All the way up, the traders are driving the move and profiting along the way. When the momentum of the move finally plays out, the price corrects back down.

There is another subtlety in the world of the specialist. When I said that he makes money buying and selling for himself in a rally, that really isn't quite accurate. What happens is this: Prudential calls the specialist and says, "Buy me 1,000,000 shares of IBM." The specialist says, "Oh you're a buyer of a million shares—what a coincidence—so am I!" This puts him at "parity" on his purchases of IBM with Prudential.

Every time he buys 10,000 shares, he gets 5000 and Prudential gets 5000. Now, long interest builds for IBM as I described above. But, unlike Prudential who buys the stock to hold, the specialist buys the stock to feed the rally; that is, he buys the stock and then sells it on the next uptick, and he does it all the way up *knowing* that the move will carry because it is right there in his book! It is no wonder that the specialist business is passed on from one generation to the next; it is the most risk-free way to make a lot of money that exists in the financial markets.

Obviously, specialists can't act irresponsibly. If they attempt to drive price movements with disregard to the interest of those whose orders they execute, they are likely to be censured and will surely lose their bread and butter commission business, as well as any future allocations of new stocks listed on the NYSE. The point is that the observable patterns that are detectable in chart watching have their basis in large part in the activity of professionals on the floor of the exchanges.

This whole discussion of the 2B and how it occurs presupposes market activity in the absence of major news or new developments in any particular security or market. To trade on the 2B observation alone without particularized knowledge can be very risky, especially in the commodities markets, which are so news sensitive. But when used in the widest context of knowledge available, this observation can make the speculator a lot of money.

THE ABCs OF SECONDARY CORRECTIONS

Elliot wave theory is, in my opinion, too subjective to be of general use in professional speculation, but there is one observation from the theory that can be highly useful in calling the bottoms and tops of secondary corrections in bull and bear markets, respectively. Elliot wave theory postulates that market price movements follow recurring wave patterns. Within these patterns, he describes an A-B-C movement as illustrated in Figure 7.15.

Secondary corrections in both bull and bear markets almost always follow this pattern. Another aspect of this pattern is that volume dries up on the BC wave. To be valid, the movement must be confirmed by the other significant averages. Exceptions occur with the advent of major news affecting the market. As the illustration shows, the C point of a secondary correction in a bull market can either test or break the low established by the A point. The converse is true for a bear market. Obviously, if you can determine when the C point has been established, that is an ideal time to go long in a bull movement or short in a bear movement.

A good way to establish a speculative position during the BC stage of a secondary correction in a bull market is to buy when prices break the trend line established in the BC wave, provided volume has been diminishing on the decline. Stops should be established at the lowest of the A and C points to protect against the ever present possibility that the exception to the rule is at hand.

If volume is relatively stable on the breakout of the BC wave trend line, then the chances for a bottom are slighter. If volume increases sharply with the movement of the BC line, there is a good chance that the movement is not a correction but the second leg of a change in the primary trend, provided that fundamental conditions warrant the change.

SUMMARY

The art of speculation consists of buying and selling stocks, bonds, currencies, commodities, options, and so on. within the intermediate-term trend. The best long

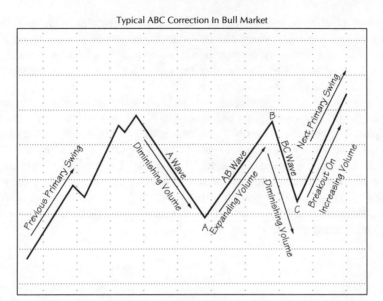

Typical ABC Correction In Bull Market

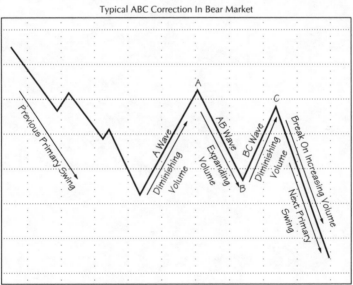

Typical ABC Correction In Bear Market

Figure 7.15 The ABCs of Secondary Corrections—a typical ABC correction in bull market.

speculative position is one taken at or shortly after the bottom of an intermediate downtrend has occurred, which can be either at the end of a bear market or the turning point of a secondary correction in a bull market. Conversely, the best short position is one taken at or shortly after the top of a bull market or the top of an intermediate correction in a bear market.

If you use the above methods as a preliminary selection criteria, a tremendous amount of time and energy can be saved. Once you become familiar with these principles, it is possible to "eyeball" the charts and quickly develop a list of likely securities, futures, or other instruments to buy and sell and to eliminate a host of others that are too indeterminate to speculate on. Once this list is developed, more particularized knowledge can be sought to choose those equities, government securities, and commodities that offer the highest reward potential with a minimum of risk. In the next chapter, a few additional technical methods are discussed that can be used to support your decisions.

8

What the Analysts
Don't Know Can Kill You

HOW IMPORTANT CAN ANCHOVIES BE?

I often marvel at the sophistication of the reports that analysts put out—so much detailed research, such complex determinations of "market value." Invariably, analysts' reports contain all kinds of interesting information, and the best of them are well-reasoned, well-written, and quite convincing. But do you know what? I haven't read one in many, many years.

When I give talks to groups of market professionals, I sometimes open up by asking the following question:

"If the tide shifts out off the coast of Peru, would you be a buyer or a seller of soybeans?"

Usually, I get looks that say, "I thought this guy was good at what he does. What the hell is he talking about?"

Then I explain that when the tide shifts outward, the anchovies that feed in the shallows off the coast of Peru move further out into the Pacific. The anchovy fishermen, whose primary market is the Japanese who feed anchovies to cattle, lose yield. The supply of anchovies dries up, and the Japanese start feeding their cattle with soybean products. The demand for soybeans goes up, and so does the price of soybean and soymeal futures. Therefore, if the tide shifts out off the coast of Peru, you should be a buyer of soybeans.

At this point, I've usually captured the attention of most of the audience, but there are still a lot of looks out there that say, "So what?" The point of the story is *not* that you should find a way to monitor the tides off the coast of Peru to trade soybeans effectively. The point is that you don't have to know everything there is to be known about a market in order to trade it. In fact, there is no way you can know everything, and it will probably be the one thing you don't know or haven't thought about that will burn you if you try to trade from knowledge of the specifics of a market. In other words, what the analysts don't know can kill you.

Like Peter Lynch explained in his book *One Up on Wall Street,* common sense is usually more useful than a myriad of facts and figures. But where Lynch and I differ is in my conviction that if you know what to look for, *the market* will tell you most of what you need to know. In particular, there are a few key technical indicators that are right more often than not and have stood the test of time throughout my entire career.

In glancing through my copy of *Technical Analysis of Stock Trends,* by Edwards and Magee, I counted over 20 different technical patterns discussed in just five chapters. With all due respect to Edwards and Magee and their fine and useful book, I do not recommend using most of these complex technical observations as a primary tool in trading. A few technical tools, however, are of tremendous value as secondary measures of the merits or pitfalls in any trade, especially in the stock market. I call these technical tools "secondary" because I *never* base any trading decision on them alone. I use them more to tell me what *not* to do, than what *to* do.

The secondary technical tools that I use most are:

1. Moving averages

2. Relative strength indicators

3. Momentum indicators (oscillators)

As I have said before, the art of speculation consists of putting money at risk only when the odds are in your favor. These secondary technical observations serve to supplement odds measurement. Of all the technical measurements that I know about, other than those discussed in the last chapter, these work the best.

UNDERSTANDING MOVING AVERAGES

A moving average is simply an average of successive numbers over a specified time period which is constantly updated by dropping the oldest number in the succession, adding the newest number, and then retotalling and reaveraging.

For example, to obtain the 10-day moving average of the daily closing of the Dow Jones Industrials, you start by summing and averaging 10 consecutive days. On the eleventh day, you add that closing number to the previous 10-day sum, then subtract the first day, and divide by 10 to get the updated average. By continuing this process on a daily basis, the average "moves" from day to day; that is, it changes in a way that takes into account the latest closing price. If you plot the daily results and superimpose it over the plot of day to day prices, the result looks like Figure 8.1.

What's the point of doing this? Moving averages tend to smooth out erratic fluctuations in market price movements, and they are useful in determining trends and trend reversals. Because they are averages over a specified period of time, they are, by definition, dampened indices which lag behind more immediate price fluctuations. The longer the averaging period you use, the greater is the dampening, or lag, effect. By studying various moving averages, it is possible to identify certain

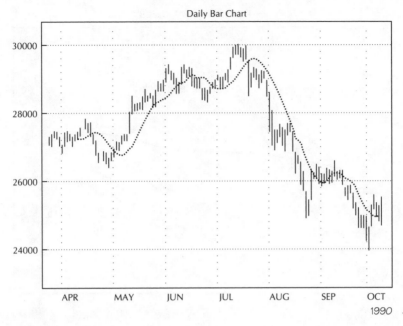

Daily Bar Chart

TQ 20/20 © 1991 CQG Inc.

Figure 8.1 The Dow Jones Industrials daily bar chart—the 10-day moving average. The solid line is the 10-day moving average for the closing prices of the Dow Industrials. Note that the moving average line lags and dampens the movement of actual prices.

repeating patterns which can be used to determine the probable course of the price trend. Some of the patterns are so well-defined that they can be used as buy or sell signals in both stocks and commodities.

Virtually every stock chart book that I have ever seen uses some type of moving average. Many individual technicians and traders use their own moving average formulations, weighting the near weeks or using exponentials in their calculations. But rather than discuss the variety and type available, let me simply tell you which ones I use and how I use them.

As far as I'm concerned, in the equities markets (individual stocks and stock indexes), by far the most useful of all the moving averages I've seen is the 200-day (that's 200–trading day or 40-week) moving average (see Figure 8.2).

I keyed into this in 1968 when I read the results of a study by William Gordon demonstrating that by buying and selling the Dow Jones Industrials stocks from 1917 to 1967 using only the 200-day moving average, an investor could have realized an average yearly simple return of 18.5%. By comparison, his study showed that Dow Theory would have realized 18.1% per year if an investor bought and sold on confirmation days of bull and bear markets.[1] In the study, Gordon used two simple rules to determine buy and sell signals from the moving average:

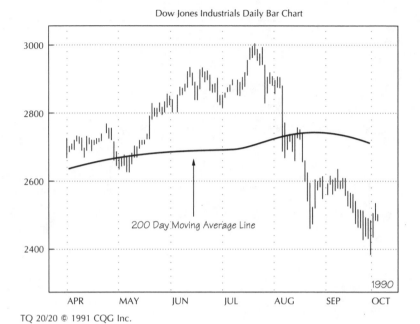

Dow Jones Industrials Daily Bar Chart

200 Day Moving Average Line

TQ 20/20 © 1991 CQG Inc.

Figure 8.2 The Dow Industrials with two hundred-day moving average.

1. If the 200-day moving average line flattens out following a previous decline or is advancing, and prices penetrate the moving average line on the upside, this comprises a major buying signal (see Figure 8.3).

2. If the 200-day moving average line flattens out following a previous rise or is declining, and prices penetrate the moving average line on the downside, this comprises a major selling signal (see Figure 8.4).[2]

You can use the long-term moving average as a predictor not only for the averages, but also on individual stocks and most commodity futures. I personally use it for two basic purposes—to confirm Dow Theory in determining the course of the long-term trend and in making specific stock selections.

When picking stocks, I *never* buy a stock when prices are below the moving average, and I *never* sell a stock when the price is above the moving average. Just pick up any chart book that uses a 35- or 40-week moving average and you'll see why—the odds of being right are way against you.

As far as using other, shorter-term, moving averages, I have only found one other set of observation that works consistently and stands the test of time. This works not only for stocks and stock indexes, but for many commodities as well.

1. When the 10-week moving average crosses the 30-week moving average and the slope of both averages is up, this comprises a buy signal, provided that prices are above both moving average lines (see Figure 8.5).

Dow Jones Industrials Daily Bar Chart

Buy Spot

1990

TQ 20/20 © 1991 CQG Inc.

Figure 8.3 The Dow Industrials, with the two hundred-day moving average for—a buy signal. If the 200-day moving average line flattens out following a previous decline, or is advancing, and prices penetrate the moving average line on the upside, this comprises a major buying signal.

Dow Jones Industrials Daily Bar Chart

Sell Spot

1990

TQ 20/20 © 1991 CQG Inc.

Figure 8.4 The Dow Industrials with the two-hundred-day moving average— a sell signal. If the 200-day moving average line flatterns out following a previous rise, or is declining, and prices penetrate the moving average line on the downside, this comprises a major selling signal.

TQ 20/20 © 1991 CQG Inc.

Figure 8.5 The Gold Futures weekly bar chart—a buy spot given by the 10-week/30-week cross rule. When the 10-week moving average crosses the 30-week moving average and the trend of both is up, this comprises a buy signal.

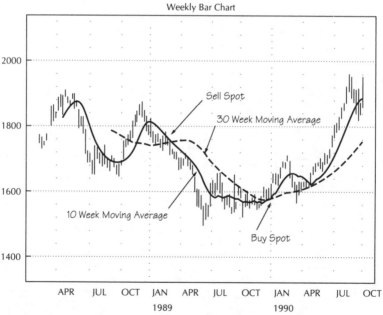

TQ 20/20 © 1991 CQG Inc.

Figure 8.6 The British Pound Futures weekly bar chart—a sell spot given by the 10 week/30 week cross rule. When the 10-week moving average crosses the 30-week moving average and the slopes are both down, this comprises a sell spot. Note that you get both a sell and later a buy on this chart.

2. When the 10-week moving average crosses the 30-week moving average and the slope of both averages is down, this comprises a sell signal, provided prices are below both moving average lines (see Figure 8.6).

Of course, as with all technical observations, these observations are never right 100% of the time. For example, you would have been creamed on October 19, 1987 if you used only the 10-week/30-week cross rule. By the time you got the sell signal, the crash was over.

For the commodity futures markets, there is no hard and fast rule about which long-term moving average works best; it varies from market to market and over time. For example, at this writing, the 200-day works well for bonds, the dollar index, and gold but not so well for the other commodities.

Basically, you've got to recognize that, as a technical tool, the validity of the moving averages is apt to change with changing market conditions. The shorter the term that you trade in, the more this is true. So, you have to experiment with different times and find the ones that work. When they quit working, you've got to change again. For example, on pork bellies, I've been using the 4-week and 11-week moving averages and I apply a rule similar to the 10-week/30-week rule I described above. Just recently, however, the relationship has started to get sloppy, so it might be time to experiment with the time periods again.

The biggest mistake anyone can make in using moving averages, or any technical observation for that matter, is to fall in love with it. By that I mean don't ever think you have found "the rule to end all rules"; no such thing exists. Every market is in a constant process of change, and any method which doesn't take change into account in a fundamental way is subject to being wrong.

In philosophy, I strongly disagree with the school of Pragmatism,[3] but when it comes to trading rules, you have to be completely pragmatic. A rule is right only as long as it works. When it quits working, you've got to kiss it goodbye and leave it alone. Otherwise, just like a bad relationship with a person, it will bring you down. I've seen it happen to people who were at one time considered to be among the best traders on Wall Street. So be careful not to get emotionally involved with any discovery you make when identifying patterns using the moving averages or any technical method.

A DIFFERENT PERSPECTIVE ON RELATIVE STRENGTH

To the best of my knowledge, the concept of relative strength was first discussed by Robert Rhea in a *Barron's* article in 1933. He didn't call it relative strength but rather the "habits of stocks and how they perform against one another." Relative strength is simply a ratio between a single stock against a stock group or an average index, or between a stock group and a larger group or average index.

Like moving averages, there are all kinds of different formulations of relative strength. Some chart books, for example, weight recent weeks more heavily than others. For example, in *New York Stock Exchange Daily Graphs,* each stock has a relative strength line which is a plot of the ratio of the stock price to the S&P 500 Index on a weekly basis, plus there is another time-weighted relative strength indicator which compares the percentage change of the stocks price to the change in price of stocks in the database (see Figure 8.7). The number varies from 1 to 99. The number 52, for example, would indicate that the stock outperformed 52% of all other stocks in the database.[4]

The idea of relative strength is sometimes difficult to understand because we are brought up with a consumer mentality. As kids, we watch our parents look for sales, and most of us carry on that tradition; we all try to buy cheap and sell dear.

For example, assuming that you like citrus fruit, if you went to the grocery store and saw that both oranges and grapefruit were selling at fifty cents per pound, you would probably buy a few of each. But if you went back a week later and found grapefruit suddenly at a dollar per pound and oranges still at fifty cents, you would probably opt just to buy oranges and wait for a better market in grapefruit. If you use this same kind of thinking in buying stocks, you are often making a big mistake.

You should never buy a stock simply because it's cheap; the chances are that it is probably cheap for a good reason. What you want is a stock that is going to

Data for chart courtesy: Daily Graphs

Figure 8.7 Relative Strength indicator as used in the *New York Stock Exchange Daily Graphs*. In this example, the line shows the relative strength of the individual stock versus the S&P 500. The number 52 is the relative strength value, indicating that it outperformed 52% of the stocks in the data base.

perform, that is going to appreciate in value faster than the average stock. Relative strength is a measure of this kind of performance. All things being equal, if you are looking to buy a stock, you should buy the *strongest* performers, as indicated by the best measurement of relative strength available.

So far, I've discussed how relative strength is *typically* used. There is another way of looking at relative strength that relates directly to my definition of a trend. Recall that when the market is in an uptrend, it makes a series of higher lows and higher highs. So, what I do is look at the Industrials average, and if it has made a higher high, then I look for stocks that have made a higher high on the same day as, or on days before the average.

These are the strongest stocks—the market leaders. If the market is in an uptrend, then these are the stocks that, everything else being equal, you would want to buy, but *not when they make the higher highs*. You buy them on reactions, during sell-offs, because the chances for fast returns are better. Strong relative strength stocks move more quickly on the upside than the other stocks in the market.

When playing the short side near market tops, I don't recommend shorting strong relative strength stocks, because if you are wrong, then you will lose more money. Nor do I recommend shorting the weakest stocks, because they often don't have far to move on the downside. I prefer to short the mid-range relative strength stocks because if you are wrong, you don't get hurt too badly, and if you are right, you can still make some hefty profits.

The time to short the strong stocks is after an intermediate-term or long-term top has occurred in both the Industrials and the Transports, and you get a confirmed change of trend in the stock by the 1-2-3 criterion. This kind of action is ideal for picking up some quick profits in the short term, because if the market continues to sell off after you get a confirmed top in a strong stock, the stock's price is liable to fall precipitously for one to three days in what is effectively a panic movement. It is best to take profits quickly on this kind of trade, however, because there will be plenty of buyers looking for a bargain in the stock because of its previous strength, and the price is apt to recover quickly.

While relative strength is an important secondary indicator, I place it lower on the scale of importance than moving averages. In other words, if the stock price is below the moving average and the relative strength is good, I weight the moving average more heavily and pass the stock up as a potential buy.

The concept of relative strength is applicable in the commodities markets as well, but the way you apply it is slightly different. If you are considering a long position in the precious metals, for instance, you would compare the relative strength of gold, silver, platinum, etc., to one another and buy the strongest of the group. For example, Figure 8.8 shows the weekly bar charts of gold and silver. A quick look shows two things: first, silver made new lows in September and gold never did, and second, gold broke its previous June intermediate high, but silver failed to break its previous March intermediate high. Obviously, gold has greater strength than silver—its relative strength is greater.

Daily Bar Chart

TQ 20/20 © 1991 CQG Inc.

Figure 8.8 December 1990 Gold (top) and December 1990 Silver (bottom) futures—relative strength comparison. A quick look shows that while gold was making new intermediate highs, silver failed to. Also, while silver made new lows in September, gold did not. Gold has greater relative strength than silver.

You can also use relative strength in the commodities to determine how to position yourself in a hedge or a spread. When looking at the grains, for example, compare the relative strength of corn to wheat. A quick glance at the daily bar charts of both shows that corn is stronger than wheat (Figure 8.9), so the best play is to go long corn and short wheat. That decision is confirmed by a plot of the daily price differential of corn to wheat (Figure 8.10).

MOMENTUM INDICATORS (OSCILLATORS)

Moving objects have a property called momentum, which is what you might call the *quantity* of motion of an object. The actual measurement of momentum is the product of something's mass times its velocity. A swinging pendulum, for example, has constantly changing momentum, which if plotted against time, would look something like Figure 8.11.

Although not in the strict physical sense, markets also have momentum. You can think of the plot of the pendulum's momentum as idealized market behavior, where prices *oscillate* around a steady center point, where the *velocity* of price

Daily Bar Chart

TQ 20/20 © 1991 CQG Inc.

Figure 8.9 December 1990 Corn (top) and December 1990 Wheat (bottom) Futures—relative strength comparison. If you realize that prices are in $\frac{1}{10}$ of a cent per bushel (i.e., 2400 equals $2.40 per bushel) a quick glance indicates that, while both corn and wheat are in downtrends, corn is outperforming wheat—it has greater relative strength.

changes is constantly changing and the reverses at the top and bottom of the plot corresponding to market tops and bottoms.

But unlike a pendulum, which has a constant mass and changing velocity, market momentum has both constantly changing mass (changing trading volume) and constantly changing velocity (fluctuating rates of change of prices). In addition, there are forces which influence the market, such as breaking major political or economic news, that can radically shift market momentum at any time.

Consequently, it is impossible to measure market momentum with complete accuracy and use the measurement to predict market turning points with certainty. It *is* possible, however, to develop correlations that closely approximate market momentum and help predict when the price trend is changing. The best of these indicators are called *oscillators*.

To the best of my knowledge, the term oscillators, which is now a standard industry term, was initially used by H. M. Gartley in his book, *Profits in the Stock Market*, first published in 1935. Like moving averages and relative strength indexes, oscillators come in a variety of formulations, but the element common to them all is that they measure the differences in some market parameter over some specific period of time. They are, therefore, measurements of the rate of change

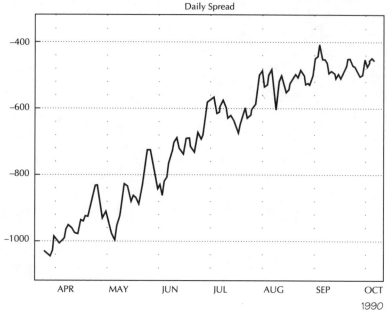

Figure 8.10 A plot of the December 1990 corn–wheat daily spread. As indicated by the relative strength comparison, a good hedge play in the grains would have been to go long corn and short wheat.

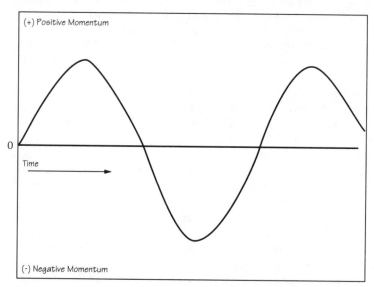

Figure 8.11 Plot of the momentum of a pendulum versus time. The plot of the momentum of a pendulum versus time oscillates around the baseline. You will notice the similarity of this pattern to that of momentum oscillators used in analyzing market behavior.

of some important market parameter such as price, breadth, moving averages, or volume; and they oscillate around a baseline, much like the plot of the momentum of the pendulum.

For the equities markets, I use two oscillators—one for breadth and one for price. For commodities, I use an oscillator based upon the difference between two moving averages.

The oscillators I use for the stock indexes, price and breadth, have remained valid since I first started using them in January 1975* (see Figures 8.12 and 8.13). The one I use for commodities is built into my quote system, and you can change the period of the moving averages until you find "a good fit" for the particular commodity you are dealing with as in Figure 8.14.

Refering to the figures, you can see that a good oscillator begins reversing when or before the market trend begins to change. In most cases, these particular oscillators are quite accurate. Typically, when the market is in an uptrend, the

---

*Actually, I did use two price oscillators for the Industrials, one short-term and one long-term, but the advent of program trading in the mid-80s invalidated the shorter-term oscillator.

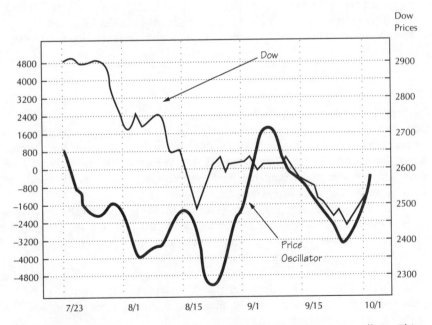

Figure 8.12 The 1990 Dow Industrials, with my long-term price oscillator. This long-term price oscillator has worked well for me since I first began using it in 1975. Note how the oscillator turns up before the market did in late September.

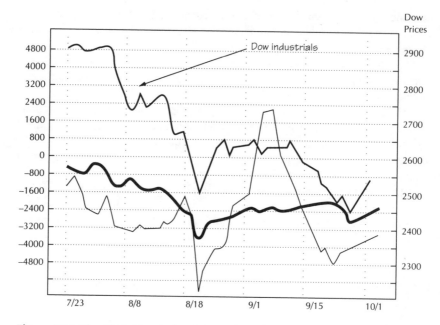

Figure 8.13 The 1990 Dow Industrials, with my breadth oscillators. The lighter line is the short-term breadth oscillator, and the darker one the long-term. Compare the movement of these oscillators with the movement of the Down in Figure 8.12.

oscillator will also be moving up. The higher the oscillator rises on the chart, the more the market approaches an "overbought" condition. Ideally, just like the plot of the pendulum, as the market approaches the top, the oscillator will "slow down," that is, flatten out and top. Then, as prices start to reverse, the oscillator will turn down and continue down until the market approaches an "oversold" condition, when the reverse of what happens at a top occurs.

Generally speaking, the higher or lower the oscillator lines go above or below the baseline relative to other peaks and valleys in the plot, the more significant they become. Now let me show you how to calculate the specific oscillators that I use and demonstrate exactly how I use them.

The best momentum measurement I use for stock market breadth is really what you might call a 10-day equivalent, net change, moving average, breadth oscillator. It sounds complicated, but it is really quite simple. Before I get into it, however, let me say a few words about breadth.

Breadth is an indicator used to counterbalance the fact that most stock average indices are weighted. The Dow Industrials, for example, is an average of only 30 stocks weighted to price. Sometimes, if a heavily weighted stock makes an unusu-

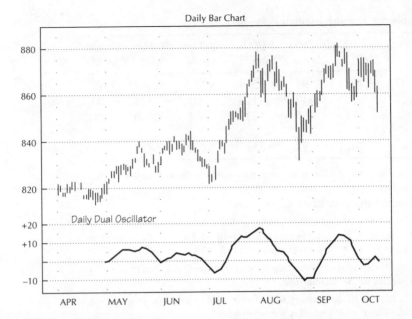

Figure 8.14 Daily bar chart of Cattle Futures, with overbought/oversold oscillator. The oscillator on the bottom is based on the difference between the 7-day and 21-day moving average. While this is a good fit for feeder cattle, it may not work well at all for other commodities.

ally extensive move, it can throw the average off as a good indicator of nationwide industrial stock performance. One way to test the validity of the averages as general market indicators is to compare them to what is called the advance/decline line (the A/D line), that is, breadth.

The A/D line is simply a plot of difference between the total number of advancing issues and the total number of declining issues of every stock on the New York Stock Exchange versus time in days. Generally, the A/D line moves with the Dow, and when there is a divergence between them, it often signals a coming change in the trend.

The breadth oscillator is simply a measure of market momentum, and it often gives you an earlier signal of a coming change in trend than does the A/D line by itself.

I actually use two breadth oscillators, one short term, and one longer term, but I generally pay much more attention to the longer term one. For the short term, every morning, first I log the net A/D number; I simply calculate, log, and plot a moving sum of advancing issues minus declining issues on the NYFE for the previous 10 days. In other words, every day, I keep a running, cumulative total of the daily difference of advancing issues minus declining issues. The process is shown in more detail in Table 8.1.

Table 8.1 Breadth oscillator numbers

Date	Today's A/D[a]	10 Days Ago[b]	10-Day Sum[c]	30-Days Ago[d]	30 Day Sum[e]	Divide by 3[f]
7/23	−1203	91	−1556	−552	−2167	−722
7/24	−2	−440	−1118	355	−2524	−841
7/25	312	465	−1271	458	−2670	−890
⋮						
10/1	761	−87	−3517	−1020	−6826	

[a]The daily net A/D—Advancing issues minus decline issues on the NYSE.

[b]The net A/D from 10 days ago.

[c]The current 10-day moving sum. Today's A/D, minus the net A/D from ten days ago, plus yesterday's moving 10-day sum. Example: For 7/24, $-2 - (-440) + (-1556) = -1118$.

[d]The 30-day sum of advancing issues minus declining issues as of 30 days prior to the current date.

[e]The current 30-day moving sum. Today's A/D, minus the moving sum 30 days ago, plus yesterday's moving sum.

[f]The 10-day equivalent moving sum. Today's 30-day moving sum divided by 3.

Table 8.2 Price oscillator calculation

Date	NY Composite 5-Day Net[a]	10-Day Moving Sum[b]	10-Day Net[c]
7/23/90	−627	63397	886
7/24	−320	63077	300
7/25	−428	62649	−482
7/26	33	62682	−859
8/3	−536	61866	−1531
⋮			
10/1	302	52238	−2586

[a]The difference between yesterday's close and the close from the previous 5th day on the New York Composite Index.

[b]The 10-day moving sum of the values in column A.

[c]The 10-day net moving sum. The difference between today's value of the 10-day moving sum, and the moving sum from ten days ago. For example, on 8/3: $61866 - 63937 = -1531$.

For the longer term, I do the same thing for a 30-day period and divide the result by 3 to obtain a 10-day equivalent average, as shown in the Table 8.2. Plotting the results gives a chart like that shown in Figure 8.13.

A quick comparison of the breadth momentum lines to the daily closing prices of the Industrials shows a good correlation between turns in the oscillators and intermediate price reversals on the Dow. You will note, however, that if you traded on the basis of turns in the short-term oscillator, you would get "whipped out" on several occasions. The long-term oscillator, on the other hand, sometimes lags changes in intermediate trend, such that trading by it alone would cost you money. That's why I use them as supporting tools. But overall, the correlation is very good and has been since I first began using it in 1975.[5]

The price oscillator I use is slightly more complex, and it is also more important in terms of the weight I place on it in evaluating the market. Again every morning, using the daily closing prices on the New York Composite Index, I begin by calculating the difference between the previous day's closing price and the closing price from the previous fifth day. Then, I add the result to the sum of the same result for the previous nine trading days, to give a 10-day running sum of the five-day price difference (see Table 8.2). A plot of the daily result compared to the Industrials average shows a highly significant correlation between turns in the oscillator and turns in the daily closing prices of the stock index (see Figure 8.13).

I use the breadth and price oscillators to anticipate coming market turning points and to confirm them when they occur. A simple look at the charts will show that the higher or lower the oscillator goes on the chart, the greater is the chance of an intermediate change of trend. Like a warning light on railroad tracks, when the oscillators approach or break through significant previous highs or lows, they are telling you that danger is ahead. They don't tell the nature of the danger, or how far ahead it lies, but they do tell you to proceed with caution or continue full speed ahead.

For commodities, as I have already mentioned, my quote system has an oscillator measurement built-in to it which is the difference between two moving averages. The nice thing about this feature is that it allows you to readily change and experiment with different time periods for the moving averages until you find one that fits the movement of the specific market you are dealing with.

This is essential in the commodity markets because, any time you are dealing with one item versus an average, the chances of conditions arising which change the nature of "normal" price behavior are much greater. Oscillators in the commodity markets are, therefore, much less reliable than they are for the stock average indices. Nevertheless, if you find the right one, they can be of tremendous value in confirming trend changes.

In fact, sometimes you can find a correlation that is so good that you could virtually make your trading decisions on them alone and make quite a bit of money. I never do this, nor do I recommend it; but it *is* possible, and I'm sure there are many traders who do it. The problem with this approach is that when you are wrong, you will often be wrong in a very big way.

Many technicians get very sophisticated with oscillators and use them, not just for the averages, but for specific stocks as well. I don't.

There is such a thing as acquiring too much information. I think you are better off using a few oscillators at most, and then only as secondary measures to affirm or deny the primary change of trend indicators I discussed in the last chapter. Frankie Joe had a trading rule which he called KISS, an acronym for "Keep it simple, stupid!" Good advice from a man who was what I like to call "a pro's pro."

MAKING SPECIFIC STOCK SELECTIONS

So far, all of the methods I've discussed apply to virtually any market, from specific stocks, to commodities, to indexes. Undoubtedly, some of you trade only individual stocks—something I used to put my primary focus on. For making stock selections, so far we have Dow Theory to make a general market call and, within that context, the technical methods I've described to pick out a group of stocks that are likely to move with or against the market. Now, we'll cover a few auxiliary methods which will help you select specific stocks. The objective, of course, is to put even *more* of the odds in your favor.

The Technical Versus the Fundamental Approach

There is a whole group of traders, some independent, some working for firms, called stockpickers—people who choose stocks for trading, speculating, or investing. Within this group, there are two basic schools of thought—the purely technical school and the purely fundamental school. My experience has been that it is a very rare purist who consistently makes money.

Most profitable stock speculators are hybrids; they combine the best of both worlds and use a combination of technical and fundamental tools. I would have to call myself a hybrid who leans toward the technical side. I combine the technical methods described in the last chapter, which are *likely* to reflect the future judgment of market participants, with fundamental statistics which consistently correlate to price movements over time.

The fundamentalists believe that, over the long term, the market prices stocks according to yield, earning power, and the value of each company's underlying assets. In other words, value is determined by those three intrinsic factors for any stock. The problem I have with this approach is that it totally ignores the subjective nature of value; it doesn't take into account that people, not computers, ultimately determine price. For the fundamentalist view to be accurate, yield, earning power, and assets would have to directly reflect the collective judgment of the marketplace. They don't. In fact, fundamentalists are notorious for being "right," but with bad timing.

One very popular fundamentalist offshoot is the Graham and Dodd approach to stock selection. Highly oversimplified, the Graham and Dodd approach says that you should buy low PE (price/earnings ratio), low book value stocks. The underlying premise is that these are likely to be the "undervalued" growth stocks, whereas the higher PE stocks have already been recognized and properly "evaluated" by the market. As long as you are in the early to late-middle stages of an inflationary bull market, this approach works pretty well—stock prices for all but the worst of companies appreciate. But over time, it can get you in trouble. Usually, when a stock has a low PE and a low book value, there are reasons for it, and the market already knows those reasons.

I find PEs and book value very useful but in a different way. If you look at PEs and book value of the indexes as a whole and compare them to historical PEs and book values, you find a good secondary indicator of overbought and oversold conditions of the averages as a whole. Then, you can compare the individual stock's PE and book value to those of the averages, and gauge, again as a secondary (perhaps tertiary) indicator, the relative performance of the specific stock to the market in terms of an overbought or oversold condition.

Rate of Change of Earnings Growth

One fundamental statistic that is excellent is the correlation between rate of change of earnings growth and the change in the stock price. In a book published in 1969, Gordon Holmes demonstrated that, "The slope of a given price trend almost always precedes the correspondent or equivalent earnings trend slope in time. The amount of time displacement is about three months."[6]

There are three things I like about this observation. First, it is *usually* true. Second, it has withstood the test of time. And third, it supports the fundamental precept of Dow Theory that the markets "discount everything." Now, how do you use this observation?

First of all, you have to establish that the correlation holds true for the stock you are evaluating. Most businesses have seasonal fluctuations which cause variations in earnings, so you should look at earnings figures for no less than six quarters before considering earnings growth as a valid indicator of future price changes. A plot of the earnings curve (lagged three months) on the same time base should give you a direct correlation between earnings growth (or decline) and price growth (or decline). The correlation should exist for the entire period considered, otherwise this indicator should be disregarded completely for that stock.

Holmes developed a rather complicated method for stock picks based on earnings growth and other factors;[7] I use earnings growth a little bit differently. In William O'Neil's New York Stock Exchange Daily Graphs, earnings are reported in quarters, with the next quarter's projected earnings included. If the correlation holds, then on the bull side, if the rate of change of earnings growth (change in earnings over time) is less than the rate of change of prices (the change in price over time, or the slope of the price trendline), then the stock is a buy. If the rate of change in earnings growth is equal to or greater than the price trend slope, then look for a better stock. The reverse holds true on the bear side.

If you trade a stock on this basis, with other technical reasons included, I want to warn you about something: so many people trade on earnings that estimated quarterly earnings reports can kill you, particularly on high PE stocks—they sometimes crash very fast. Find out when the actual earnings figures come out, and if the stock is near its highs, get out before the reports come out. If they come out less than expected, the stock can easily gap down and your accumulated profits will disappear!

The whole idea of looking at yield and PEs is to identify stocks with strong growth potential. Actually, however, rate of change of earnings growth is the primary number to look at for finding growth stocks. Yield, for example, is dividend divided by price. Obviously, a high yield can result from a high dividend being paid by a company with a depressed stock price. But why is the price low? Because earnings are poor!

Both Citicorp and Traveler's had declining prices but increasing yields for six months or so as of July 1990. The companies have kept up their dividend payment while the stock price has been falling. Since the stock prices have fallen in greater proportion than earnings, the PEs of both stocks have also fallen. What you have in this situation is two stocks with low PEs and high yields. Does that make them a good buy—a bargain?

I don't think so. What if both companies continue to perform badly? PEs and yield can be very misleading, if not viewed in the context of earnings growth. I often think in terms of the phrase, "Wherever a stock price goes, there it is!" It is a good reminder that it is highly unlikely that you will spot an underpriced stock before the rest of the market.

Let me give you an example which illustrates why earnings growth is such an important aspect of picking stocks. Eighty percent of all companies listed on the NYSE pay out 30 to 65% of their earnings in dividends—those that earn money. Assume the stock of a young company is selling at $10 per share, is currently earning $1 per share, is paying a $.50 dividend (50% of earnings and a 5% yield), and has a rate of earnings growth of 25%. Both the PE of 10 and the yield of 5% are mid-range, and say little about the stock as a buy. But the 25% rate of earnings growth tells a lot more!

With a 25% growth rate, the company's earnings will double in 2.9 years. Assuming the same percentage dividend payment, if you buy the stock now, your yield will double in roughly three years, and double again three years after that. If the stock continues in its rate of earnings growth, you will pay out your investment, *in dividends alone,* in less than eight years, not to mention the equity appreciation you would most likely enjoy. Picking stocks based on yield and PEs alone will tell you nothing about this kind of potential.

Other Fundamental Considerations

There are a few other fundamental considerations which I use to make a final decision if, on balance, everything else is equal in choosing between two stocks.

First, given two equal bullish charts, I would pick the lower PE stock as a buy. Conversely, if both charts were equally bearish, I would pick the higher PE stock as a short. Graham and Dodd lives as a minor consideration!

Second, in a buy, I would always choose to buy the stock of a company in a less leveraged position over a company in a more leveraged position; the greater the leverage, the greater the susceptibility to a credit crunch. The converse is true in a sell. Third, whether buying or selling, I always trade the stock with the most shares on the market to ensure liquidity.

As a final consideration with respect to the fundamental approach, part of being a speculator in the stock market is being able to judge whether or not a new product or service offered by a new or established company will be accepted favorably by the market. In these kinds of cases, the traders in the stock markets are sometimes wrong, and either fail to anticipate consumer demand for a great new product or overanticipate a new product that bombs.

I don't very often participate in these kinds of speculations, but they are speculations nonetheless. The reason I don't is that there is no way to measure the odds. This is where I think simple common sense comes into play. If a new product is great, tastes good, is unique, is well marketed—if you believe it is going to take off big for common sense reasons—then by all means, buy some stock if you can afford to lose your investment.

A Few Extra Words about Technical Methods

Aside from the technical tools in this and the last chapter, there is one more thing I want to add about the technical evaluation of stock charts. Basically, all of the tenets of Dow Theory apply to individual stocks; they just aren't quite as valid.

In any statistical study, the more samples you have, the more repeatable the results are likely to be. A single stock has many of the characteristics of a market average index. For example, the sum of all knowledge about that stock is expressed in the movement of the price. Volume relationships are much the same. The psychology of the stock cycle is much the same. Most things are the same. But the first premise of Dow Theory is that it is not infallible. The same is true for individual stocks, only more so. Also, you have to draw all inferences for individual stocks without the benefit of another index for confirmation. Nevertheless, it is useful to apply Dow Theory's technical observations to individual stocks.

CONCLUSION

At this point, we are equipped with a simple but powerful set of technical tools with which to approach analysis of price movements in the financial markets. We move from the general principles and concepts of Dow Theory, to primary technical considerations, to secondary technical considerations, to some more particularized technical and fundamental considerations for individual stocks. In the next chapters, we will add some powerful, common sense, fundamental economic considerations to our speculating arsenal.

9

The Way The World Really Works: The Basics of Economics

THE JIGSAW PUZZLE

Imagine trying to put together a 10,000 piece jigsaw puzzle that had no picture or pattern for reference. Assume that all the pieces were the same shade of gray, and each was cut in a similar pattern with only slight variations. The process of solving the puzzle would not only be unendurably tedious, but the only result would be a meaningless gray smear in the shape of a rectangle. Do you think you would seriously attempt to solve such a puzzle? I doubt it. Although you may question the motivation of the designer, you would probably shrug it off, leaving it to those eccentric few that could find some obscure purpose in its solution.

Most people view contemporary economics like the hypothetical jigsaw puzzle —tedious and unrewarding—and economists as eccentrics looking for a solution to an unendurably complex puzzle. It is difficult to see the relationship between running a business or pursuing a career and economic theory as it exists today. But it can be a financially fatal error to shrug off economics as pointless if you want to make money in the financial markets. It is the designs of theoretical economists and the alleged solutions to economic problems instituted by bureaucrats and congressmen that largely determine the long-term course of business activity and the direction of price movements.

If you already watch the markets, you have seen equities, debt, and futures prices respond dramatically to news of the level of the new budget deficit, to the Federal Reserve Board's policy regarding the availability of money and credit, to reports on the Treasury Department's policy regarding the value of the dollar abroad, or to rumors of new trade legislation. The markets concede that the government holds the club that can break the back of American business. A huge part of successful speculation and investment now rests on anticipating the nature and effects of government fiscal policy, monetary policy, and interventionist legislation on specific markets and on the general business cycle.

Our economy operates according to market principles, but the government sets the stage—and it's a secret, rotating stage subject to change at any moment. But if you understand the errors in the economic theory that motivate the stage managers, you can anticipate the new set and position yourself to act profitably. Therefore, understanding economics has *everything* to do with successful speculation and investment; it provides the foundation for any good system of market forecasting. Let me put that last statement in perspective.

I went to New York City and Queens College to study economics but found it almost completely worthless except in a reverse sense; that is, I gained knowledge of what is wrong with conventional economic thinking rather than what is right.

My formal schooling gave me an understanding of the predominantly Keynesian ideas that our government uses in making policy decisions. Studying on my own, however, I discovered that the conventional wisdom taught in most universities was contradicted by thinkers such as Adam Smith, Ludwig von Mises, Frederick Hayek, Henry Hazlitt, Ayn Rand, and others. I learned that Keynes was little more than a sophisticated mercantilist and a bubble builder.[1] I identified the contradictions inherent in Keynesian economics and discovered the *right* economic principles in the Modern Austrian School of Economics.[2] And I began to see the profit potential of riding the government bubble in the initial stages of inflation, jumping off early, and being on solid ground when the bubble bursts, waiting to pick up the pieces.

I don't think you need formal schooling to obtain the economic knowledge needed to succeed in the financial markets. In fact, I encouraged a brilliant young man who trades for me not to go to college by offering him a job and telling him that he could learn what he needs to know about the markets much better and faster on his own than he could in most university systems. Through observation and experience, he is learning how the world really works and is rapidly becoming a fine trader.

On the other hand, I know of a securities analyst, an economics major with five years' experience at a major firm, who, when asked if she thought the U.S. government debt would ever be paid off, replied, "No, it will probably continue to grow." When then asked how long the debt could continue to grow without lenders losing confidence in the government's ability to repay, she replied, "I don't know, but eventually they'll just have to write it off. After all, its just paper!" Just paper!!?? Incredible!! She'll watch in horror in the next bear market, when bonds and stocks keep making lower lows. Unfortunately, judging from the countless number of people I have talked to with similar views, this kind of thinking is the rule rather than the exception, and it is traceable to a poor or misguided understanding of basic economic principles.

You can't reverse cause and effect. The so-called economic "gurus" in Washington can't create prosperity with the stroke of a pen on a new bill in Congress. Economics isn't a mystical realm nor the province of geniuses or specialists with some kind of special insight akin to religious revelation. Many policy makers are little more than political cowards who are afraid to tell special interest groups that they can't have something for nothing. Instead, they develop elaborate schemes to try to cheat reality by overspending, while evading or ignoring the inevitable results of their programs—inflation or recession. And they do it in the name of economic principles.

In his so-called "new economics," John Maynard Keynes formalized and gave quasi-scientific status to economic fallacies that are as old as civilized man. He provided a rationalization for government intervention into free markets, for government control of the supply of money and credit, and for policies of irresponsible deficit spending and inflationary expansionism. With very few exceptions, the intellectual community has taken his fallacies as axiomatic principles and expanded them into a hopelessly complex system of terms, symbols, and mathematical equations. It is no wonder that most people are either bored or intimidated by the study of economics.

If you are bored or intimidated by economics, it is partly because politicians and members of academia have for years been declaring that our society and the interworkings of the markets have become too complicated for the average man to cope with on his own. The "complex economic issues" of our modern world, they contend, must be carefully weighed against one another, and a balance must be struck between the "ideal" and the "practical."

They foster the view that only government, supported by countless task forces, high-paid consultants, and innumerable subcommittees and bureaucratic agencies can find the right set of "compromises" to manage the mixed bag of interests in our nation. They allege that the government should manage the economy by inflating the supply of money and credit to encourage production, while simultaneously taxing the "excess profits" of the most productive industries; by deficit spending to provide the "underprivileged" with "equal opportunity," while forcing the businesses that might have been able to employ them to provide minimum wages, matching social security contributions, and unemployment insurance; by imposing trade barriers to encourage domestic industry, while simultaneously providing "developing" third world countries with low cost loans or outright grants so that they will be our "friends"; by subsidizing the price of wheat, sugar, soybeans, milk and other agricultural products to "maintain the independence and competitiveness of the American farmer," while giving away the surpluses or selling them at a loss to foreign nations; and the list goes on and on.

My true reaction to this view is not fit for print, so I'll temper it by saying: "Don't let them kid you!" If you balance your checkbook each month and understand that you can't operate with a negative balance indefinitely, you already know more about economics than most government policy makers. They and their countless contradictory programs and laws, which cost American producers (by producers I mean not just industries, but anyone who earns a living) a huge percentage of their income each year, are just shapeless, colorless pieces in a jigsaw puzzle with no meaningful solution. But with the right knowledge, you can make those pieces fit into *your* puzzle; you can turn government irrationality into dollars in the bank.

As a trader, speculator, or investor you make money by buying and selling market instruments in anticipation of price changes or value appreciation and depreciation. To do this well, you have to acquire a basic understanding of why people exchange things, what a market is, who participates in it, how a price is arrived at, why price changes occur, what will bring them about, when they will occur, and so on. In addition, because government intervention into the markets causes more price volatility than any single factor, you have to understand how government policy affects market conditions. Like a journalist seeking the truth in writing a story, you have to ask and answer the questions: Who? What? When? Where? Why? and How? Answering these questions on a general, fundamental level is the province of economics. Answering them in particular for a specific market is the province of market forecasting. Economics provides the fundamental ideas needed for accurate market forecasting.

Armed with the right basic economic principles, you can develop a logical method of market forecasting, rip through the masses of data, and discard the trash that will burden you when making decisions. You can start with a single correct idea, observe market data, and derive conclusions that are both sensible and accurate. You can listen to the opinions of the analysts and "experts" and test their conclusions according to basic premises that are unchanging in their validity, knowing that where there are contradictions, there are mistakes. In short, you can compete effectively with people who have much more particularized knowledge than you do.

It's not how many facts you know but the truth and quality of what you know that counts. I know a man who I personally watched answer every single question on Jeopardy—*correctly*—and yet he blew out as a trader. He spent countless hours developing ingenious but faulty strategies to predict market behavior. I admire the man's raw intellectual capability, but he has a problem when it comes to trading—he has never identified the basic principles which govern market behavior.

The purpose of this chapter is to identify and define the basic principles and terms of economics so that later, I can show you how to apply them to anticipate changes in the business cycle and make money with your knowledge. Like the picture on the cover of a jigsaw puzzle, these principles act as the guidelines for piecing together the puzzle of market forecasting.

ECONOMICS ACCORDING TO ROBINSON CRUSOE

I place economy among the first and most important virtues and public debt among the greatest of dangers; we must make our choice between economy and liberty; or profusion and servitude. If we can prevent the government from wasting the labors of the people under the pretense of caring for them, they will be happy.

—Thomas Jefferson

In this statement, Jefferson used the term "economy" in two slightly different senses. When he said economy was "among the first and most important virtues," he meant *careful and thrifty* management of public revenue. When he said we have to choose between economy and liberty, he was addressing the question of where the focus of government should be—whether government *should expand its purse and provide public services or focus on protecting life, liberty, and property.*

Jefferson understood better than any political leader in world history that government "profusion" can only be paid by "the labors of the people." He knew that a growing government budget and an extension of the services government offers "under the pretense of caring for [the people]" can only come at the expense of private property and individual liberty.

Unfortunately, over the last two centuries the people of this nation, through the selection of their political leaders, have chosen profusion over liberty to the extent that many of us now labor about 1 day in 3 to pay for government extravagance. And even that is not enough. With deficits consistently higher than $100 billion a year, future generations will inherit a financial burden that, if not arrested soon, will be impossible to bear. Jefferson has probably worn holes in his funeral clothes turning over in his grave.

We've reached this state because bad ideas, not just economic ideas but philosophical ideas, have been adopted and put into practice. Americans have been duped into thinking that there is no absolute right and wrong—only a balance of relative elements, that life is enormously complex and nothing is simple, and that therefore it is best to leave economic policy in the hands of the "experts."

I am not writing a philosophical treatise, but nothing is more absolute than life or death—and life means *economic* survival. I won't tell you that everything is simple, but I will tell you that most things are not as complex as they seem. I can't describe every mistaken economic notion and then refute it, but I can supply you with the basic definitions and principles that I *know* are right and appeal to logic and the size of my bank account, not the conventional wisdom, for confirmation. So let me start from scratch by answering the question, "What is economics?"

Economics is the study of a branch of human action. According to economist Ludwig von Mises, "It is the science of the means to be applied for the attainment of ends chosen[3].... [It] is not about things and tangible material objects; it is about men, their meanings and actions."[4] In other words, it is the study of the instruments, methods, and actions available to human beings for attaining their goals. This definition serves as the first principle of economic analysis and market forecasting; understanding it is a prerequisite for integrating all other principles into a unified, coherent system and profiting from your knowledge.

Most economics texts would define economics more like this: the study of the "production, distribution, and use of income, wealth, and commodities."[5] While it is true that economics is concerned with these things, this is *not* a true definition. It implies, for example, that income and commodities already exist and that they stand apart from wealth. It assumes a level of development such that distribution is a major concern. In short, it assumes that people exist at a high level of sophistication in society, when in fact that very sophistication is the *result* of fundamental economic principles that apply first to the individual, even if he is alone on an island.

Consider, for example, Daniel Defoe's character Robinson Crusoe. His actions demonstrate concretely and clearly the fundamentals of individual economic behavior that lead to the formation of a market economy. Stranded on an island visited only by cannibalistic savages, Crusoe first devised a method of acquiring more food than he immediately needed and storing it so that he could redirect his efforts toward achieving other necessities. He used the time he saved to build shelter, provide for his defense against the natives, and manufacture clothing. Then through industry, ingenuity, and management of time, he simplified the process of acquiring essentials and went on to produce other luxuries as time allowed.

The keys to the process of increasing his standard of living were *evaluation, production, saving, investment,* and *innovation.* He *evaluated* the ends and means available to him and chose the alternatives that best addressed his needs. The *value* of each thing that he sought was set by his judgment according to his perception of what was most needed, the means available to obtain it, and what it would cost him to get it relative to the alternatives. He *produced* the essentials necessary for survival and *saved* enough of them so that he could *invest* his energy into developing other products that he needed or desired. The *price* he paid at each step was the time and energy he spent according to his own evaluation of his needs. What he gained on balance in the exchange was his *profit.* If he made mistakes, and his efforts were futile, he suffered a *loss.* His actions were a matter of *exchange,* the exchange of a less desirable state for a more desirable one. At every step, he managed his time; he made choices based on the consequences of his options in the short, intermediate, and long term. As he became more and more sophisticated through *technological innovation,* the cost of essentials (in terms of time and energy spent to achieve them) diminished and he could afford to spend more of his time in the pursuit of "luxuries."

The concepts I've emphasized in explaining Crusoe's actions are generally associated with actions and results in a market economy. In fact, a market economy is simply the result of the same concepts applied in a social context. Evaluation, production, saving, investment, and innovation are *requirements* for man's survival and growth according to his nature as an individual, rational human being.

Properly considered, economics is the study of the means available to sustain life as a human being, and because people are social creatures, a major emphasis must be on surviving through association with others. But the fundamental focus must be on the requirements of one individual standing alone, for a society is simply a collection of individuals.

What is a Market?

The fundamental means of survival available to a group are the same as they are for one person. The only significant differences arise from the degree of complexity with which the actions of production and exchange are performed. The individual acting alone can exchange one state of affairs for another, but only through the expense of his own energy.

Within a free society, he can exchange the product of his effort (his property) for the products and services of others, gaining enormous benefits through the division of labor, specialization, and the innovation of others. Thus, a market economy makes survival easier, but through more complex means than any one person can achieve alone. Economic activity is more complex in terms of the resources and choices available; but in terms of survival and growth, it is much simpler. Crusoe couldn't have survived by acting as the janitor on his island, but there are many people who make a decent living washing the windows of skyscrapers in New York City.

Given knowledge as elementary as Crusoe's, and if protected from coercion by others, people attempt to trade their property by voluntary consent to their advantage. They evaluate the products and services offered for trade, and based on their ability to strike a bargain, choose those that are deemed most needed or desirable. On each side of the trade, one person exchanges something judged to be of lesser value for something judged to be of greater value. The trade is a matter of individual judgment, of each person's estimate of the value of holding one item versus another. The process of evaluation is necessarily subjective; that is, it depends on each person's specific preferences, judgment, values, and goals.

The fact that value is subjective—that people value things differently—both drives people to trade and makes it possible for both sides to profit.[6] The farmer who has excess corn but not enough meat values his surplus corn less than the rancher who needs corn to fatten his cattle—the opportunity for a trade exists. As more and more people associate and get involved in the process of *exchanging their surpluses,* trading becomes more complex. The interaction of numerous individuals, the social device of production and trade through free association, is called a market.

A market is the means people use to engage in the voluntary exchange of property according to the law of supply and demand. This definition applies equally to a local flea market and to the New York Stock Exchange. The system of exchange may be simple or complex, but the defining characteristic of a market as such is that it is composed of a group of individuals engaged in trade—engaged in the process of trying to exchange property in their self-interest.

THE ROLE OF MONEY

Money is necessary only after members of the marketplace have achieved a high level of productivity and long-term control over their lives. In its essential form, money is simply a commodity which is so generally desirable that it is acceptable to virtually anyone in an intermediate exchange. It is no less a commodity than pickled herring, but it has a longer shelf life (durability), has a universally recognized value, is divisible, and is portable. Money so simplifies the process of exchange that direct barter becomes unnecessary. It makes economic calculation possible; it provides a means for people to translate the inherently subjective hierarchy of their economic values into numeric terms. And it provides a means of quantifying and saving the surplus of products over consumption. By accepting dollars or gold (or whatever the accepted medium is), an individual relies on its buying power in the future, whether that be minutes, days, or years. Thus, money is a product which serves as a medium of exchange and a store of value, but which is no more and no less subject to the laws of supply and demand than any other product or service.

Another form of money arose from a sophistication in the extension of credit. Credit is a market innovation created to utilize the otherwise idle savings of individuals. In the early history of credit, when gold and/or silver were the accepted money, the metal itself was loaned (usually secured by specified collateral) in return for a promise to pay the original amount borrowed plus interest. Then a new innovation was created — the money certificate or bank note.

Lenders discovered that a certificate promising to redeem to the bearer a specified amount of gold or silver was a suitable and convenient medium of exchange. Once these certificates were recognized as acceptable due to the soundness and reputation of the financial institution which issued them, it didn't take a genius to realize that more certificates could be issued than actual deposits of hard currency, and *fiduciary media*[7] were created.

As long as the issuer carefully scrutinized the prospects of repayment and maintained a reputation of soundness with depositors, it could *create* money substitutes (bank notes and money certificates) by extending credit beyond the limits of its hard currency deposits. In this way, and for the first time, the rate of growth of wealth could be accelerated beyond that possible by loaning hard currency — all based on the lender's judgment of the borrower's ability to produce and trade in the future.

When the government stayed out of it, the growth of fiduciary media was regulated primarily by market factors.[8] That is, the bank was ultimately liable to redeem *all* outstanding notes in gold or silver, so the quantity of precious metal deposits provided an objective standard and a check on the limit of credit expansion. Like any other business, some banks prospered and other banks failed; and some depositors earned interest on their savings and other depositors lost everything. But overall, the innovation of extending credit beyond actual savings dramatically accelerated the growth of wealth.

Today, *fiat* money — paper declared to be legal tender by the government — is the accepted medium of exchange. Fiat money is similar to fiduciary media in the sense that the currency itself has no use except as a medium of exchange, but it is different in that there is no objective value backing it. In a fiat money system the government, not market factors, determines the supply of money and credit. The objective limits are gone, replaced by the subjective limits imposed by government bureaucrats.

The banking system holds reserves not as precious metals, but as demands for government notes[9] secured by the power to tax and print money.[10] By stipulating fractional reserve requirements for lending, buying, and selling government money market instruments, and manipulating interest rates, government central banks set the limits of credit availability. These limits largely determine the level of borrowing by businesses and consumers, which in turn sets the rate of growth or decline of the money supply.

Even though the supply of money and credit are government controlled, market principles still govern the purchasing power of money and the cost of credit. Money and credit are still subject to the law of supply and demand, but the supply side of the equation is manipulated. And savings are still the basis for sound business expansion through the prudent extension of credit.

Credit, if properly managed, accelerates the growth of wealth because it provides the most efficient use of savings and the potential productive capacity of individuals and institutions. Money saved is a claim on unconsumed goods. Savers choose to forgo immediate consumption in favor of future consumption or investment. Through the advent of credit, they can make a deal, either directly or through the institution holding their money, to let others borrow their savings for consumption or investment in return for a promise of greater purchasing power in the future. Borrowers use the loan to purchase unconsumed goods either for consumption or investment, but either way they are obligated to *create* enough new wealth to pay back the loan plus interest. The lending institution creates new money when it makes the loan, but if the money is not repaid out of newly created wealth, then *actual* savings are consumed.

What Is Wealth?

Wealth is simply an accumulation of products and services which are both available and wanted for consumption. The only way to create wealth is to produce more than is consumed, which is made possible through technology. Technology is an applied science, and science means knowledge. People increase their productivity by acquiring new knowledge and applying it. In many ways, our lives are so abundant that this fact is easy to forget. We take for granted the efficiencies introduced in the market through innovations such as specialization, the division of labor, and mechanization. These were all *discoveries*, ideas in the creative minds of individual people that were transformed into reality. In a market economy, everyone gains from the creator's discovery. The efficiencies gained through technological innovation cascade through the market so that each person can produce more in less time. As each person produces more, he or she can consume more, according to the law of supply and demand.

No matter how sophisticated the products and services become, no matter how many people get involved in the process, the principles that Crusoe employed on his island remain immutable. To live, one must *evaluate* what is required or desired to enhance life, and *produce* in order to acquire it. The *price* one pays is what one must give up in order to acquire the desired item. To accumulate wealth, one must *save* so that time and intermediate products can be *invested* in acquiring other goods. To diversify one's labor requires *innovation*, which increases the time efficiency of one's industry.

ECONOMICS AND HUMAN NATURE

Business is like a man rowing a boat upstream. He has no choice; he must go ahead or he will go back.

—Lewis E. Pierson

A free market economy is a human invention based on a view of humanity as consisting of independent, rational beings capable of providing for their own survival. It is an invention, but one which arises spontaneously, as a natural result of individuals acting reasonably and uncoerced in a social setting. Governments don't create markets; they take them away through forceful intervention. If government leaves its citizens alone, markets arise automatically, almost as if they have a life of their own.

As evidence, I offer the fact that even in societies where production and trade are tightly controlled by autocratic or collectivist regimes, "black" markets are rampant and are most often silently sanctioned and even patronized by the authorities. For example, a recent television program about Poland explained how the local government in a small city took a few acres of land and divided it into small plots (smaller than the back yard which many American suburbanites take for granted) and distributed them to families so they could grow vegetables for their own consumption. Almost immediately, the rights to use the plots were trading on the silently sanctioned black market for amounts far exceeding the average yearly earnings of a Polish family. The reason? Fresh fruit and vegetables were (and I presume still are) practically nonexistent in the state-run markets but sold on the black market for premium prices. A family that acquired a few plots instead of one and produced small crops for sale in the private market could more than double their yearly income.

While such "gray markets" spring up any time trading in a highly desired item is restricted by any government, the idea of markets *as such* is condemned in collectivist regimes. For example, in the Soviet Union, a completely different set of principles is derived from the study of "the means applied to the attainment of ends chosen." Human beings are viewed not as independent beings existing for their own sake, but as a disposable natural resource designed to serve the greater whole—the state or the collective. By this view, to act as Crusoe did to improve his standard of living is *self*-fulfilling and therefore opposed to the fundamental communist tenet "from each according to his ability, to each according to his need." In any issue, the "common good" is the standard of value; and the "collective wisdom," as interpreted by self-appointed guardians, is the final judge of truth and falsehood. [11]

For them, the concepts of value, price, investment, and innovation have completely different meaning and focus. Bureaucrats attempt to set value by government dictate, and price by decree. State planners invest resources without regard for profit. They try to make people work without personal incentive or potential for substantial self-improvement. And the result is a society of people so tired of living at a subsistence level that its political leaders are, at this writing, in the process of removing many market constraints for fear of total economic collapse and political rebellion.

I bring up what may seem to be political issues for a very important reason. You can't separate economic thinking from a view of the nature of human beings. The dominant philosophic view of humanity in any culture will determine the nature of its political structure and therefore the nature of its economic activity. The closer that philosophic view comes to being correct, the more successful economic policy will be. The extent that people are viewed as rational beings, not infallible but nevertheless capable of providing for their own survival with actions based on the independent exercise of their minds, is the extent to which the society will be free and unfettered by government intervention. And the extent to which a society is free is the extent to which it will be successful in terms of a general and increasing rise in the standard of living of its people (i.e., in terms of the accumulation of wealth).[12]

Just so you don't think I'm getting too abstract, let me give you just one example of how I applied this thinking and profited from it. There has been a strong socialist-collectivist element in France for most of the twentieth century. But in 1981, François Mitterrand, an ardent socialist, surprised the world by winning the Presidential election over the relatively moderate incumbent, Valéry Giscard d'Estaing. The *New York Times* wrote about Mitterrand with high praise, even though his platform was predictable for a socialist.

He promised to create full employment and prosperity by nationalizing major segments of industry including the banking system, imposing heavy taxes on the rich, introducing massive social welfare programs, and stimulating the economy by inflating the currency.[13] I knew (and so did many others who understand economic realities) that Mitterrand's attempts to control market activity would lead to disaster, and that the value of the French franc relative to the dollar would collapse.

I immediately went short the franc—it was 4 to 1 on the dollar—and covered approximately three weeks later when it was at 6 to 1 (it eventually went to 10 to 1), making a very substantial profit with virtual certainty that I was right. I knew I was right because, paraphrasing Aristotle, "something cannot be and not be at the same time and in the same respect." This translates in economics to "you can't get something for nothing." By 1983, the effects of Mitterrand's policies were apparent. Prices were increasing at a 12% annual rate. The government had huge budget and balance of trade deficits. The people had suffered a general decline in the standard of living. The franc fell even further relative to other currencies. And unemployment was at 10% of the work force. Amazingly, Mitterrand still holds his office today! I suppose this is to be expected, for as our founding fathers stated in the preamble to the Declaration of Independence: "All experience hath shown that mankind are more disposed to suffer while evils are sufferable, than to right themselves by abolishing the forms to which they are accustomed."

Unfortunately, there are strong collectivist elements in every nation in the world, including the United States. To some extent, people are universally regarded as being responsible not just for their own lives, but also for the welfare of others.

The purpose of government, according to collectivist ideology, is to provide for the common good through forceful redistribution of wealth from those who produce to those who can't (or won't), or to those who don't produce as much. Consequently, markets in the United States and worldwide are, in varying degrees, regulated and controlled.

In particular, the supply of money and credit is totally in politicians' hands, and therefore the markets are largely at the mercy of bureaucratic whim. But just as a good detective can apprehend a criminal by taking on his mindset, so it is possible to apprehend the course of government policy by taking on the mindset of key figures in power. The extent to which they are collectivist is the extent to which they will intervene in the markets and create imbalances of varying forms. By examining the effects of their interventionist policies on production, savings, investment, and innovation and by analyzing the impact on supply and demand in the various markets (assuming of course the government doesn't change its policies in mid-stream, which it often does), you can predict the direction of price movements.

To anticipate future economic policy, you must understand the policy weapons available, as well as the character and intent of the men in crucial positions of power. In the United States, the most fundamental policy weapons are taxes, the level and method of funding deficit spending, the Federal Reserve Board's control of money and credit, and specific laws restricting production and trade. The chief personalities to observe are the President, the Fed Chairman, the Secretary of the Treasury, and key Congressional leaders. By understanding first what these men *can* do, and then anticipating what they *might* do based on their view of the nature of human beings, you can position yourself to profit from future government action.

Analyzing effects is much simpler than anticipating new policy. As Adam Smith put it in his book, *The Wealth of Nations:*

> That state is opulent where the *necessaries* and *conveniences of life* are easily come at.
> . . . To talk of the wealth of nations is to talk of the abundance of its people. Therefore,
> whatever policy tends to raise the market price diminishes public opulence and the
> wealth of the state, and hence it diminishes the necessaries and happinesses of people.

Government interference in the economy has consequences directed by distinctly market principles. One simple principle is: *Price controls cause shortages, and price supports cause surpluses.* For example, when Ronald Reagan was elected in 1980, the domestic oil production industry was enjoying a government-stimulated boom brought about by tariffs on imported oil, an artificial shortage induced by the OPEC cartel, and a complex system of price controls and tax benefits created by the Carter Administration which put a price limit on "old oil" but let the price of newly produced oil float. There was a drilling frenzy—everyone was speculating on oil wells.

After his election, Reagan announced a plan to deregulate the oil industry. Shortly thereafter, I got a call from a stock broker friend of mine who urged me to buy Tom Brown, an over-the-counter oil stock that had enjoyed a mercurial rise from $2 a share to about $68 a share. I told him, "Jimmy, it's over for the oil industry; I might want to *short* that stock." He pleaded with me not to short it because Tom Brown was a friend of his, so I didn't, but I did short many other oil stocks.

I told Jimmy that the oil cartel in the Mideast would soon collapse from competitive pressure and that Reagan's proposed deregulation would absolutely kill the domestic oil industry as free competition drove prices down. He slowed down his purchasing but held on to his positions hoping to close them out in 1981 for tax reasons. By January 1981, however, his oil portfolio was down about 25%. The S&P 500 index, which was heavily weighted by the oil stocks, topped in November 1980. Tom Brown eventually dropped back to about $2. Needless to say, I profited handsomely by acting on very simple principles.

Now let me project into the future a little bit using the same principles. The recent increase in the legal minimum wage will decrease the profitability of fast food stores and other retail outlets, forcing some out of business and others to lay off workers. Automation devices will enjoy increased use as they become relatively more valuable due to the increased cost of labor. Unemployment among the unskilled labor force and youth will increase, and the demand for government assistance programs will increase. "[I]n the name of caring for the people" the government will once again contribute to the impoverishment of the nation. Government intervention doesn't circumvent the laws of supply and demand; it simply maldistributes factors on both sides of the equation.

To reiterate, economics is important because it describes the instruments, methods, and activities human beings employ to achieve ends or goals. The focus of economics must be first on the individual acting alone, and then on the individual acting in a social setting. The principles that apply to one person apply equally to any group and to society as a whole. For economic principles to be correct, they must be based on a view of humans as independent, thinking beings in pursuit of their own fulfillment. Any other view will lead to contradictions—mistaken judgments that result in failure when action is taken based on them. Like Robinson Crusoe, everyone must understand the concepts of evaluation, production, savings, investment, and innovation in order to survive and flourish as human beings. For the trader, speculator, and investor, a more detailed knowledge of these principles is an indispensable tool for market forecasting, particularly for evaluating the effects of government intervention on price movements.

PRODUCTION BEFORE AFFLUENCE

Opportunities multiply as they are seized; they die when neglected. Life is a long line of opportunities. Wealth is not in making money, but in making the man while he is making money. Production, not destruction, leads to success.

—John Wicker

Suppose you went to work for someone, and every day you just sat and drank coffee, read the comic strips, and doodled on company stationery—that's it. How long do you think you would last? Not long, for sure. Your employer would justifiably fire you for not contributing anything of value to the business—for not *producing* anything.

It is an inescapable fact that human beings have to produce in order to survive and prosper. Production is the act of bringing something new into existence, by recombination and rearrangement of natural and/or man-made elements, which is designed for a specific purpose. By the phrase "bringing something new into existence" I don't mean to imply that something can come from nothing. What was a fish, the fisherman turns to food; by his actions and innovation he brings food into being. What was steel, copper, aluminum, plastic, textiles, and so on, the auto maker turns into a car. The film producer combines the director, actors, writers, and crew to make a film for entertainment, advertisement, or education. The doctor attempts to produce the health of his patient. The stock trader brings into being an evaluation and an exchange. You get the idea.

The act of production can be simple or complex—from gathering food to the manufacture of plastics from refined oil derivatives. The products can range from biological necessities to abstract ideas—from food to poetry—but in each case, something new is created that is intended to serve a predefined goal or end. There are some all too influential pressure groups that condemn production beyond a certain point. They say that through "overproduction" humanity is progressing farther and farther away from its "natural state" and speak of the "simplicity and beauty" of the few remaining food-gathering tribes in remote regions of the world. For example, the organization manual of Friends of the Earth declares, "The only really good technology is no technology at all," further declaring that economic development is "taxation without representation imposed by an elitist species upon the rest of the natural world." (I wonder where the *artificial* world is.) Others refer wistfully to the fabled "Garden of Eden" as man's ideal state and hold that productive work is mankind's punishment for seeking knowledge of good and evil.

Can you imagine living your life totally dependent on fickle mother nature, spending each day hunting and gathering food in never ending repetition? Can you really imagine living in a "paradise" where no thought and no action were required, in which "to produce" was inconsequential and irrelevant? What would be your source of pleasure and happiness if all your provisions for survival and all decisions were predetermined—if alternatives were neither necessary nor possible? Whatever this sort of "paradise" would be, it could hardly be called a "human" existence, and I would have no desire to take part in it. I have to wonder why some people regard a beaver dam as "natural," but not the New York skyline—both are the result of animals acting according to their nature.

The basis of production is, in Ayn Rand's words, " the application of reason to the problem of survival."[14] People survive through the use of their minds; by identifying their requirements and desires, ordering them according to the evaluation of their relative importance, discovering the means to achieve them, and taking productive action. Unlike other animals, people *create* their environment by remolding nature in accordance with its laws. They can lift themselves out of nature's harshness, make scarce necessities abundant, prolong human life, and open whole new frontiers of challenge and opportunity. But they can do so only as long as they are free to produce.

I have carefully defined production to include *all* purposeful action that results in the attainment of a goal or value in an attempt to dispel a mistaken notion, widespread in economic thinking, that only action which results in the creation of material goods is "productive." Many economists divide industry into the productive sector and the service sector, as if those who provide services aren't productive. Some lament the growth of automation and mechanization saying that it is forcing labor to move into the service sector and that therefore the pool of skilled and educated labor will continue to decline. Services, they declare, act only to redistribute wealth rather than generate it. This is a very short-sighted and mistaken view that arises from a mistaken concept of economic value and wealth.

An economic value is *anything* that fulfills a need, is recognized as such, and is attainable—which includes both commodities and services. I use "need" here in the widest sense to mean that which is required, desired, or wanted; and I assume that only one person can determine need—the individual. If enough individuals desire and are willing to pay for the same economic value, then it has *market* value.

It is a business's goal to recognize or create market value and profit by satisfying consumers' desires. In pursuing this goal, businessmen use mechanization, automation, and other innovations to make more products and services available to more people at a cheaper price. The laborers who are temporarily displaced by technological improvements may move into the service industry, but they may also be absorbed by the manufacturers of the complex capital goods which make mechanization and automation possible. No matter which, both are a new source of wealth. The savings gained in mechanization are invested in new products and services, and the net wealth of the nation is increased. You might call it nature's way of upgrading and improving mankind. New, more economical methods of production replace old ways, forcing people at all levels of society to upgrade their knowledge and skills in order to compete in the markets.

While there are strong factions, especially in organized labor, that would prefer stagnation to growth, those who embrace change and continually expand their knowledge are likely to grow, not only financially, but also personally. Continually thinking, learning, and producing are fundamental requirements for gaining a sense of self-esteem and self-worth. If this fact were more widely understood and applied, it would contribute to a healthier, happier, and more productive culture.

The idea that the service industry is unproductive is totally unfounded. Beyond attaining the subsistence commodities of food, shelter, and clothing, there are an unlimited number of options available for individuals to dispose of the products of their efforts; to use their wealth. If they choose to spend money in an expensive restaurant, they are consuming their wealth, but in so doing helping to pay the construction workers who built the structure, the landlord who owns it, the furniture manufacturer who built the tables and chairs, the wages of the waiter who serves them, and so forth. Their consumption supports, in part, the ability of countless others to produce.

Economists often divide the nation into "producers" and "consumers" as if they were a different species, perhaps even at odds with one another. While this division has some value for analytical purposes, actually every producer is a consumer and every consumer is a producer (unless you are talking about someone who spends away an inherited fortune or who lives on the government dole). The man who works in an automobile assembly plant contributes to creation of the finished product. Even though his role is as an intermediary in the process, he is nonetheless productive. The same is true for a waitress in a restaurant—she creates a portion of the atmosphere and service that is paid for. These people are wage earners, producers who trade their product for wages, and then in turn trade their wages for the goods and services of others. For each individual, the simultaneous role of producer-consumer—the chain of action consisting of produce and trade, produce and trade—is the *only way* people can legitimately achieve their ends in a free market economy.

To produce is to create *potential* wealth. Wealth is an accumulation of unconsumed goods, whether products or services—anything that is considered to be of value by individuals in the marketplace. In this sense, a waiter's as yet unused services (if he is employed at a profitable restaurant) are wealth. The fact that today we generally measure wealth in monetary terms does not change its essential nature. An accumulation of money is simply an accumulation of claims on market goods and services, but one which varies in value over time.

The measure of success in the marketplace is the ability to accumulate wealth by either creating or anticipating the demand for one's products or services at a price that will sustain not only survival, but economic growth. Production is the first step in this process; saving is the next.

SAVINGS, INVESTMENT, CREDIT, AND WEALTH

Savings is investment.

—Henry Hazzlit

While production is the prerequisite to survival, savings is the prerequisite for economic growth. To accumulate wealth, the first step is to produce more than is required for immediate consumption. Then, two alternatives are possible: the surplus can be stored for consumption at a later date, which is called plain saving; or the stored product can be used either to enhance future productivity or for sustenance while working toward ends that take longer to achieve, which is called capital saving or capital accumulation.

With plain saving, products are set aside but sooner or later will be consumed leaving nothing in their place. With capital saving, goods are accumulated which are designed for either improving the production process or creating new products altogether. It is capital savings which leads to the improvement of man's material condition and frees him to further enhance life, not only by learning and producing more, but also by enjoying leisure and recreational activities. Capital saving is an investment in the future, and in this way, savings is investment.

Saving is an act of choice based on a discounting of the value of consuming future products against the value of consuming existing products. The ratio of the value assigned to existing products and the value assigned to future products is called originary interest[15] — it is a measure of the *interest* in consuming now versus consuming later. The higher originary interest is, the lower will be the rate of capital savings, and conversely, the lower it is, the higher will be the rate of capital accumulation and therefore the rate of growth of wealth.

Originary interest shows itself in the financial markets through the rate of growth or decline of capital goods,[16] which is directly tied to the level of individual savings and the supply of and demand for credit. Capital accumulation *is not* directly tied to the interest rate. The market interest rate is the cost of credit of which originary interest is only one component. But originary interest is the underlying driving force which determines whether people will consume now or later. It varies from person to person and is dependent on a wide range of conditions. The reason for this distinction will become apparent when I discuss the effects of monetary policy on the business cycle in the next chapter. Ultimately, the decision to save is based on the ability and desire to forgo consumption now in exchange for higher returns in the future; it is the choice not to consume today at the expense of growth tomorrow.

The engine of growth is new technology, which arises from creative innovation and the investment of knowledge, time, energy, and resources gained through savings. Technology is applied knowledge, and innovation is an act of creation. Therefore, technological innovation is the act of creating new ways to apply knowledge. The first fisherman who thought of catching fish with a net was an innovator, and the net was his new technology. In effect, the net was a form of savings — a capital good used to simplify the process of production.

The first net fisherman had to save in order to acquire the knowledge, time, energy, and materials to construct the net. Once he created the net and learned how to use it, he saved enormous amounts of productive energy by making each of his working hours more fruitful. He could not only provide fish for himself and his family, but could trade his surplus for the products of others. Fish became less scarce because they required less labor to attain, and therefore his neighbors could afford to specialize in producing other necessities to trade with him for his fish. This example, on a primitive scale, shows how the efficiencies gained from one man's saving, innovation, investment, and capital accumulation filter through the community and make everyone more productive.

At each step in the progress of civilization, we inherit the knowledge of other people and improve on it. This too is a form of savings that leads to growth. We inherit the canoe and make a sailboat. The sailboat becomes a steamship. The steamship becomes a diesel-powered supertanker. And so on. Underpinning the whole process is the savings and preparatory work arising from earlier generations and ultimately from the creativity of individuals. If our fishing ancestors had simply consumed their nets and canoes without bothering to invest the time to replace them; if our ancestors hadn't passed down the knowledge of how to grow wheat and make flour; if human beings, like other animals, were pure consumers, civilization as we know it would not exist. It is savings, of products and of knowledge, which makes investment and growth possible.

It is easy to see at a primitive level of social development how savings makes investment possible. It is not so easy to see the process at work in a complex market economy. For example, when a manufacturing company borrows money to invest in capital goods such as new and more efficient machinery, it is difficult to see where savings comes into play. It is so difficult in fact, that economists like John Maynard Keynes convinced (or at least provided a rationalization for) other influential economists and government policy makers that production and savings are not the prerequisite for growth.

In Keynesian terms, *aggregate demand,* as measured in dollars of disposable income, is the driving force behind production. Put a few extra dollars into everyone's hand, he said, and they'll spend it, thereby increasing demand and inducing industry to produce more (assuming of course that businesses don't respond simply by increasing prices). Savings on the other hand, promotes "underconsumption," takes away from aggregate demand, diminishes the GNP, and stifles growth. According to this view, government can guarantee prosperity by pumping money into the economy through deficit spending and easy credit policies and by encouraging spending rather than saving. The problem for Keynesian thinkers is simply one of careful management of government spending and of the money supply.

I mentioned earlier that money serves as a medium of exchange and a store of value, and that when someone saves money he or she is withholding claims against unconsumed goods and services. On the surface of it, based on these two observations, it may seem that saving is unproductive, that in fact savings and investment are not directly tied. You might argue that by not buying anything, the saver reduces demand for the products available on the market, diminishes the profits of industry, and therefore contributes to a decline in business activity. Nothing could be further from the truth.

Consider the two basic types of savers: the miser who stuffs money into the mattress, and the typical saver who puts money into a bank or into some other instrument such as bonds, gold, or stocks. There aren't many Scrooges in the world who hoard money in mattresses for no other reason than for the love of holding it. But to the extent that this happens, the result is a reduction in the supply of money in circulation relative to other commodities, producing a downward pressure on prices and an increase in the purchasing power of money. Remember that money is a commodity no more and no less subject to the laws of supply and demand than any other commodity. If its supply is diminished, its value relative to other products will go up. Wealth cannot be equated with a quantity of money without regard to the purchasing power of money.

In the last few decades of the nineteenth century, industrial expansion and the standard of living in the United States grew at the fastest rate in the history of the world, before or since. But an economist measuring wealth in terms of dollars wouldn't necessarily recognize this. Over a 20-year period, during the height of the expansionary period, the gold- and silver-based money supply remained relatively stable, and the general level of prices *fell* about 50%. In fact, throughout the eighteenth and nineteenth centuries, except during war time when the government financed expenditures through the issue of paper money, declining prices were the rule, not the exception.

Today, because we are so completely indoctrinated to our government's inflationary monetary policy, this seems almost bizarre. But if you think of money as a commodity, then it makes sense. Just as businessmen today attempt to account for continually rising prices in their pricing and return calculations, so businessmen used to anticipate the effects of falling prices. Businesses actually increased profits during periods of declining dollar revenues, because the value of the dollar was constantly increasing. The difference is that market factors, not the government, were the principle determinant of the supply of money and credit.

Many modern economists equate falling prices with economic decline. The reason is that since the late 1920s the only time the general level of prices has declined is during periods of depression or recession. A careful examination of these periods will show government intervention at its worst. For example, in the 1930s, the Federal Reserve Board reduced the money supply by one-third while Congress simultaneously passed legislation to maintain prices at 1920s levels. Farmers were paid to burn potatoes and plow under cotton crops to create high prices. (Many farmers in the 1930s used mules for plowing, and mules have a reputation for being dumb. But to plow under a crop, the mule had to walk directly on the plants, and it was said that the mules refused to do it. One editorialist suggested that the mules knew more about economics than the government.) Merchants were rewarded with a "Blue Eagle" insignia in their windows if they adhered to artificially high government price guidelines, and Roosevelt in his "fireside chats" encouraged consumers to shop only at Blue Eagle stores and to snitch on merchants who violated the guidelines. Labor legislation empowered and encouraged unions to increase their wage demands and stopped industries from instituting wage reductions. The result was that real wages increased during a period of declining output and widespread unemployment. For some reason, it never dawned on government officials that a decrease in the money supply would necessarily result in lower prices! The result, of course, was the most prolonged recession in U.S. economic history.

Our government's spending and monetary policy alternates between inflationary booms driven by easy credit policies, followed by busts resulting from the tightening of money and credit to control inflation. It is our government's policies of deficit spending and control of the money supply through the Federal Reserve system that make it virtually impossible for modern Americans to imagine prosperity during a period of price declines. But wouldn't it be incredible to be able to put money in the bank and actually have its purchasing power *increase* without worrying about price inflation? Can you imagine how fast the prices of high-tech items would drop when you combined the effects of technological improvements, competition, *and* deflating prices because of the increasing purchasing power of the dollar? The major point is that business declines are not caused by, and do not necessarily have anything to do with, declining prices.

The miser, at worst, by removing money from circulation can have only a limited effect on prices and the markets. Assuming that the money supply is static, prices will eventually adjust to a higher level as the result of his actions. If the money supply is continually increasing relative to other goods and services, as is presently true, then his money will lose purchasing power. If a miser stuffed a million dollars into his mattress in 1940, it would today be worth only $120,000 in terms of relative purchasing power. So the miser really only hurts himself with his hoarding.

There are many alleged justifications for government regulation of money and credit, but among the most influential is Keynes' argument that saving is unproductive—that business declines are caused by "underconsumption," which means hoarding. For years, saving has been equated with hoarding, but I have just shown that the most foolish of misers really does no damage except to himself by stuffing money into his mattress.

The average saver is not a miser, but rather puts money into the bank or into other institutions and instruments which make savings available for use in the credit market. This kind of saver entrusts another person or institution to keep his money in return for the benefits to be derived from their management of his savings. It is this kind of savings that provides the fuel for an expanding economy. In addition, the higher the level of savings, the lower the cost of credit—it's a simple matter of supply and demand.

The principle is no different than Crusoe saving food so he would have time to build shelter. It just happens on a more abstract level and at a more accelerated pace through the process of credit transactions.

A credit transaction is an agreement to loan either goods or claims on unconsumed goods (money) to another person or group in return for repayment, usually plus interest, after the passage of some time period. The exchange is based on the lender's confidence in the borrower's ability to pay out of future production. If the borrower makes good on his loan, he exercises his borrowed claims (he spends the money) but also produces enough new wealth to replace them with claims of greater value (the principal amount plus interest). The positive difference between the value borrowed and the value returned is the lender's return for not consuming now.

If the borrower defaults, what actually happens is that the claims for the goods are exercised, the goods are at least partially consumed, and not enough new wealth is produced to replace them. The creditor is left with the burden of redeeming what value remains of the debtor's holdings. The difference in market value between what is loaned and what is redeemed is a loss—wealth is consumed—the goods no longer exist in their formerly marketable form.

A credit exchange is neither a gift nor a grant; it is a trade just like any other on the market. The borrower, whether an individual or a group, earns and builds credit by consistently producing and meeting obligations undertaken in exchange agreements (contracts). The money may be borrowed for investment or consumption, but either way the exchange is money or goods for a promise to pay. The lender chooses to loan the money rather than consuming it himself or investing it in his own pursuits, and in so doing puts confidence in the borrower's ability to repay.

The transaction is one based on a difference in time-preference between the creditor and the debtor.[17] The creditor, more precisely the depositor of savings, chooses to delay investment or consumption on his own account until some later date, and the debtor chooses to consume or invest beyond his current means and pay out of future production.

In a complex market economy, the majority of economic transactions involve credit of one form or another. Merchants receive their products from wholesalers with 30 days or longer to make payment. Auto dealers borrow money to buy inventory based on their ability to sell it profitably. Corporations borrow money through bond issues to finance business expansion. Stock speculators buy on margin. But no matter what form credit takes, it represents a claim on unconsumed goods traded by one party in return for a promise to pay by another. The lender chooses to forgo consumption until some future date, and the borrower chooses to consume now and pay for his consumption in the future.

I have already touched on the fact that when a bank makes a loan it doesn't actually lend away savings, it creates new money. Nevertheless, it *does* put actual savings (in the form of capital) at risk. On the upside, borrowers create enough new wealth to pay back the loan and still profit or at least break even. But on the downside, if they default, then existing goods (savings) are either consumed or rendered useless. When a business borrows money to invest in new equipment or machinery, two things happen: The business commits a portion of future profits to savings, and the lending institution puts actual savings at risk. In this way, no matter what the government's fiscal and monetary policy is, credit is tied directly to savings.

If I seem to be overemphasizing the fact that when you borrow money, what you are borrowing is someone else's claim on unconsumed goods, then it is only because I have been faced countless times by people who don't understand the relationship of savings, credit, investment, and wealth. Savings provide the basis for the extension of credit. Credit provides the fuel which accelerates investment in capital goods. And the accumulation of capital goods accelerates the rate of growth of wealth. But anytime a loan is "written off," someone somehow, now or later, pays the full price out of savings; that is, goods are consumed but *not* replaced.

There is a widespread and very dangerous misconception that because the government and the banking system can create money from what seems like nothing, they can also clean the slate of bad loans with an eraser without paying the price in real goods and services. The treasury in particular is viewed as an unlimited resource, bound only by public confidence. And like the "unsinkable" Titanic, the sick irony is that the government is floundering from the continuing demands of special interest groups for handouts when, by normal standards of prudence, the treasury should be considered bankrupt.

There is nothing magic about government borrowing and government "guaranteed" notes and loans. When the government sells a bond or T-bill, the purchaser refrains from consuming and lets the government consume in return for a promise to pay in the future. But unlike commercial borrowing, the government's ability to repay is backed not by its ability to produce in the future, but by its ability to *tax* in the future; which means that government borrowing is incurred at the expense of your and your children's future real income—their productive ability.

Government income, whether generated from taxes, borrowing, or inflation of the money supply is by its nature a burden on the productive capability of the nation. It is a forced redistribution of wealth that shifts the balance of normal market factors. Most government activity is inherently consumption oriented, and does not produce anything.[18]

The fact that government lending and borrowing are "guaranteed" changes nothing. The guarantee is based solely on the ability to tax and/or print money. And if debt is paid by printing money, the result is a debasement of the dollar's value through inflation, which is simply another (and much more perverse) form of taxation. You can't get something from nothing, but you can get nothing from something. Sooner or later, the debt incurred by deficit financing of government expenditures has to be paid in full, and so does the cost of a business expansion built and dependent upon easy credit. Whether the price takes the form of higher taxes, inflation, a general business decline (recession or depression), or some combination of the three, the price is always the same—wealth is consumed.

SUMMARY: THE CLOSEST THING THERE IS TO A FREE BREAKFAST

America never ceases to amaze me. I have a fax machine in my office that cost about $1600, and about once a week I marvel at what it can do. Somehow images on paper are turned to electric impulses that can be transferred over miles of phone cable to another machine where they are turned back into the same images.

I'm totally ignorant about chips, digitizers, transducers, and so forth, but for a mere $1600 I can reap the benefits of the creative minds and the countless hours and dollars that went into research, development, and marketing of that product. And I'm sure that if I had waited, I could have gotten a better product even cheaper.

On a simpler level, I can eat two eggs with toast and juice, and if I cook it myself, it costs me less than a dollar. Just think what it would cost if I tried to produce the same breakfast by growing wheat, grinding the flour, cultivating the yeast, raising the orange trees, raising the chickens, and so forth. It is simply fantastic—the closest thing there is to a free breakfast.

It's fantastic, but it is not an accident or a miracle; it is the result of productive people trading property by free association in the marketplace. Without government intervention, our economy would experience natural minor cyclical adjustments as the markets changed to accommodate new technologies, changes in consumer preferences, and shifts in credit; but production and prosperity would maintain an ever-increasing upward trend. But we have, and always have had, government intervention. As a result, we have a business cycle subject to major swings, both up and down. Everybody loves the upside, but very few know how to protect themselves from the downside.

As a businessman, the only way I know to protect myself from financial disaster in crashes, recessions, or depressions is through the ability to anticipate long-term market turning points and position myself accordingly. This means being leveraged and long at market bottoms and liquid and short at market tops. To do this requires an understanding of the basic economic principles I have described and the principles discussed in previous chapters.

In this chapter, I have presented the basic economic concepts required to understand the effects of government intervention on the markets. In the next two chapters, I'll show how the government, through deficit spending and the Federal Reserve System, intervenes with monetary and fiscal policy; and I will demonstrate how this intervention is the key determinant of the long-term trend of the economy. The objective is to demonstrate how to apply the fundamental principles of economics to stop the interventionists from consuming your capital, while making money in the process.

10

Booms and Busts: Who Holds the Pump and Who Holds the Needle?

The wavelike movement affecting the economic system, the recurrence of periods of boom which are followed by periods of depression [recession], is the unavoidable outcome of the attempts, repeated again and again, to lower the gross market rate of interest by means of credit expansion. There is no means of avoiding the final collapse of a boom expansion brought about by credit expansion. The alternative is only whether the crisis should come sooner as the result of a voluntary abandonment of further credit expansion, or later as a final and total catastrophe of the currency system involved.[1]

—Ludwig von Mises

BOOMS AND BUSTS: THE BUSINESS CYCLE

Since the mid to late eighteenth century, the debate has raged as to what causes broad cyclical fluctuations in the market economy. In the context of this book, I want to answer that question so you can make money, not only during market upswings, but also in the downswings when many businessmen and most investors are losing money or are at least giving back a large part of previous gains.

I started this chapter with the quote from von Mises because I have never read a more accurate and well-formulated answer to the question of what causes the business cycle than his. In spite of his rather obtuse style, his answer is simple. But like Einstein's simple formulation, $E = mc^2$, there is a lot of knowledge underlying the statement.

If you can understand the content of von Mises' statement with all its subtleties

133

and apply it to the U.S. and world system of money and credit, you will be better equipped to foresee major market turning points than, say, 90% of speculators in the markets.

In the statement, von Mises implies that to understand the business cycle, you have to understand the relationship of money, interest, credit, and the effects of credit expansion on the economy.

THE NATURE OF THE BUSINESS CYCLE

Almost everyone knows the nature of pyramid schemes such as chain letters, and most of us don't participate in them because we rightly assume that either the founders of the schemes are crooked or that there is a good chance of ending up at the top of the pyramid with everything to lose and nothing to gain. The business cycle is like an extremely elaborate pyramid scheme that repeats itself over and over again, introduced not necessarily by intention, but through widely accepted errors in economic thinking.

The phenomenon known as the business cycle didn't really begin until the middle of the eighteenth century. Before that, there were depressions, but their causes were easily discernable. A king would need money to wage a war or simply to fill his purses and would send out his marshalls to confiscate money (taxes). Naturally, this would cause a slump in commerce because it deprived people of their ability to carry on "business as usual."

Or perhaps during war, one nation would deprive another of an essential re-source, the way the North deprived Britain of cotton during the American Civil War, and cause a slump in industries dependent on that item, leading to a general economic decline. Whatever the source, it was relatively easy to identify the event which caused the economic downturn. Without these external, or *exogenous,* events, economic activity went along in more or less a straight line with steady but moderate growth.

Starting in about 1750, however, there emerged a recurring cyclical fluctuation in the economic activity of industrialized nations that wasn't so easy to explain. There were two coincident developments during this period of history: the industrial revolution, which began in England and spread throughout the western world; and the rise of central banking, specifically, central fractional reserve banking controlled by government regulators. Since these were the only new significant economic developments, political economists began to explore the possibility that one or the other of these two factors were responsible for the business cycle.

Two basic schools of thought emerged. One group, the mercantilists, assumed that there was something inherent, or *endogenous,* in the market economy which caused cyclical fluctuations in business activity. For this group, their focus was to find these causes and then use government control to eliminate them and provide a stable environment for business expansion. The other group, led by the classical economist, David Ricardo, explained the business cycle by analysis of the effects of paper money and credit expansion on trade.

In their terms, the business cycle is caused by the exogenous factor of government intervention in the money and credit markets. Unfortunately, the endogenous school triumphed, culminating in the economics of John Maynard Keynes, which in variant forms still dominates world economic thought today. Consequently, central banks, operating on the fractional reserve system, exist in every major industrial nation in the world—and so do booms and busts.

I realize that it is not enough to say that because central banks exist and booms and busts exist, that central banks are the cause. But before I explain exactly how central bank expansion of money and credit causes the boom/bust cycle, let me give an example from history, an example which repeats over and over again, just with different players.

Although the business cycle didn't develop until the mid-eighteenth century, central banking began in 1692 with the foundation of the Bank of England. Almost simultaneously, in The Royal Commonwealth of Massachusetts, the first fiat money was issued (money with no redeemable value in the precious metals). Obviously, even this early in banking history, some government advisors had recognized the short-term benefits of credit expansion and fractional reserve banking. Perhaps the best illustration of this is the so-called Mississippi Scheme, which occurred in France in the early eighteenth century.[2]

During his long and lavish reign from 1643 to 1715, King Louis XIV put the finances and economy of France into total disarray. After a period of prosperity (centered primarily in Paris and the immediately surrounding regions) brought about by extravagant royal spending, by the time of Louis XIV's death in 1715, both domestic and foreign commerce were on the decline, and the solvency of the French government was in question.

The national debt was 3 billion livres[3] (in the forms of *billets d'etat,* or government securities), the tax revenue was 145 million, and the government budget was 143 million, excluding the interest on the outstanding 3 billion debt. There was a debate whether the government should just declare bankruptcy and start from scratch, but the politicians of the time feared revolution and looked instead for a more expedient solution.

The government's first feeble attempt to remedy the problem was to devalue the currency through a recoinage, depreciating the currency by 20%. New coins were issued weighing ⅘ of the old coin, but with the same face value, and the populace was ordered by law to make the exchange. The net effect was to bring 72 million livres into the state treasury and to throw the commerce of the nation into a state of further disarray and economic depression.

To calm the public outcry which arose in response to the devaluation, the government slightly cut taxes and launched a reform program to eliminate widespread corruption among tax collectors. These measures drew public attention away from the crisis state of the country's finances but did little to bring the government into a state of solvency.

There emerged onto this scene a wandering Scotsman named John Law. An avid gambler and ladies' man, Law had fled from Scotland to the European continent after killing a man in a duel over a woman. In Europe, he found a home for both his gambling skills and his twentieth century ideas about money, credit, and government finance. Law was a firm believer that an entirely metallic currency system, unaided by paper currency, was inadequate for the commercial needs of a country and actually limited economic growth. In other words, like John Maynard Keynes, Law believed that prosperity could be bought through carefully managed credit expansion and inflation of the currency. (I have to wonder if some of the wild oats that Law was reputed to have sown ended up in the Keynes family tree.)

Law lobbied the Duke of Orleans, his friend and the regent of France,[4] and convinced him of the need for a private central bank to employ his currency and credit theories and bring France back to the fore as an economic power.

In 1716, the regent issued a royal edict authorizing Law and his brother to establish a bank, under the name of Law and Company, to be capitalized through the sale of 12,000 shares at 500 livres each, purchasable one-fourth in specie and the remainder in *billets d'etat*. The regent authorized Law's bank to issue bank notes instead of coin and decreed the notes as acceptable, at full face value, for payment of taxes (in effect, they were declared legal tender in a limited sense).

Law was no neophyte to banking. The son of a Scottish banker and an avid student of money, credit, and trade, Law knew that he had to establish public confidence in his bank's notes for the entire scheme to work. He immediately announced that all notes from his bank were payable on sight in the coin current at the time of issue. The public, reasonably fearing further devaluation of the coin, naturally favored holding Law's bank notes to coin and, almost immediately, the notes sold at a premium to the precious metals.

Public confidence in Law and his bank notes grew rapidly, the notes trading as high as a 15% premium to the metal coin, and branch bank offices were opened in five major French financial centers. During the same period, the *billets d'etat* were trading at a discount of 78.5% or more.

At this point, one could reasonably argue that Law's actions were based on sound economic principles. Above all, what France needed at the time was to restore confidence in the currency and credit of the nation. Law's fully backed paper currency did just that.

In effect, he offered his depositors an insurance policy against devaluation of the coin. As long as people believed in the credibility of Law's bank and his ability to redeem his notes in specie, his notes were literally "as good as gold." With confidence restored in the currency, both foreign and domestic commerce enjoyed a resurgence. Taxes were paid with greater regularity, and the debt of the nation was slowly but surely being retired.

But the Duke of Orleans, who really didn't understand what was happening, thought that paper currency was the magic cure for all of France's economic woes. Seeing what he thought was an opportunity to quickly retire the overwhelming government debt, the regent made two fatal errors in 1717.

First, he authorized Law to form a company with exclusive trading privileges in the Louisiana Territory along the entire west bank of the Mississippi River, which was thought to be rich with deposits of gold and silver. The company was capitalized through the sale of 200,000 shares with a par value of 500 livres each, which could be purchased with *billets d'etat* at face value, even though they were trading at roughly 16% of their original value at the time.

Second, the regent made Law's bank public, declaring it the Royal Bank of France. Totally blind to the consequences of his policies, the Duke then caused, over a period of a few years, the issue of over one billion livres in paper currency. Whether Law agreed with this policy is not known, but when the bank was operating under his authority, the paper issue had never exceeded 60 million livres.

The billion livres weren't just handed out on street corners throughout France; they were given out as loans. In other words, there was a huge and rapid credit expansion resulting in an inflation of the paper currency. In addition, in a further attempt to retire the still outstanding *billets d'etat,* another recoinage was ordered in which 5000 livres of a new and smaller coin were exchanged for 4000 of the old coins plus 1000 livres in the *billets d'etat* at their full face value.

The immediate consequence of the credit expansion was a speculative boom. Businesses and merchants that borrowed money bought domestic and foreign goods, domestic production was expanded, imports increased, and construction (especially around Paris) picked up. Leading the way in this boom was Law's Mississippi Company. The Duke of Orleans granted the company the exclusive rights to trade in India, China, and the South Seas, and to all the possessions of the French East India Company. The name of the company was changed to The Company of the Indies, and Law promptly arranged the sale of 50,000 new shares at 500 livres per share to be bought 100% with *billets d'etat* at their nominal value, while promising a 200-livre per year dividend to all stockholders.

There was an immediate speculative frenzy for the new stock issue. Believing Law to be a financial miracle worker, thousands of people filled the streets outside Law's residence, trying to get shares of the stock that was increasing in value daily. The regent saw an opportunity to retire the entire remaining national debt and authorized another issue of 300,000 shares to be sold at 5000 livres each, again payable in *billets d'etat*.

You might think that such an enormous increase in the stock issue would have quelled the frenzied speculation. It didn't. The credit expansion simply fanned the fire and soon the price of the stock was rising as much as 10 or 20% in the course of a few hours. Stableboys and housemaids became rich overnight, and the general sentiment was that the magical source of prosperity would never end. Amazingly, the paper currency maintained its integrity for several years, but slowly and surely, the gold and silver which supposedly backed the paper began to drain out of France into foreign countries.

As with all credit driven booms, the paper inflation caused prices in France to increase, making foreign products cheap relative to domestic products. As imports increased, specie payments to foreign governments also increased, creating a drain on the nation's stock of gold and silver. In addition, people who knew that gold and silver reserves at the Royal Bank were but a fraction of the paper circulation quietly began converting paper to coin and transporting the coin to foreign banks.

By 1720, the scarcity of coin was so great that it was becoming impossible to carry out foreign trade, which was carried out with hard currency. In an effort to stop the run on gold and silver, coin was decreed depreciated first to 5% below, and then to 10% below the paper, and specie payments at the bank were limited to 100 livres in gold and 10 in silver.

These stopgap measures held back the coming storm until Law made a fatal error in February of 1720. At his suggestion, a decree was issued forbidding anyone to hold more than 500 livres in coin, and also forbidding people from buying up precious stones, jewelry, silver settings, and so forth, under penalty of a heavy fine and confiscation of the holdings. The decree encouraged the public to inform on lawbreakers by providing an incentive reward of one-half the recovered amount. Rather than restore public confidence in the paper currency, this measure totally destroyed it and brought the country to the brink of revolution.

By May 27, 1720, the bank was forced to stop making payments in specie and the price of Law's stock was tumbling. The bubble burst, and the pyramid tumbled in what I believe was the first recorded stock crash in history. The stock of the India Company plummeted and the value of the paper currency depreciated relative to gold and silver in spite of every effort by the government to achieve the opposite. Commerce was in total disarray, and every measure the government took aggravated and prolonged the problem. Law, once a national hero recognized as the savior of the glory of France, became the scapegoat for the entire problem and was nearly murdered by angry crowds. He eventually left the country, carrying with him virtually nothing of the vast fortune he had amassed.

A council was formed to restore order to France's financial system. Their audit found that rather than being diminished, the government debt had risen to 3.1 billion livres. The corruption they found within the government financial offices was unbelievable, and some of the guilty were sentenced to life imprisonment at the Bastille. Eventually, order and solvency were restored to some degree, but as history shows, the same mistakes were made again and again, contributing to the impoverishment of the people and the growing division between the landed aristocracy and the working man. Eventually, these and other problems led to the abortive French Revolution and the eventual reign of Napoleon.

This story is such a wonderful microcosm of the effects of credit expansion on an economy that I couldn't help but tell it. Every boom/bust cycle in market history follows a similar, but not as dramatic or condensed, pattern. The pattern goes something like this. After a period of economic decline—a bust—economic activity is sluggish and there is a social clamor for the government to "do something." While the market is in the process of a necessary adjustment, some ingenious economic guru links up with the government and offers a plan for recovery.

Invariably, the plan calls for an end to inflation, a balancing of the budget, decreasing government deficits (if they exist), and stabilization of the currency relative to foreign currencies. BUT (and there always is a but), the policies to achieve these noble ends always involve some form of interference in the workings of the free market and eventually amount to little more than a new credit expansion that results, sooner or later, in another boom and bust cycle.

Why does central bank credit expansion necessarily cause a boom/bust cycle? Simply put, it results in a misallocation of resources and confuses economic calculation to such a degree that either, like a drug addict, higher and higher doses of credit expansion are required to stay one step ahead of the inevitable consequences, or the economy goes into cold turkey—a recession or depression. But to fully understand what happens, you have to go back to the economic fundamentals; you have to understand the effect that credit expansion has on originary interest.

Recall from the last chapter that Von Mises defined originary interest as the ratio of the valuation of present goods to the valuation of future goods, or "the discount of future goods as against present goods."[5] It is originary interest, as expressed by individuals exchanging in the marketplace, that determines the level of spending on consumer goods versus the level of plain and capital savings. In other words, originary interest determines how much of the available supply of goods in the marketplace is to be devoted to immediate consumption versus provisioning for the future. Its expression in the market is as a *component* of the market rate of interest.

The market rate of interest tends toward the level of originary interest held by a predominance of market participants. It is important to realize, however, that in the continuing operation of the market there is no fixed, constant level of originary interest. Rather, it varies from person to person, market to market, and within each market according to changes in valuations brought about by changing conditions and opinions. But there is a tendency, brought on by the competition of entrepreneurs, to drive originary interest to a uniform level.

To understand how credit expansion causes the boom/bust cycle, you have to understand the distinction between originary interest and the gross market rate of interest. The gross market rate of interest has three components: originary interest, an entrepreneurial component, and a price premium. The entrepreneurial component is the portion of interest which gives the creditor incentive to lend money for investment. In effect, the entrepreneurial component entitles the creditor to a portion of profits gained through the investment of his money. The price premium is an allowance, either positive or negative, for anticipated changes in the purchasing power of money. To put it in somewhat oversimplified terms, originary interest is the subjective value that the market places in consuming now versus consuming later, the entrepreneurial component is a premium which varies according to the creditor's confidence in getting his returns, and the price premium varies according to the creditor's assessment of the purchasing power of money in the future versus the present.

All three components of the gross market rate of interest operate in every credit transaction; they are all constantly changing, and they all affect one another. As with any other market, the final determinant of the nominal interest rate on each loan is supply and demand. In a free market, entrepreneurs and promoters attempt to make profits by selling products at a price exceeding production costs plus the gross market interest rate. The role of the gross market rate of interest is to show entrepreneurs and promoters how far they can go in withholding the factors of production from immediate consumption for the purpose of creating more products in the future. The market rate of interest guides entrepreneurs to make the best use of the limited amount of capital goods available, which are provided by the savings of market participants.

Credit expansion by central banks, under certain conditions, can completely reverse this role. Assume for the moment that the credit expansion takes the form of making more money available for banks to lend, as happened in France during the Mississippi Scheme fiasco. In cases like this, money has a driving force of its own, and the loan market is directly affected before any changes occur in the prices of commodities and labor.

At first, no change in originary interest occurs, but the entrepreneurial component of the gross market rate of interest rate drops due to the apparent availability of new capital for investment. Although no additional capital actually *does* exist, when entrepreneurs put pencil to paper, the increase in the supply of money available makes it appear that it *does* exist. Previously unfeasible projects now appear to be feasible. In the early stages of a credit expansion, there is no way for the entrepreneur to distinguish between money available and capital available—the whole basis for economic calculation is distorted.

Artificially lowering the market rate of interest has no real relationship to the supply of capital goods available or to the current level of originary interest. But because of the distortion of increased credit availability, decisions are made as if they were directly related. As a result, capital goods are diverted away from their best use, encouraging poor investments and eventual capital consumption.

In addition, the role of the price premium component of interest rates in economic calculation is totally subverted. Because the money supply expansion directly affects the loan market before it affects prices, there is a lag time before the price premium can possibly reflect the inevitable rise in prices which will occur as a result of the money supply expansion. Consequently, the price premium component of the gross market rate of interest is artificially low in the early stages of the credit expansion and creditors unknowingly make loans at too low an interest rate.[6]

In a fractional reserve banking system,[7] credit expansion always causes an inflation in the money supply, as I will discuss in detail shortly. Advocates of an inflationary expansion argue that the price increases which occur from money supply inflation affect commodities before they affect wage rates. Consequently, they say, producers' costs go up, consumer prices go up, and the wage earners and salaried people, who have less tendency and ability to save than other classes in the market, are forced to restrict expenditures, and savings are made available for capital expansion.

On the other hand, they say, entrepreneurs and businesses, who have a greater tendency to save, enjoy the benefits of higher prices and increase their savings in greater proportion than consumption. As a result, there is a general tendency toward an intensified accumulation of new capital paid for by the diminished consumption of wage earners and salaried people. This *forced savings* lowers the rate of originary interest (lowers interest in immediate consumption) and therefore, because of an increase in capital investment, accelerates the pace of economic progress and technological innovation.

While this may be true at times, and indeed has happened at certain times in the past, it is an argument that overlooks several important facts. First, it is not necessarily true that wage rates always lag commodity prices. Labor unions in the 70s, for example, caught on to the effects of inflation and bargained for real increases in wage rates above and beyond the rise in the Consumer Price Index (CPI)—the so-called "wage-price spiral." There is also no guarantee that entrepreneurs and businesses will always necessarily save more than wage earners and salaried people. But perhaps the most important fact that this argument overlooks is that inflation introduces forces in the market that tend toward capital consumption.

Inflation—an increase in the money supply caused by central bank credit expansion—falsifies economic calculation and accounting. When the central bank makes a greater supply of money available on the credit market, it makes additional loans available that otherwise would not have been. The nominal interest rate—the actual average percentage interest rate—might not change, but because more money is available in the loan market, the gross market rate of interest is lowered. Consequently, loans are made that would not have been made prior to the expansion. This is exactly what the Fed is trying to accomplish now (2/91).

To entrepreneurs, who deal and think only in dollar terms, the availability of credit makes formerly unfeasible projects *appear* feasible. For them, credit is a claim on unconsumed goods to be invested in new projects. As more and more entrepreneurs embark on new projects, business activities are stimulated and a boom begins. But there is an inherent problem from the outset of the boom. At any point in time, the goods and labor available for business expansion are finite, or scarce. The increased demand for these scarce items caused by the credit expansion creates a tendency for a rise in the prices of producers' goods and the rates of wages.

With the increase in wage rates, there is a corresponding increase in demand for consumer goods, and their price begins to rise as well. This happens in stages, affecting different sectors of the economy at different times and to different extents. For many businesses, rising prices of their products on the consumer market give the false appearance of real gains on their accounting ledgers.

Encouraged by these illusory gains, these businesses calculate that they can now afford to consume more, and they too contribute to the rising prices of consumer goods. Producers' prices are affected first and the most dramatically, but the rising prices of consumers' goods reassure the businessmen that their capital expansion program will pay for itself in spite of the rising costs of production.

Von Mises was the first economist to realize how this whole process occurs. It gets a little bit complicated here, but I urge you to stick with this analysis, because understanding it will help you avoid losing money by being fully invested at bull market tops.

In Von Mises' terms, call p the amount of capital goods available on the eve of credit expansion, r the replacement capital which must be saved from the gross proceeds of production with p, and g the total amount of consumer goods that are produced from p. Further, assume that the economic condition prior to the credit expansion was a progressive one that produced surplus capital (capital savings) of p_1 and p_2 which, without the advent of the credit expansion, would have been employed to produce the incremental quantity g_1 of goods produced previously and the quantity g_2 of newly developed goods.

Without the credit expansion, the result would be that p (the existing capital) would produce $r + g$ (the necessary replacement capital plus the goods that p produced for consumption) and capital savings of $p_1 + p_2$ (new capital to increase existing production plus capital to invest in new projects). Growth would come from using $p_1 + p_2$ to produce $g_1 + g_2$ (more existing products plus new products), and technological innovation would accelerate the process. But instead of this happening, the central bank, trying to stimulate employment and production, puts money into the system creating additional credit availability.

Enticed by the credit expansion, entrepreneurs decide to produce an additional quantity, g_3, of goods previously produced, and embark on new ventures designed to produce g_4 of newly developed products. To produce g_3 and g_4, additional capital goods, p_3 and p_4, are needed. But as I already mentioned, the capital available for business expansion is limited to p_1 and p_2; p_3 and p_4 don't even exist, they just seem to! The entrepreneurial decision to produce g_3 and g_4 is based on an illusion brought about by the credit expansion.

Looked at this way, the *actual* quantity of capital goods at the disposal of entrepreneurs for planning is $p_1 + p_2 + r$, but the *apparent* capital available is $p_1 + p_2 + p_3 + p_4 + r$. Entrepreneurs act as if they could produce $g_1 + g_2 + g_3 + g_4$ with the apparent capital available and, because of the lack of real capital available, a bidding war ensues for $p_1 + p_2 + r$. Prices for producers' goods rise and may, at first, outstrip the rise in consumers' goods prices, causing originary interest to decline in the near term.

During this period, the increased interest in producing for the future may actually bring about the generation of real new wealth. But eventually, as the credit expansion continues, the rise in prices of consumers' goods outstrips that for producers' goods. The rise in wages and profits (largely apparent, not real) intensifies the demand for consumers' goods before the capital is in place to provide them. Consumer prices rise. If consumer prices continue to rise, eventually people want to own consumer goods as soon as possible to avoid paying more for them in the future. In other words, there is a tendency to raise originary interest, which means there is a tendency toward increased consumption in the immediate term versus provisioning for the future. Capital, in the form of savings, is consumed. This often reaches the point where people like Donald Trump will borrow as much as possible to own items which they believe will cost more or be worth more in dollar terms in the near future.

From an arithmetic standpoint, interest rates may rise as a result of the increased demand for loans. But the entrepreneurial and price premium components of the interest rate necessarily lag behind what is required for the "proper" allocation of capital. Banks assume that their higher rates are enough to compensate for the effects of changing prices, so they continue loaning to businessmen, confident that the business expansion will continue indefinitely.

In fact, however, their confidence is a false one because they fail to realize that they are fanning the flames of the bidding war for scarce capital. As entrepreneurs, judging that they can meet the increased costs of production through increased sales, continue to borrow money to expand production, interest rates continue to rise, as do the prices of both producers' and consumers' goods. Only by a continued increase in the supply of money *created* by the banks can the boom continue.

But soon, even that is not enough. If banks continue their expansionist policies, eventually the public becomes aware of what is happening. They see that the real purchasing power of their money is on the decline and a flight to real goods begins—the originary interest in holding goods skyrockets and that of holding money plummets. It is at this stage that runaway inflation, such as that which until recently existed in Brazil and still exists in Argentina and other nations, takes hold. Von Mises calls this stage of credit expansion a "crack-up boom."

Normally, however, things never go quite this far. Consumers on fixed incomes cry to politicians about the rising cost of living. Politicians blame someone else and urge the central bank to put on the brakes. The central bank responds by restricting credit availability. Entrepreneurs, unable to afford the now scarce loans, abandon new projects as they realize that they are doomed to failure. Banks stop lending because they realize that they have already overextended themselves. Loans are called in. The monetary expansion stops.

At this, the turning point of the boom, prices begin to fall as businessmen, hungry for cash to service their debt, sell off inventories. In particular, the price of producers' goods usually falls precipitously and to a greater extent than consumers' goods, such as in 1929 to 1933, when retail sales dropped 15% while the sales of capital goods dropped about 90%. Factories close. Workers are laid off. And as confidence in the economy wanes, the entrepreneurial component of interest rates jumps to excessive heights which further accelerates the deflationary process. Accompanying this process is usually some kind of news which turns the already existing crisis into a panic, often reflected in a plunge of stock and commodity futures prices. The bust occurs.

Typically, after such a crash, economists decry the failure of capitalism and declare that "overinvestment" was the cause of the bust. This is a huge mistake and the most misunderstood aspect of the boom/bust cycle. It is not overinvestment, but what Von Mises calls "malinvestment" that causes both the boom and the bust. It is the fact that lowering the gross market rate of interest through credit expansion encourages entrepreneurs to attempt to employ $p_1 + p_2 + r$ (the actual capital) as if it were $p_1 + p_2 + p_3 + p_4 + r$ (the apparent capital) that causes the problem. It necessarily brings about investment and distribution of resources that is out of whack with the real available supply of capital goods.

It is like trying to build the foundation for a 5000 square foot house out of concrete sufficient for a 2500 square foot house—either you alter the plans or you spread the concrete so thin that it won't support the structure.

As I discussed in the last chapter, to increase wealth requires the savings of surpluses for investment in future production. Technological innovation accelerates the rate of growth of wealth but is possible only through the application of saved capital. Most often, during a credit expansion, part of $p_1 + p_2 + r$ is invested in innovations which accelerate the real rate of growth of wealth, offsetting some of the negative effects described above. But this is only a damper.

The nature of the distorted investments brought about by the credit expansion must sooner or later collapse, and wealth will be consumed. It may be true, and most often is, that by the end of the boom/bust cycle, the actual standard of living and overall wealth in the economy is greater than at the beginning. But it is certainly not greater than it would have been during the same period without the irresponsible credit expansion.

As a speculator participating in markets influenced by credit regulation by central banks, you must be able to identify the stages of the boom/bust cycle. To do this, you have to understand the different forms that credit expansions take. Specifically, you have to understand how both the Federal Reserve Board and the Treasury contribute to money and credit inflation. Since central banks in all nations operate in basically the same way, once you understand how the U.S. system works, you will have a grasp of how all central banks work. Then, you will have the basis to understand and potentially to predict the economic outcome of politicians' attempts to coordinate both national and international monetary policy.

THE STRUCTURE AND ROLE OF THE FEDERAL RESERVE SYSTEM

In the title of this chapter, I posed the rhetorical question: "Who holds the pump, and who holds the needle?" In France during the Mississippi Scheme, the answer was John Law and the Duke of Orleans. In the United States today, the parallel answer is the The Federal Reserve Board and the Federal Open Market Committee (FOMC). These organizations monopolistically control the supply of money and credit in the entire Federal Reserve System which now includes, de facto, nearly all depository institutions in the country.

The economic power that they wield is absolutely mind boggling. It is so great that we have become a nation of Fed watchers, clinging to the obtuse proclamations made by the Fed Chairman and other key Board and FOMC members as we look for some indication of forthcoming policy. A single statement made by the Fed Chairman can literally reverse the stock market trend, as happened on July 24, 1984, when then Chairman Paul Volcker announced, "The Fed's [restrictive] policy was inappropriate." That same day, the stock market made its low, and a new bull market began.

Ironically, an agency which can literally swing the market with a sentence was established by the Federal Reserve Act of 1913 to *stabilize* the workings of the money and credit markets.

In the words of the legislation, the purpose of the Federal Reserve is to "give the country an elastic currency, to provide facilities for discounting commercial paper, and to improve the supervision of banking." By 1963, the Fed's acknowledged objectives had expanded "to help counteract inflationary and deflationary movements, and to share in creating conditions favorable to a sustained, high level of employment, a stable dollar, growth of the country, and a rising level of consumption."[8] (Note the emphasis not on *production* but on **consumption**—pure Keynesianism.)

Today, the Fed is virtually another branch of government which attempts to coordinate its policies with Congress, the President and the Treasury, and the central banks of foreign governments. But the primary function of the Fed is to act as the central bank of the United States. Let's first look at its operation in this role.

As the nation's central bank, the primary function of the Federal Reserve is to:

> ... regulate the flow of bank credit and money. Essential to the performance of this main function is the supplemental one of collecting and interpreting information bearing on economic and credit conditions. A further function is to examine and supervise State banks, ... obtain reports of condition from them, and cooperate with other supervisory authorities in the development and administration of policies. ... [9]

The Fed's big stick is its power "to regulate the flow of bank credit and money," which means, plain and simple, to inflate or deflate the supply of money and credit.

Before I go on, let me briefly define what "the Fed" is. The Federal Reserve System has three basic components: the Board of Governors, the Federal Open Market Committee (FOMC), and the Federal Reserve Banks. As an agency of the Federal government, the organization of The Federal Reserve System is mandated by law, but little else is. The Board and the FOMC—the seven board members occupy seven of the twelve seats on the FOMC—unilaterally establish and implement the monetary policy of the United States. It is these two components that people generally refer to when they use the words, "The Fed."

The Board consists of seven Presidentially selected appointees, confirmed by the Senate, who serve 14-year terms. The terms are arranged such that one expires every even-numbered year, and a member may not be reappointed after serving a full term. The Federal Open Market Committee consists of the seven Board members plus five presidents from the twelve Federal Reserve District banks, one of whom is always the president from the New York Bank. The other four members serve one-year terms which rotate among the other 11 district banks.

The FOMC is responsible for establishing and implementing the monetary policy of the United States. While the Board has unilateral control over the discount rate and reserve requirements (within bounds prescribed by law), it attempts to set its policies according to objectives established by majority vote at FOMC meetings.

The meetings are currently held eight times per year. The committee decides its own schedule and ad hoc meetings may be called at any time. In addition, the FOMC decides upon a plan of open market operations to attempt to achieve its policy objectives, and the plan is carried out by the Federal Reserve Bank of New York.

Open market operations consist of buying and selling of government securities by the Fed on the open market. These transactions have an immediate and direct impact on the reserves held by the banking system and therefore on the availability of credit and the rate of growth of the money supply. It is through this process that the Fed expands or contracts credit availability and manipulates interest rates. Let me explain this process in detail.

HOW MONEY AND CREDIT AVAILABILITY IS CREATED AND CONTROLLED

In the last chapter, I described how in the early stages of banking history, lenders discovered that they could issue more gold- or silver-backed bank notes than their actual holdings of gold and silver. As long as the public had confidence in the institution's ability to redeem the bank notes in coin on demand, then the bank could *create* paper money, or fiduciary media, which was acceptable in the marketplace as a medium of exchange. I also showed, through the description of the Mississippi Scheme, the disastrous results which can come from pushing this process too far — price inflation and ultimate economic collapse.

The basic principles are the same in The Federal Reserve System, with one huge exception — there is *nothing* backing the dollar except a government law declaring it to be legal tender. This is called a *fiat* money system. The value of the dollar is totally dependent on the market's faith and confidence in its purchasing power, which is ultimately determined by the supply of and demand for currency in relation to other goods and services available in the market.

As a substitute for precious metals, which were used to serve as one of the checks of paper money expansion, the Fed establishes *reserve requirements* which, since the passage of The Monetary Control Act of 1980, must be adhered to by all depository institutions in the United States.[10]

Reserve requirements are a percentage of *reserve liabilities* that must be held by depository institutions in the form of *reserve assets*. Reserve liabilities consist of transaction deposits, time and savings deposits, and net liabilities to foreign banking offices (Eurodollar liabilities). Reserve assets consist of vault cash (actual dollars and coin) held by the depository institution and *reserve deposits* held at the Federal Reserve District Banks. In essence, reserve requirements act as the depository institution's only objective check on credit expansion, and therefore on the expansion of the money supply.

For example, if a commercial bank has transaction deposits (deposits with un-limited checking privileges such as checking and NOW accounts) of $100 million,

Table 10.1 Reserve Ratios, May 1990

Type of liability	Reserve ratio (%)
Transaction accounts	
$0-40.4 million	3
More than $40.4 million	12
Time and savings deposits	
Personal	0
Nonpersonal, by maturity	
Less than 1½ years	3
1½ years or more	0
Net liabilities to foreign	
banking offices. (Eurocurrency liabilities)	3

it must currently have at least $12 million in vault cash and/or deposits at the Federal Reserve Bank in its district. The $100 million is the reserve liability and the $12 million is the reserve requirement as calculated according to the current *reserve ratios* established by the Board of Governors (see Table 10.1).

In terms of money creation, there is an inverse relationship between reserve ratios and the amount of money a depository institution can create. For example, a reserve ratio of 10% means that for every dollar of added reserve assets in the system, 10 dollars of new money can be created. In more realistic terms, if the Fed buys government securities of $250 million in a week, with a reserve ratio of 10% this creates a potential for $2.5 billion increase in the money supply. Conversely, the sale of $250 million in securities creates a potential contraction of $2.5 billion in credit availability.

This is difficult to see if you try to think in terms of all depository institutions, their transactions on the market, and their transactions with the Fed District Banks. But it is relatively easy to see if you look at a model of a hypothetical country; let's call it Newmoney, with a Central Bank and a fractional reserve system.

I'm going to take you through the credit expansion process step by step, and show you how the Fed, or any Central Bank, can literally create or destroy money at the stroke of a pen. For simplicity, I'm going to show only the affected portion of the balance sheets, so don't look for a balance between assets and liabilities. On a complete balance sheet, obviously, both sides would balance.

Assume for simplicity that the only kind of deposits in the Newmoney are demand deposits (checking accounts), that there is a total of $1 billion in those accounts—all as loans—and that the central bank has established a 10% reserve ratio. Also assume that the banking system in Newmoney stays loaned up to the maximum allowed by the central bank. Then, the relevant portions of the consolidated balance sheet of the Newmoney Central Bank and the consolidated balance sheet of all depository institutions in Newmoney would look something like this:

Simplified segment of the consolidated balance sheet of the Newmoney Central Bank

Relevant Assets (thousands of dollars)	
Government securities	150,000
Relevant Liabilities	
Newmoney Central Bank Notes	100,000
Reserve Deposits	95,000

Simplified segment of the consolidated balance sheet of all Newmoney depository institutions

Key Assets (thousands of dollars)	
Loans	1,000,000
Vault cash	5,000
Reserve Deposits at Central Bank	95,000
Government and other securities	150,000
Key Liabilities	
Demand Deposits	1,000,000

Notice that the combined reserve assets of commercial banks (vault cash plus reserve deposits at the central bank) of the depository institutions equal exactly 10% of their reserve liabilities (10% of demand deposits). At this point, the bank's hands are tied. No new loans can be made because the loans would become demand deposits and put the banking system in violation of the 10% reserve requirement.

But let's assume that the Board of the Central Bank meets and decides that the unemployment rate is too high in Newmoney and that to stimulate new business and new jobs, they want to increase the availability of credit.

To do this, they engage in open market operations and purchase Newmoney government bonds from the banks to the tune of $50 million. When they buy these securities, they write checks against themselves (out of thin air) that the banks then deposit in their reserve accounts at the Central Bank. The transaction occurs with nothing but ink.

The banking system as a whole now has $50 million more reserve deposits. So now their balance sheets look like this:

Simplified segment of the consolidated balance sheet of the Newmoney Central Bank

Relevant Assets (thousands of dollars)	
Government securities	200,000
Relevant Liabilities	
Newmoney Central Bank Notes	100,000
Reserve Deposits	145,000

**Simplified segment of the consolidated balance sheet
of all Newmoney depository institutions**

Key Assets (thousands of dollars)	
Loans	1,000,000
Vault cash	5,000
Reserve Deposits at the Central Bank	145,000
Government and other securities	100,000
Key Liabilities	
Demand Deposits	1,000,000

Now the banks have *excess reserves* of $50 million; that is, they have $50 million more on deposit with the Central Bank than they need to meet the 10% reserve requirement for existing demand deposits. That means they have enough excess reserves to support another $500 million in loans ($50 million divided by 10% equals $500 million). Being generous and patriotic men that want to see full employment and economic growth, the bankers promptly approve all sorts of new loans.

When the banks make the loans, they *create an asset and a liability which automatically balances on their ledgers*. In this case, when the $500 million in loans are made, the banks credit the borrowers' demand deposit accounts by $500 million and credit their asset sides with loans so that the affected portion of the consolidated balance sheet now looks like this:

**Simplified segment of the consolidated balance sheet
of all Newmoney depository institutions**

Key Assets (thousands of dollars)	
Loans	1,500,000
Vault cash	5,000
Reserve Deposits at Fed District Banks	145,000
Government and other securities	100,000
Key Liabilities	
Demand Deposits	1,500,000

So, by purchasing securities on the open market worth $50 million, the central bank set a chain of events in motion that increased the money supply by $500 million—$500 million of new money was *created*. The exact reverse would happen if the central bank *sold* securities in open market operations.

I want everyone who is reading this to understand that this is a simplified version of what actually occurs, not only with the Federal Reserve System, but with every central banking system in the world. The actual workings are more complex; but I could show in a more detailed discussion how, no matter how many banks are involved, the potential impact on the supply of money and credit is virtually identical to what I just described in the hypothetical country of Newmoney. For you doubters out there, it's a good mental exercise.

In net effect, when the Fed purchases securities, it creates, on paper, the money with which it buys those securities—it simply writes a check on itself. That new money, in turn, enters the banking system and may be used to increase reserve assets held by the banking system. The increase in reserves assets creates the potential for an increase in the money supply through credit expansion equivalent to the reserve increase divided by the *net* average reserve ratio. When you leave Newmoney and enter the real world, things then start to get a little more complicated.

If you look back at Table 10.1, you will see that reserve ratios in the Federal Reserve System currently vary from 0 to 12% depending on the type of liability. If you buy a 10-year, $10,000 certificate of deposit from your bank for cash which has been stuffed in your mattress, the reserve ratio is 0 for that item (it is a time deposit with over 1 ½ years to maturity), and the banking system as a whole can potentially expand its loans by $10,000/.12, or $83,000! When the Fed buys securities, the exact same thing can happen.

The net reserve ratio—an equivalent ratio which would give you required reserves for deposits as a whole—depends on where the market chooses to place its money. But to give you an idea of the relationship of required reserves to depository liabilities as a whole, the data in the May 7, 1990, issue of *Barron's* shows the broadest measure of the money supply, M3, at $4.066 trillion, while total reserves deposited in Federal Reserve District banks equalled only $60.3 billion. Of that 4 trillion plus number, actual currency equaled only $228.4 billion, which means that the rest consists of deposits (liabilities) in accounts of one form or another at various institutions.

So the ratio of reserve assets to monetary deposits as a whole is almost 1 to 70. Even assuming that M3 is not an accurate measure of the total money supply, the same issue of *Barron's* reported that the Fed then held $233,966,000 in government securities. Assuming a net average reserve ratio of 10%, that gives the 12 men who make up the FOMC the power to add over $2.3 trillion in potential credit availability to the system—over half of M3!

Are you beginning to understand why open market operations are such a powerful tool of monetary policy?

Plato, the Greek philosopher, believed that the common man was incapable of governing his own life and affairs. Ideally, he thought that philosopher kings should rule the world. In a sense, Plato got his wish. The members of the FOMC are the philosopher kings of the U.S. economy, and as the sovereigns of the most powerful industrial nation on earth, they wield enormous power over the world economy as a whole. They are the kings, and the markets are the subjects—free to act only within the confines of sovereign dictate.

Just 12 men on the FOMC—the members of the board and five district bank presidents—vote to set policies which critically constrain and alter free market action. They set objectives in terms of and take action based upon broad, aggregate economic statistics such as unemployment figures, capacity utilization, the Consumer Price Index (CPI), the Producer Price Index (PPI), the growth and rate of growth of the money supply (as measured by M1, M2, and M3), the trade balance figures, indices of the money supply (M1, M2, and M3), reserve balances, and many other indicators. They constantly monitor these macro indicators and alter their strategy—in secret at the FOMC meetings—according to what they agree, by consensus, is needed to better achieve their policy objectives.

Now I've simply got to put in an aside here. When the FOMC meets, they purposefully withhold their decisions from the market. Yet, the 12 members of the committee all bring aides to the meeting. Most of the committee members are married and have families, as are most of the aides. In addition, secretaries and staff must type up and duplicate the minutes. Now, in a country where the National Security Council can't sneeze without the press getting wind of it (no pun intended), do you really think the decisions in the meeting stay completely a secret? I don't. And in fact, that gives me an idea.

Instead of raising taxes and doling out welfare, why doesn't the government secretly distribute the minutes of the FOMC immediately after the meeting to committees responsible for the development of depressed areas of the country. They could train these committees to trade in the markets and use the secret knowledge to get a jump on the rest of us who trade government securities. You could virtually end poverty in depressed areas! Of course, I'm not serious, but in my opinion, a select few are getting the jump anyway!

Who holds the pump and who holds the needle? Without a doubt, the Fed does, in the form of Open Market Operations and the other policy weapons available to them to control the supply of and demand for money and credit. In order of increasing importance, the Fed has three principle tools of monetary policy: setting reserve requirements, setting the discount rate, and performing open market operations.

As a speculator, you need to understand the nature of these tools and how the Fed uses them in order to accurately assess the likely direction of future market movements. Let me discuss each of these weapons in turn.

RESERVE REQUIREMENTS, FED FUNDS RATE, AND THE DISCOUNT RATE

In terms of the mechanical workings of reserve requirements, little more needs to be said than what I brought out in my discussion of the Newmoney banking system. But it is important to understand the different ways banks can achieve their reserve requirements and how the Fed uses its hand within this context both to affect the supply of money and credit and to monitor the activity of lending institutions.

The Board uses reserve ratios to establish reserve requirements that can only be met by holding sufficient reserve assets—vault cash and deposits with the Federal Reserve District banks. Because money is constantly moving in and out of individual lending institutions, a particular institution may have a deficit or surplus of reserve assets in the short term. In the case of a deficit, a bank or lending institution has one of two choices: either it borrows the excess reserves of another institution on a short-term basis, or it can borrow from the discount window at the Federal Reserve bank in its district.

The market for borrowing the excess reserves of other institutions is known as the Fed Funds market, and the prevailing interest rate charged is known as the Fed Funds rate. This "borrowing from Peter to pay Paul" market and the interest rate which accompanies it is very important to watch. Although it is ostensibly designed to facilitate banks with a short-term reserve deficit, what it actually does is enable the system as a whole to stay loaned up to the fullest extent possible.

In fact, it is such an important market that until 1979 the Fed based its open market operations primarily upon trying to achieve a target Fed Funds rate, thinking that the interbank interest rate would determine the ease or tightness of borrowing for reserves, which would in turn set the standard for the credit market as a whole. But if you review the Carter years (1976–1980), you'll find near runaway inflation, followed by interest rate controls, followed by a credit crunch, followed by deregulation and 22% interest rates!

Obviously, targeting a particular level of the Fed Funds rate was a totally inadequate tool for controlling credit availability. Like any other item in the marketplace, supply and demand determines how much credit expansion will occur. In the Carter years, people willingly borrowed and banks willingly loaned money at high interest rates because they thought rates might go still higher. In late 1990, however, there were plenty of excess reserves in the system, but banks simply weren't making loans.

Until 1979, in addition to trying to control the Fed Funds rate, the Fed also attempted to use the discount rate as means to control credit expansion. The discount rate is the interest rate that the Federal Reserve District banks charge lending institutions for borrowing reserves directly from the central bank. In theory, the discount rate was supposed to be set by the board of each Fed District Bank, subject to review and approval by the Federal Reserve Board. In practice, however, the discount rate is now uniform throughout the system and is established by the Federal Reserve Board with District banks automatically approving the Board's "recommendation" as a formality.

There are several differences between the discount rate and the Fed Funds rate. First and foremost, discount window borrowing is inflation of the most blatant form. When a bank borrows from the discount window, the Fed writes a check against itself, creating money that then serves as new reserves for the borrowing bank.

The borrowing bank pays interest (the discount rate) on the borrowed reserves and the system as a whole is able to expand loans by approximately 10 times the amount borrowed. The discount rate is always lower than the market rate of interest so, just like I used to do when I started trading options, the borrowing bank "makes the middle" when it makes new loans secured by reserves borrowed through the discount window.

But there is a catch. Borrowing from the discount window flags the borrower as being possibly overextended. No one wants a federal agency breathing down its throat and monitoring its activities, so lending institutions are limited in the number of times they can go to the discount window. Basically, when they borrow from the discount window, they are given a silent, but not so subtle message, "Clean up your act, bad child, and provide the reserves you need from your own sources."

By comparison, the Fed Funds market is much more free. As long as banks can successfully "make the middle" and pay off their loans to fellow banks, they can borrow reserves in the Fed Funds market. During the late 70s, Fed credit was running amuck because the board was reluctant to sell enough securities to make the Fed Funds rate rise to a level that discouraged interbank borrowing for credit expansion.

It was all Volcker could do to get the Board to approve a ½-point raise from 10½ to 11% in the discount rate (a 4 to 3 vote), much less encourage open market securities sales to increase the Fed Funds rate.

What the Fed failed to realize during the 70s is that interest *rates* aren't the sole determinant of the supply of and demand for money and credit. It goes right back to Von Mises' explanation of the three components of the gross market rate of interest and how they change during the boom/bust cycle.

If, during an expansionary period, originary interest is low because of rising prices, if the price of the premium component is perceived by the market as being a bargain because interest rates are continuing to rise, and if the entrepreneurial component (no matter how high interest rates are nominally) is perceived as sur-mountable in profit/loss calculations, then the markets will borrow as much money as they can!

In other words, no matter what the actual interest rate number is, if both the supply of and demand for credit exists, money will be loaned and the credit expansion will continue. Another reason the Fed couldn't quell the credit expansion of the 70s was that only Federal Reserve member banks were subject to reserve requirement restrictions. This meant that unregulated lending institutions could create money, which in turn ended up as new deposits in Fed member banks, further fueling the credit expansion. In addition, the foreign liabilities (such as Eurodollars) of member banks and other institutions were exempt from the same reserve restrictions as domestic liabilities, and dollars created abroad were entering the system and further stimulating the growth in the money supply.

We were in the latter stages of a boom fueled by credit expansion, prices were rising in every sector, and the sentiment was that prices would continue to rise indefinitely. People were making paper fortunes in real estate, the commodities markets, stocks, you name it, and there was no end in sight; simultaneously, the average worker on fixed income was infuriated by the government's inability to put a lid on rising prices. It was Law's Mississippi Scheme on a grand scale.

Still, as long as interest rates were on the rise, a loan today was better than a loan tomorrow because the markets realized that the purchasing power of the dollar was declining. Politicians kept the pressure on the Fed to keep interest rates low so they could keep their constituents happy. Those in government who were aware of the dangers of what was happening were afraid to act for fear of collapsing the house of cards and ruining Democratic hopes for the next election.

By the last quarter of 1979, the U.S. economy was universally engaged in a flight to real goods. Gold skyrocketed in price, peaking at nearly $875 per ounce in the futures markets in early January 1980. Nobody wanted to hold paper money. Rather, they bought stocks, futures, real estate, or gold, held it for a year, or even a few months, and then turned it over for a 20% gain! Magic! Instant wealth! Doesn't this ring a bell—something like the Mississippi Scheme?

Fortunately, there was enough prevailing economic wisdom to realize that we were heading for a "crack up boom" similar to what existed in Germany in the 30s and what exists in some South American countries today. On Tuesday, October 12, 1979, Paul Volcker returned prematurely from an International Monetary Fund/World Bank meeting in Belgrade, Yugoslavia and announced an emergency meeting of the FOMC to take place on the following Saturday (The Fed likes to meet and make announcements at times when the markets can't react immediately to their pronouncements.)

At 6:00 P.M. on that Saturday, Volcker convened a press conference in which he outlined a plan that would revolutionize the Fed's approach to monetary policy.

Volcker announced that the discount rate would be raised from 11 to 12% and that new, restrictive reserve requirements would be imposed on banks' foreign liabilities. Both actions demonstrated the Fed's resolve to bring inflation under control. But the real kicker was Volcker's proclamation that from then on, the FOMC would control the money supply directly by controlling reserves through open market operations rather than by shooting for target Fed Funds rates. At this point, Volcker was engaging in psychological tactics to cool the speculative fever. After the election in 1980, the real tightening would come.

My point in telling this whole story is to show that the philosopher kings really do control the economy and with very limited knowledge. The Fed has been experimenting with our economic lives by trial and error. But before I go into that aspect of the Fed, let me discuss open market operations in more detail.

Open Market Operations

Any open market operation—the purchase or sale of securities by the Fed—has a direct dollar for dollar influence on the amount of reserves available in the system; a purchase increases reserves, and a sale decreases reserves. If you understand how a gold-backed monetary system works, the Fed's power with open market operations is tantamount to the Fed sitting on millions of ounces of gold and injecting or removing it from the banking system at will—a power that would be considered monopolistic if wielded by the private sector.

There are several types of open market operations, and each has a slightly different effect on credit availability and monetary growth. Some operations are more hidden than others and some are very blatant. If you understand the different types and monitor the Fed's activities, you can not only get an idea of the direction of monetary policy, but even more important, you can gain insight into the psychology of the men on the Board and the FOMC. And since it is the minds of these men that largely determine the direction that economic activity will take, it is essential to understand the direction of their thinking.

There are two basic approaches to open market operations: long-term and short-term. For trying to achieve long term operating objectives, the primary tool is the outright purchase or sale of securities, usually U.S. Treasury issues of bills, notes, and bonds. If the objective is to increase reserve availability, the manager will purchase securities from dealers in an auction process until the desired amount of reserves are added. If the objective is to remove reserves, the manager will sell securities to dealers, again in an auction process. Another method of withdrawing reserves is to let securities held in the system's portfolio mature without replacement.

To compensate for short-term deficits in reserves caused by things such as increased seasonal demand for currency (as in the Christmas buying season) and other short-term technical factors, the Fed uses repurchase agreements (RPs), often called repos by the market. In a repurchase agreement, the Fed buys securities from dealers with the agreement that the dealers will buy them back within a specified period (the period can vary from 1 to 15 days but is usually 7) at a specified price, usually with the dealer having the option to terminate the agreement before maturity.

The flip side of repurchase agreements is *matched sale–purchase transactions*. "Matched sales," as they are called, consist of a contract for an immediate sale of securities (usually T-bills), and a matching contract for purchasing the same amount of securities from the same dealer at a later date (usually not exceeding seven days). Matched sales are a way for the Fed to remove reserves from the system on a short-term basis in response to seasonal or other technical factors.

Described like this, these operations seem innocent, even reasonable. But at the risk of repeating myself, you need to be aware that all open market operations represent the creation or destruction of ink deposits in banking accounts. When additional reserves are created, the banking system has the capacity to increase the money supply by making new loans. In Von Mises' terms, the gross market rate of interest is lowered, regardless of the nominal level of interest rates.

Conversely, if reserves are pulled out of the system by the sale of securities, the banks will lose credits in their reserve accounts at the Federal Reserve Banks. If the contraction reduces reserves to such a level that lending institutions have a net deficit in reserves, loans will be called in, inventories will be reduced, and a business contraction will ensue—the gross market rate of interest is raised even if nominal interest rates remain unchanged.

Repos and matched sales, while short-term tools, can have a significant long-term impact. If the Fed regularly engages in repos such that there is a consistent balance of securities held under repurchase agreements, then from the standpoint of the banking system as a whole, these balances are tantamount to outright purchases.

The Fed Funds market is very efficient. It is in any bank's *interest* to loan excess reserves, even if on an overnight basis. A continuous balance of reserves added to the system by repurchase agreements can have an important impact on the Fed Funds market and the Fed Funds rate. It is also significant if the Fed discontinues a regular policy of supplying short-term reserves through repos. This is a somewhat hidden way of tightening "a little bit." The converse is true for matched sales or changes in matched sales balances.

The most apparent and readable of all Fed policy actions are outright purchases and sales. The news wires report these immediately when they occur, and their effect is usually predictable.

Perhaps the best indicator of the *effects* of Fed policy, however, isn't the quantities of outright purchases and sales but the level and changes of the level of *free reserves* in the system.

Free reserves equal excess reserves minus discount window borrowings other than extended credit.[11] This number, which is reported every Sunday in *Barron's* and other financial publications or can be obtained directly from the Fed, is a key measure of the degree of ease or tightness of Fed policy. As an approximation, if the free reserve number is *positive*, then you can multiply the number by 10 to calculate the approximate current potential credit availability on the market. A *negative* number means that a credit contraction is in progress. But, the number doesn't have to be negative to indicate Fed tightening.

The Fed can tighten while maintaining a positive level of free reserves. It is helpful to think in terms of Von Mises' formulation of the gross market rate of interest. If the level of free reserves declines, then the gross market rate of interest increases, regardless of the nominal interest rate.

This means that less capital is apparently available for investment than before. The converse is true if the level of free reserves increases, other things being equal. To get the best reading, what you should look for is changes in *levels* of free reserves in conjunction with changes in the Fed Funds rate, the discount rate, the rate of growth or decline of the adjusted monetary base,[12] the rate of growth of the money supply, and the CPI and PPI numbers.

One thing you can count on is that, on balance and in the long term, Fed policy will be expansionary, the money supply will continue to expand, and the purchasing power of the dollar will continue to fall. According to the U.S. Department of Labor and the Bureau of Labor Statistics, what cost $1.20 in December 1988 cost only 30 *cents* in 1961 and only 10 cents in December 1913. But the Fed's expansionary monetary policy isn't the only reason that the dollar's value is diminishing. Our government's continuing policy of deficit spending is to blame as well, and it is important to recognize the impact that deficit spending has on the business cycle.

Deficit Spending and Its Effects on Money and Credit

Here are some hard facts. The last time the U.S. government didn't operate at a deficit was 1969, when it reported a surplus of approximately $4 billion. Since then, the trend has been toward an ever upward spiral of deficit spending so that the March 1990 deficit—the deficit for one month—was larger than that for the entire 1975 fiscal year.

According to *Grant's Interest Rate Observer,* at the end of fiscal 1989, gross federal debt totaled $2.866 *trillion*, not to mention the $4.124 trillion face value of government insurance programs, and the $1.558 trillion in outstanding federal credit. Government outlays in 1989 were 22.2% of GNP, and that was a seven-year low! The interest expense on federal debt was 3.3% of GNP and hasn't been below 3% since 1983. As of September 30, 1988, the net worth of the country was estimated by the Comptroller General to be *negative* $2.4526 trillion, omitting public lands and mineral rights except at nominal values.[13]

In large part, these numbers speak for themselves. The U.S. government is a debt junkie, and if the trend continues, the doses are eventually going to become lethal.

Suppose you have two credit cards, each from a different bank; and each month you pay the balance of one card by charging it to the other card, while simultaneously spending more than your paycheck each month. The respective banks, unaware of your practice, keep increasing your line of credit because you always pay in full—you're a good and valued customer in their eyes.

While the banks don't know what's happening, you start waking up in the middle of the night with anxiety attacks about the increased amount of interest you pay each month, wondering how long it will be before the scheme blows up in your face.

That's basically the way our government has been operating for the last several decades. It borrows money from two main sources: the public, or the Fed itself; and it borrows more money in each cycle to pay its debts.

If you listen to politicians talk about deficits and their impact on the value of the dollar and the business cycle, you'll be nothing but confused. The party out of power always blames deficits for chronic inflation, while the party in power declares that deficits have nothing to do with inflation.

Both statements are wrong. If the Treasury sells its bonds to the public to fund the deficit, money is *transferred* from the public's hands to the government's hands. The government then spends the money, putting it back into the public's hands, albeit redistributed. There is nothing inherently inflationary in this process—no new money is created as a direct result of the securities sale.

On the other hand, if the Treasury sells securities directly to the Fed, the money used to pay for them is "printed"—the Fed credits the Treasury's account with the purchase price of the bonds, plus it increases its inventory of securities for open market operations. This process is *obviously* and directly inflationary, but it is not a common practice. But there is a more subtle way that deficit spending *induces* inflationary policies by the Fed.

If the government is a debt junkie, the Fed is the pusher providing the supply of the deadly substance—credit. It works something like this: If the government needs to sell $100 billion in government securities to the public (including the banking system itself), the Fed buys $10 billion of securities on the open market to enable the banking system to lend the $100 billion needed to finance the new Treasury issue.

It's a rich and self-fulfilling scam—no different in principle from the Mississippi Scheme. When the government operates this way, it guarantees a supply of credit for itself in the short term and financial trouble for all of us in the long term.

There are many mistaken notions which beset economic thinking about government debt. One of the biggest is that government deficit financing has no effect on credit availability in the private sector. To support this assertion, some analysts point to the 1982–83 period, when deficits were not only high but on the rise, while nominal interest rates fell.

In fact, a study I carried out in January 1983 shows a *characteristic* inverse relationship between deficits and nominal interest rates; interest rates virtually always drop during periods of high deficits and rise as deficits decrease. But this doesn't mean that deficits have no effect on credit availability. It is a huge mistake to equate low nominal interest rates with the real *interest* in borrowing money.

The main reason for the inverse relationship of interest rates and deficit spending is the policies of the Fed. During periods of recession, unemployment rises, businesses cut back production and borrow less, and profits diminish, with the net effect that government revenues decline. Simultaneously, the demand for government social services and guarantee programs increases because of economic hardship. Consequently, the level of government deficit spending increases during times of economic recession.

Acquiescing to anti-recessionary political pressures, the Fed then pumps money into the system by purchasing huge quantities of government securities on the open market, creating excess reserves and artificially driving down the gross market rate of interest. The low interest rates are a mere facade that mask the lack of real capital available for borrowing.

Nevertheless, the low nominal interest rates draw entrepreneurs in, and a stimulated recovery begins. As the recovery gains momentum and the level of borrowing picks up, the demand for credit increases relative to the supply, and interest rates begin to move up. Jobs are created, tax revenues increase, and the deficit, or at least its rate of growth, declines.

Another important impact deficit spending has on the credit markets is dictated by the law of supply and demand. The economic facts of the matter are that any time the government borrows money in the market, it is taking potential resources out of the private sector and putting them into the government sector.

Money borrowed is a claim on unconsumed goods, and at any point only a limited amount of unconsumed goods are available on the market. Therefore, when the government borrows money, it gains a claim on unconsumed goods that would otherwise be available to the private market. Nothing can change this simple fact. When the Fed pumps so much money into the credit market that interest rates remain unchanged or even drop in the face of massive government borrowing, it simply masks or waters down what is actually occurring—the artificial lowering of the market rate of interest, the distortion of economic calculation, and the misallocation of resources.

An historical example of this process began in 1969. The Fed reduced the rate of growth of the money supply, interest rates shot up, and the country went spiraling into recession. Credit demand faded, and interest rates began to decrease. Because tax revenues diminished and government spending increased, the budget figures moved from a surplus in 1969 to a deficit of $2.8 billion in 1970 to $23.4 billion in 1972!

The discount rate moved steadily downward from 6% in 1970 to 4.5% in 1971. Then the credit expansion began to have its expected impact. Business activity increased. Employment was stimulated. Company earnings began to improve. As a result, Federal tax revenues increased, and the deficit plummeted to $4.7 billion by 1974.

Consumer prices were also affected—they soared! The CPI (1982–1984 = 100) moved 10 full points from 35.6 in 1969 to 46.6 in 1974—over a 28% increase in just five years!

Faced with rising consumer prices, the Fed once again put on the brakes and, once again, recession struck. From 1974 to 1976 the discount rate dropped from 8% to 5¼% while the deficit soared from $4.7 billion to $66.4 billion. And the cycle continues today.

Another prevailing fallacy is that tax increases are a cure for deficits. As Parkinson's Law states, "Expenditures rise to meet income." The net level of taxes has increased in every administration since the Kennedy administration, while deficits have grown to all-time highs. The only way to cut deficits is to cut the budget.

As if direct deficit spending isn't bad enough, there is another growing burden which James Grant calls "the latent deficit"—all the contingent liabilities and government guarantees accumulated since the New Deal. The face value of U.S. government insurance programs has grown from $662 billion in 1979 to $4.214 trillion in 1989. Direct loans, loan guarantees, and GSEs (Government Sponsored Enterprises) have grown from $200 billion in 1970 to $1.558 trillion in 1989.

To put some of these figures in more concrete terms, almost 75% of all farm loans are facilitated by the government, and approximately 88% of housing mortgages are federally supported by some means.[14]

I don't want to sound like a prophet of doom, but this process has to stop sooner or later. When it does, because of the huge scale of what has been happening, we are going to see the most severe economic correction—bust—in history, provided the government lets the correction run its course. But depending on how the Fed, the Executive, and Congress handle the problem, we could continue for a long time to come with spurts of stimulated economic growth followed by short, sharp recessions which slow down the expansionary, inflationary process.

As a speculator in this kind of economic climate, you have to be constantly aware of the downside possibilities. You have to carefully monitor Fed and Treasury activities and pronouncements and be prepared for the market's response.

HOW TO PREDICT THE TREND AND CHANGES OF TREND BASED ON FED AND TREASURY POLICY

Market forces—supply and demand—ultimately determine the long-term price trend of any market. But part of the supply and demand equation in any market is the supply and demand for money and credit. Whether you are trading stock indexes, individual stocks, or commodities, both Fed and government fiscal policies dramatically affect money and credit and therefore the price trend.

My biggest wins have come from the ability to predict the consequences of government policies (combined with other methods, of course). But my biggest losses came when I assumed that the government would behave rationally.

For example, in July 1982 I had one of the largest long positions of my life. We were in a bear market, and Dow Theory gave me a buy signal. I went long the world, and within three weeks was up $385,000.

But on July 23, Bob Dole came out with a tax bill proposing the largest tax increase in the history of the world. I made the mistake of believing Reagan's campaign promise not to raise taxes and assumed the bill would never pass. The market fell 12 out of the next 14 days, and by the time I got out of the position, my profit had turned into a loss. I posted a loss of over $93,000 for the month, the second largest losing month of my career. (Actually, the losses were about twice that; the $93,000 was just for Interstate.)

The market bottomed on August 12, when the news arrived on the market that the Fed would ease. The psychology of what happens in this kind of case is really amazing, if you think about it. The federal government, operating at a deficit, increases taxes at the tail end of a bear market to help alleviate the burden of deficits.

The Fed, fearing that the increased tax burden will drive the economy deeper into recession, realizes that the only way the tax bill will do any good is if business is stimulated into recovery, so they pump money into the system, which drives down interest rates, and business begins to expand. In essence, by expanding credit, the Fed provides the government with the resources to pay the bill of the new tax law. And people call this a *free market* economy!

Another case where I lost money by believing in politicians occurred in November 1984, after Reagan's reelection. His proposed new tax law was presented as "simplified" and "revenue neutral." I believed him, and was long more than ever in my life—pages and pages of calls on stocks. It turned out that "revenue neutral" meant that the government was going to take money from corporations and give it to individuals, and the market went down nine of eleven days. I lost over $349,000 that month, by far the largest monthly loss of my career, and, again, my actual total losses were almost double that.

My failure in these two cases was not thinking like a politician, but at least I learned something. I learned that you can count on politicians to take the expedient route, the "pragmatic approach," no matter what their expressed intentions are. I became almost cynical as I watched an avowed gold standard and laissez-fair advocate, Alan Greenspan, take the chairmanship of the Federal Reserve Board and turn into an expert at saying nothing with far too many words—the hallmark of every "good" politician. I watched the federal budget grow and deficits soar under an administration that ran on a campaign of "limited government" and "a return to free market principles." I watched the economic bubble inflate, driven by the most rapid credit expansion in U.S. economic history. By mid-1987, I was poised, waiting for the needle that would pop the bubble, and the rest is history.

Make no mistake about it, the Fed is a *political* institution subject to the pressures of the lobbyists and constituencies of Congress and the President. Why? It's the nature of the beast. Any man who tries to remain aloof from those pressures will lose both his influence and, eventually, his position. It is naive to expect the Fed to act as a truly "independent agency." In large part, the members of the Fed are forced to act on the basis of the short-term, pragmatic policies of the party in power, not on the basis of sound economic policy. A trading rule that you won't see in the chapter on trading rules is: "Never go long politicians—and the Fed is a group of politicians."

Predicting the long-term trend based on government fiscal and monetary policy is basically a matter of thinking in fundamental economic principles in the context of the nature of the business cycle. The central problem is one of being vigilant and of assuming a politician's mindset when evaluating the pronouncements of the President, the Secretary of the Treasury, and key members of the Fed. There are really only two long-term possibilities—prices are going to trend up, or they are going to trend down. And the turning points will occur when the Fed changes its policies to accommodate government fiscal policy or to actively reverse a market downtrend. At the risk of being redundant, I will repeat the Von Mises quote I used at the beginning of this chapter. By this time, the meaning should be more clear:

> The wavelike movement affecting the economic system, the recurrence of periods of boom which are followed by periods of depression [recession], is the unavoidable outcome of the attempts, repeated again and again, to lower the gross market rate of interest by means of credit expansion. There is no means of avoiding the final collapse of a boom expansion brought about by credit expansion. The alternative is only whether the crisis should come sooner as the result of a voluntary abandonment of further credit expansion, or later as a final and total catastrophe of the currency system involved.

CONCLUSION

In this chapter, we have seen that the business cycle is the result of credit expansions and contractions, induced by government fiat, and controlled in monopolistic fashion by the Federal Reserve and the fiscal policy makers in government. We have also seen that as long as the government controls monetary policy, there will be booms and busts. And as long as there are booms and busts, there will be an opportunity for the speculator to make money both on the upside and the downside. It is ironic that as an advocate of a purely free market, most of my knowledge would become obsolete if the Fed were put out of business and we went on the gold standard. But, unfortunately, I don't see that happening, at least not in my lifetime.

As long as government induces these cyclical fluctuations by manipulating the money and credit markets, it is the speculator's job to profit from it. By monitoring both government policy and the policy makers, you can often anticipate their actions and therefore predict the economic consequences. It all goes back to what I spoke about in the first chapter—thinking in principles.

When Fed policies and government fiscal policies fly in the face of basic economic principles, draw conclusions based on the fundamental economic principles involved, and you'll be right. The problem from there is one of timing—timing how long it will take the markets to recognize and react to the effects of faulty government policy. And that's where knowledge of Dow Theory, technical methods, and all of the essentials I've talked about so far—come into play.

11

Managing Money by Measuring Risk

THE TRUE MEANING OF RISK

Suppose I told you that it is possible to objectively measure risk in the stock market. For those of you who are pros, I know what you're thinking: "B.S.—NO WAY!!" Now, assume that you were long the stock market as of October 9, 1989, and I told you that the odds were then better than seven to one that the market would fail. If you had known these odds and *believed* them, would you have changed your investment strategy at all? If you were long at that point, I think you would have.

The fact is that there *is* a way to measure risk in the stock market in *quantitative* terms; there *is* a way to determine the probability of the market going up x% versus going down y%. It's not a "system"; it is a consistent method of gauging the likelihood that the current market trend will continue or fail. It is an approach that allows a speculator or investor to change his or her basic focus from the determination of "value," which is subjective and constantly changing, to *objective* risk.

But what is risk? When I started my career on Wall Street in 1966, I knew a lot more about playing poker than about the markets, but I also knew that there were many similarities. Both require skill and luck, but more skill than luck. Both require knowing how to manage money so that even if you lose a few hands, you'll still be around to play in the next one. And both involve *exposure to the chance of losing money,* which is the meaning of *risk.*

In my late teens, instead of making minimum wage bagging groceries, I made a decent income playing poker. I was good at poker because I knew how to measure and manage risk in the game. Instead of focusing on the size of the pot—the value approach—I only stayed in when the odds were in my favor; my focus was on the risk involved if I stayed in the hand. Risk involves chance, and chance involves odds. Odds take two forms: either those set subjectively by a professional

163

oddsmaker, or those that are measurable according to probabilities based on a statistical distribution of limited possibilities.

In poker, odds are measurable, concrete, objective. For example, assume you are sitting at the right side of the dealer in a game of five-card draw poker with five players. With a $10 ante, there is $50 in the pot after the first round. If the first player bets $10 and everyone has called but you, then there is $90 at stake in the game—your potential reward is 9 to 1 (even though $10 of the $90 is yours, you have to consider each betting round separately in risk/reward terms). Assuming that you have four hearts and want to draw for a flush (the chances of a flush being a winning hand are a minimum of 1.0037 to 1), your chances are 1 in 5.2 that you will draw another heart—your risk is 5.2 to 1. With a risk of 5.2 to 1 and a reward of 9 to 1, the risk/reward for the current round is 1.73 to 1 in your favor. With a risk/reward of 1.73 and a probability of .9963 that a flush will win, the adjusted/risk reward is 1.73 × .9963, or better than 1.72 to 1 in your favor.

If you employ this kind of strategy consistently, you may lose individual hands. You may even have a bad run of luck now and then, but you will win much more money than you lose over the long haul. I don't consider this gambling. Gambling is taking a blind risk. Speculation is taking a risk when the odds are in your favor. That is the essential difference between gambling and speculation.

Naturally, because my focus on risk had worked so well for me in cards, when I came to Wall Street I sought a method of objectively defining the odds of being right or wrong when speculating in the stock market. But when I asked pros whom I respected how they determined risk, I got chuckles and comments like, "You can't *measure* risk in the markets. It's not like cards. It's not a mathematical business. The market is a random walk game," or "The efficient markets theory invalidates risk/reward analysis."

Instead of talking about measuring risk, they spoke about *distributing* risk, or even more often focused on "values," saying things like "Find value, buy value and hold it, and you'll do well over the long term." This advice went against my grain; I didn't want risk exposure unless I could *objectively* determine that the odds were in my favor.

The advice of market professionals is more sophisticated today than it was in the late sixties, but it is not substantially or predominantly different. Most professionals today think in terms of distributing financial resources according to some relative measure of performance or value. For example, Alpha and Beta are typical tools used in stock portfolio management. Alpha is a measure of quality which compares the performance of an individual stock relative to the market. An Alpha value of 1 means that the stock has, on average, outperformed the market by 1% per month, so if the market moves up 10% in six months, that stock should move up 16%. Beta is a measure of volatility. A stock with a Beta of 2 should be up 20% when the market is up 10%, or down 20% if the market is down 10%.

Most money managers buy stocks according to some set Alpha and Beta combination, plus other relative factors such as price-earnings ratios, book value, and yields; and they call this "risk evaluation." But think about it. What do these measurements really have to do with risk? What do they tell you about the current trend of the economy or the effects of a change in Federal Reserve policy? What do they tell you about the likelihood that the market as a whole might be subject to a sustained and/or dramatic decline? The answer is: "Very little!"

I am by no means implying that these measures are worthless, far from it. But to use them as primary tools in speculation or investment assumes that value is an objective, static concept. Value implies evaluation, which means that individual human minds determine it. What something is worth depends totally on what individuals in the marketplace *decide* it is worth. Value can change and often does . . . rapidly. Consider the case of Penn Central.

In early 1970, Value Line Investment Service announced that the company was "worth" $110/share (as measured by the value of its underlying assets) and that it was "undervalued" at $74/share. By this measure, the stock price should have soared. It went to $2/share! The analysts who calculated the value of the company's holdings failed to take account of the fact that those holdings would deflate in value during a recession. They assumed that the market's standard of valuation would remain unchanged.

More recently, in June 1990, some analysts were saying that Citibank was "undervalued" at $24½. The last time I looked it was at $14. What they assumed was that Citibank was too big to fail, that there wouldn't be a recession, and that therefore Citibank's previously bad loans would turn into good loans. All of their conclusions rested on the *assumption* of this occurring, and did not take into account the risk of a market downturn.

In a market downturn, the Citibanks, the Trumps, and any entity that is highly leveraged against assets that depend on dollar appreciation through continued inflation are subject to decline and possible failure.

Now consider the concept of buying and holding "value." The problem with this view is that there is only one true measure of value—the market. For example, IBM has been a standard for such "value." But if you bought "Big Blue" in January 1983 or later and held it until November 1989, then you would have been *losing money* during the third largest upward stock market movement in this century! Why *ever* "hold value" by being invested in a declining issue? Why experience all that pain when you could have made money instead?

The problem with the conventional approaches to market involvement is that none of them address one simple and fundamental question: "What are the odds that the current market trend will continue?" In other words, what is the *risk* of being long or short in the current market? Alpha, Beta, value, yield, PEs, book value—all of these measures have merit, but only as secondary considerations when you have a firm grip on the *most likely* direction the market trend will go. What is first necessary is a primary standard to gauge the risk of market involvement in general. So, how do you measure the risk of being long or short in the stock market?

A REVOLUTIONARY APPROACH TO RISK ASSESSMENT

Answering this question eluded me for several years. In order to measure something, you have to identify a quantitative relationship established by comparison to a standard unit reference value. In the financial markets, this presents a perplexing problem: How do you establish a standard to measure risk and determine the probability of success without being arbitrary and subjective in the process?

Markets aren't like a deck of cards with a limited number of permutations possible; they are composed of individuals engaged in the pursuit of their own unique set of desires or values that are by their nature subjective—unique to the situation and frame of mind of each person. So it would seem that to gauge market behavior accurately, to predict the likelihood of success of any investment, you would have to be practically omniscient—be able to poll every person's mind simultaneously and be certain how they would react to coming events. It is *impossible* to predict the future of price movements with *absolute certainty*. The best we can do is deal in probabilities, so the question becomes: By what standard do you measure probabilities in the financial markets?

Any time you speak in probabilities, you are speaking of the *odds* of something occurring based on a statistical distribution of possibilities. Insurance companies use statistical data, such as mortality tables, to set insurance premiums. For example, the current odds of a 24-year-old white female dying in New York are 50,000 to 1. The average life insurance premium for a $100,000 policy for this group is $100 per year. According to the statistical odds, the *probable outcome* is that the insurance companies will gross $500,000 in premium payments for every $10,000 they pay out to the beneficiaries of 24-year-old white females who have died. That is odds of 50 to 1 in the insurance company's favor—not bad odds management. It is no wonder that most well-managed insurance companies are so profitable (the ones that didn't fill their balance sheets with junk bonds and real estate).

There is nothing certain about the life expectancy of any one individual, but that doesn't mean it is impossible to define a standard with which to gauge the odds of an individual person living to a certain age within a given standard of health—insurance companies make such measures their business. The same type of reasoning can be applied to the stock market. In 1974, I began a two-year, intensive study of stock market movements dating back to 1986, that I keep current to date. What I found is that market movements, like people, have statistically significant "life expectancy" profiles that can be used as the standard for the measurement of risk exposure. Let me explain.

After I missed the October lows in 1974, I started asking myself some questions so I wouldn't make the same mistake again, questions like: "What exactly is a trend? How high or low does it usually go? How long does it usually last?" Drawing on Charles Dow's identification of the three concurrent market trends—the short term, lasting from days to weeks; the intermediate term, lasting from weeks to months; and the long term, lasting from months to years—I went back in history and classified every price movement in the Dow Jones Industrials and Transportation

(Rails) averages, logging their extent (how much they moved in percentage terms from the previous highs or lows) and duration (how long they lasted in calendar days) in statistical distribution tables.

Using Robert Rhea's classification methods (along with some of my own refinements), I identified primary movements (the long-term bull or bear markets), intermediate primary movements (the legs that make up primary movements in between secondary reactions), intermediate secondary corrections (*important* intermediate movements that move contrary to the primary trend), plus some other less important classifications (the hardest part of this process was in distinguishing between secondary reactions and minor movements against the trend). The result was a set of statistically significant bell curve distributions for the extent and duration of all market movements since 1896 such as shown in Figure 11.1.

In a bell curve distribution, statistical samples tend to bunch around the *median* or midpoint of the distribution. For example, the current median extent for bull market primary intermediate swings on the Dow is 20%. Of the 112 bull market primary swings since 1896, 57 of them, or 50.89%, have reached an extent of between 15% and 30%, while the minimum move was 4.3% and the maximum was 116.6%. Twenty-five percent of the moves went to highs above 30%, and 33.04% of the

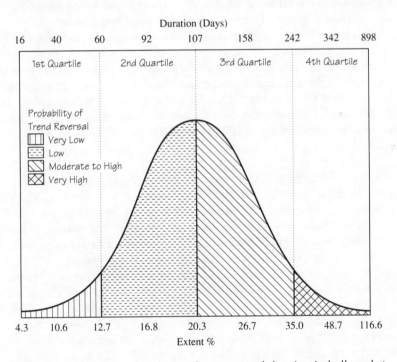

Figure 11.1 Frequency distribution for extent and duration in bull market primary swings on the Dow Industrials since 1896.

moves failed below 15%. Based on these criteria alone, you would be wise to bet that a primary swing would appreciate somewhere between 15% and 30%. But of course, you would never use these criteria alone.

Think about how life insurance companies go about gathering their information. The first question they ask is age. Then they factor in job hazards, medical history, family history, and so forth. But the mortality tables are the standard of reference, the starting point of evaluating the risk of insuring the customer. In the same way, I use my distributions as a means to establish the base probability that a market movement will reach or go beyond a given extent and duration. *I absolutely do not use them to predict the exact levels the current market movement will reach or how long it will last!* Market turning points occur when the tide of market participants' judgments changes . . . period. This is usually driven by fundamental economic factors, the policies of the Federal Reserve Board, major world events, and so forth, as I discussed in the last chapter.

To use extent and duration profiles to predict in advance exact market turning points would be like having an insurance company tell you when and how you will die on the day you buy your policy. I don't mean to be morbid, but just as each individual person dies in a different manner, context, and point in time, so markets die. But who are you most likely to see on stage next year, Meryl Streep or George Burns? What these profiles *do* tell you is the base probability, in the context of history, that the current stock market trend will continue or fail.

Returning to the insurance analogy, if two men, one 18 years old and one 75 years old (the median age that American men die), both in good health, went into an insurance company to apply for a term life policy, then the younger man would pay a very low premium and the older man would pay a very high premium. The premiums would be set such that the risk, according to the statistics, of the person dying before he pays the entire policy value plus interest is very low. But if the older man had a temperature of 102 and were a heavy smoker, he wouldn't be sold a policy at all.

Consider the examples of the October 1987 crash and the October 1989 mini-crash in a similar context. The primary intermediate movement leading to the crash of 1987 began on 5/20/87. By 8/25/87, the Industrials had increased 22.9% in 96 days, while the Transports had increased 21.3% in 108 days. These were nearly the exact *median* levels, both in extent and duration, of all bull market intermediate movements in history. In life insurance terms, the market had reached the median life expectancy, meaning that 50% of all intermediate movements in history ended before this one—it was a likely candidate for retirement. From this standpoint alone, caution was warranted, so it was time to examine the medical history.

The market was no Jack LaLanne. There were divergences; the Dow made a new high in August, but the advance/decline ratio did not—a bearish indication. PEs were at an average of 21 times earnings, the highest levels since 1962, when they were at 22. The average book value to price ratio was nominally higher than 1929. Government, corporate, and consumer debt were at unprecedented levels, and all the rest that I've discussed before. In October 1987, the market was not only no Jack LaLanne, it was an alcoholic, with pneumonia, that smoked three packs of unfiltered Camels a day.

Consequently, I was out of the market and looking for an opportunity to short it. The first sign was on October when I read in the *Wall Street Journal*: "Fed Chairman Greenspan said interest rates could become 'dangerously high' if inflation worries 'mushroom' in financial markets. Greenspan called such worries unwarranted but hinted the discount rate may have to rise to allay them." The next day, stock prices plunged a record 91.55 points for no immediately apparent reason other than Greenspan's pronouncement. On October 15, Dow Theory gave me a sell signal, and I went short thinking that the patient's heart could fail with even the slightest excitement.

The heart attack occurred when Germany and Japan failed to heed James Baker's request to stimulate their economies (inflate) to protect the value of the dollar. In response, Baker announced to the world on Sunday, October 18, that he "would let the dollar slide." I knew at this point that the financial markets would collapse from the dollar devaluation. When the market gapped down on October 19, I shorted the opening of the S&P 500 futures and made a substantial profit for my account in that position alone. The bittersweet part of it is that I had independent traders working for me at the time (free to make their own decisions) who were caught long, and some of my profits were offset by their losses.

The point in describing my thinking before the crash of October 1987 is to show how watching extent and duration criteria can clue you in to the potential health of the market—they act as a caveat telling you to pay close attention to what is happening fundamentally. Sometimes they tell you more than that. For example, I was essentially out of the market from May until October of 1989; partly because I was busy organizing my new money management firm, but also because I feared the downside possibilities. By 10/9/89 the net appreciation primary intermediate up move on the Dow, which began on 3/23/89, was 24.4%. During the same period, the Transports had moved 52%, fueled by takeover stocks. Let me put this into the framework of my statistical base.

The median *net* appreciation, or yield (the net percentage move if you buy and hold from the bottom of one intermediate correction to the next), for primary intermediate movements (primary swings) in bull markets is 10%. Further, only 15 of 112 such moves in history yielded more than 24.4% (the gain that was current in the existing primary swing as of October 9). Even more important, only 8 of 174 upward movements in both bull and bear markets had matched or exceeded the Transport's 52% gain. In other words, the odds, based on history, that the market would fail ranged from 7.46/1 to 21.75/1! That told me to close any longs and look for a shorting opportunity. Measured by statistical criteria alone, to be long in October 1989 was one of the poorest risks on record. And once again, the fundamental and technical factors were on the side of the statistics.

The new high set by the Industrials on October 9 was unconfirmed by the Transports—a bearish indication. As of Friday, October 13, the Japanese and the Germans had raised interest rates, making it more expensive for their companies and citizens to buy American products on credit. The Fed had reduced the money supply and credit availability (as measured by free reserves) over the previous two reporting periods, and with the CPI already at an annual rate of approximately 5.5%, they did not have much room to ease in order to stimulate business activity, which was already sluggish. Northeastern real estate and the regional banks holding the mortgages were already in recession. The bottom had already fallen out of the junk bond market. In short, the patient was once again old and sick and another stroke was imminent—not a good time to write an insurance policy at any premium rate. It was certainly no time to be long. I was fortunate to be short at the right time and in the right instruments, but it was my statistical profiles that clued me in to the downside possibilities.

Anybody who knows me knows that I don't mind playing the short side. But I want to emphasize that this approach to risk assessment is equally valuable to pension fund managers, who must be long to some extent in the stock market. Suppose the fund manager is trying to determine what percentage of capital to allocate to the stock market, with 60% being an aggressive position and 20% being the minimum allowable position according to the investment charter of the fund. If the stock market is in the third primary swing of a bull market, then the statistics say that the median extent and duration for third primary swings are 139 days and 18.8% respectively. If the market had appreciated 12% in 103 days, the manager would know from the profiles that 16 of the 23 third primary movements in bull markets had lasted longer. On that basis alone, the manager should commit no more than 69% of the maximum 60% to stocks. In other words, on the basis of the statistics alone, they should commit a maximum of 41.4% of the portfolio to stocks.

I want to emphasize again that this is only a starting point, a basis from which to evaluate the risk of market involvement. If under these same statistical circumstances, inflation was at 1%, PEs were at nine, interest rates were at 5%, and earnings were soaring, then the manager would underweight the statistics and invest the full 60% in stocks.

This concept of risk measurement has been absolutely instrumental to my success in the markets, particularly in positions involving either long-term or intermediate-term market turning points. It allows me to place my primary focus on risk, which is the basis of my approach to speculation. But no matter how you make market calls or stock selections, market life expectancy profiles provide an objective base context within which to gauge the risk of market involvement. They add a unique and powerful new dimension to risk assessment.

ALLOCATING CAPITAL WITH ODDS MANAGEMENT

As mentioned in Chapter 2, my primary focus is to minimize risk, while simultaneously putting enough capital in the right place to make consistent profits. What it takes to do this is a prudent system of money management.

Money management is the art of allocating financial resources and timing entry and exit to and from the marketplace to achieve business goals. A solid approach to money management must consist of three crucial components: (1) a method of assessing risk/reward, (2) a means with which to determine the probability of success on any given trade (whether short-term, intermediate-term or long-term), and (3) a system of asset allocation. And, since you are dealing with money, these three components must, at least predominantly, be reduced to objective, measurable criteria.

I have already discussed my statistical profiles and how I use them to measure risk. Also, if you recall, I pointed out that my risk/reward criterion is at most 1 to 3, and I demonstrated how I determine that ratio technically on the charts. Basically, it amounts to looking at the chart, evaluating where you think the market can *probably* go—the target point, establishing the point where the market proves that you are wrong—and your exit point, and then calculating the following ratio:

$$\text{Risk/Reward} = \frac{\text{Purchase Price} - \text{Exit Point}}{\text{Target Price} - \text{Purchase Price}}$$

This ratio expresses technical risk/reward in terms of maximum probable losses versus probable potential profits. Properly considered, risk/reward from any dimension is always a ratio of probabilities. Where it gets tricky is in establishing a way to quantify probabilities when dealing with other than technical factors. When assessing risk/reward, a whole range of information, including both technical and fundamental economic principles, comes into play. Let me illustrate how to combine these factors by examining a position I took in gold in October 1989.

I bought gold on 10/27/89, the day the market gave me a confirmation of a 1-2-3 change of trend in the intermediate term by breaking above the previous rally high of 376.70. At this point, there was also a *probable* change of the long-term trend by the same criteria—both the break in the trend line (condition 1) and the test and failure of the previous low (condition 2) had already occurred.[1]

In the intermediate term, because I had a *confirmed* change of trend, the market would prove me wrong if prices fell back through the buy spot, so I set my mental stop slightly below that point, at 375.70. The target point in the intermediate term was the 7/25/89 high of 399.50. So my technical risk/reward ratio was:

$$\frac{376.70 - 375.70}{399.50 - 376.90} = \frac{1}{22.6}$$

When I looked at the long-term chart (the weekly bar chart), things looked even better in terms of the potential levels gold might reach. There, I could see a target price (resistance) at 433.50. After that, there was another resistance point at 469.50, one at 502.30, and if I looked at an even longer-term chart (at a monthly bar chart), I saw prices in the 800 range. I won't bother calculating the risk/reward of each point for you, but you can see that the ratios were extremely favorable.

From a technical standpoint, trades this obviously good don't come along too often. The only problem is to figure out the probability of success and establish your entry and exit point(s). What do you do: Play the intermediate term, or buy and hold for the long term?

To help answer this question, what I did was to assume the most conservative case. That is, since the intermediate trend had already changed by definition, I assumed that this would be an intermediate trend lasting from three weeks to three months. Next, I went back in history to 1981 and tabulated the extent of every upward move in gold lasting from three weeks to three months.

I found that, of 18 such moves, the minimum movement was 9.4%, the maximum movement was 68.8%, and the *median* movement was 15.2%. Based on the low of 360.60 in the December futures, this told me that there was a *very high probability* that gold would rally at least 9.4%, which is a change of $33.90 per ounce, to a price of $394.50. In addition, it told me that 50% of all moves within the last nine years rallied more than 15.2%, which for the December futures would be $54.81 per ounce to the 415.40 level.

What does all this tell you in terms of asset allocation? The extremely low technical risk/reward factor, the high historical probability of the move going to at least 394.50, and the fundamental factors all supported taking a long position on October 27. When all the factors are strongly in favor of a position like this, then it is time to become aggressive.

This means that, in the early part of the move, you should use optimum leverage. My choice was to put approximately 10% of all my managed portfolios in gold by buying calls on the gold futures, calls on some gold stocks, and some of the gold stocks themselves (the stocks for my less risk-oriented clients). Once prices broke through the 400 level, I began scale-selling at a very substantial profit, with the intention of holding a smaller, long-term position, still highly leveraged, until the market proved me wrong.

Why did I sell at all? Because after prices reached the intermediate target level, the risk/reward of holding the position increased substantially. The justification for staying involved at this point has to be a conviction that the long-term trend will keep going up. I held a smaller long position with a portion of profits, and guess what? I was wrong and lost the money. Although I was dumbfounded at the fact that gold failed to sustain its rally, my principles of money management saved me.

Let me tie this process directly to the principles of my business philosophy.

First, by using leverage and by picking a buy spot that allowed a small loss as an exit point, I did not expose capital to a high degree of risk. If, by some odd circumstance, prices had failed back below the trend change confirmation point, then I could have most likely closed the position with a loss of at most 1 to 2% on my accounts. Then, if it rallied again, I could still afford to take another position. In short, I set the trade up to preserve capital.

Second, when prices reached the target level, I took enough profits to lock in a substantial gain in accordance with the goal of consistent profitability.

Third, I used a portion of profits to hold a long position for the pursuit of superior returns. I was wrong in the long-term call, but I still ended up net profitable on my overall position. In my mind, that's successful speculating through smart money management. By allocating capital according to the risk of involvement, by setting preliminary exit points to lock in your profits, and by using only a portion of profits to pursue the larger gains, you'll stay at the table even when you lose some hands.

Allocating Capital

Unfortunately, there is no simple formula to plug into a computer that will tell you the best way to allocate capital in the markets. For example, I can't take my historical data and buy the stocks that make up the Dow Industrial and Transports averages according to some linear risk relationship. To do so would be to defy the nature of the markets. What you have to do is make a judgment call based on the widest context of knowledge possible, combining all aspects of your knowledge to form your best estimate of coming events.

Suppose we were in a strong bull market that had already exceeded its extent and duration medians; inflation was at 2%; the world was at peace with no potential conflict in sight; corporations in general had little debt and high earnings; and every major country had a balanced budget, little or no debt, and operated on a free, gold-based banking system. Nice thought, isn't it? In such a case, you would obviously want to be 100% invested.

In effect, what you do is build a risk assessment scoreboard that tabulates all the driving market forces and weigh each factor separately to decide how much and in what way to put capital at risk. If you decide to invest at all, then you use the same facts as a context to choose those instruments that are most likely to achieve your goals.

What I've said so far is all very general, so let me get more specific. When you are assessing the risk of being involved in the stock market, you have to ask yourself the following questions:

1. What is the long-term trend? Is it up, is it down, is it drawing lines, or is it changing?

2. How does the current long-term trend fit within the context of history in terms of extent and duration? Is it young, old, or middle-aged?

3. What is the intermediate trend, and where does it fit within the context of history?

4. What does Dow Theory say about the current market? Are there divergences? What does the volume tell you? Is breadth moving with the trend?

5. What do the moving averages say—buy, sell, or hold?

6. Do oscillators tell you that the market is overbought, oversold, or in the middle of a move?

7. What is the health of the economy?

   a. Where is inflation and what is the Fed's policy toward it? What are the levels of national, civil, corporated, and private debt? What is the rate of growth of credit availability as measured by free reserves? What is the rate of growth of the money supply? Where are interest rates? How are the markets receiving new issues of government securities?

   b. How strong is the dollar relative to foreign currencies, and what is the likelihood that it could be debased? How strong are the yen and the deutsche mark and are those governments likely to take action to protect them?

   c. What is the prevailing attitude of the American consumer: produce and save, borrow and spend, or somewhere in between?

   d. What economic sectors are strong? Which ones are weak? Are any stock groups driving the market, giving it the appearance of health when in fact the tide could easily turn at the slightest bad news?

   e. What potential problems exist that could cause a sudden change of the economic climate?

8. What predominant fallacies exist that can be used to advantage, especially when the market changes?

Once you answer these questions, you then have the basis to decide when, where, and how much money to invest in the markets. And when you decide to make your move, you've got to do it in a very disciplined way. That's where rules come in, the subject of the next chapter.

12

There Must Be Fifty Ways to Lose Your Money

THE $4017 HAIR DRYER

One day in 1979, I was day trading the commodities when I got a call from my friend, Susan. I was long 40 wheat contracts, and the market was moving, so I had to watch the position intensely. I had a mental stop set to get out and limit my losses. Anyway, Susan calls me, she's hysterical—crying, sobbing, sniffling—to the point that I can't understand what she is saying.

Naturally, I was concerned. I thought that maybe she and her husband had been fighting, that some real crisis had occurred. Then the truth came out.

Through sobs and sniffs I heard, "Mmm . . . my hairdryer, it's . . . ittsss . . . it's broken!"

I just couldn't believe my ears. "Your HAIRDRYER! Is THAT why you're so upset!" I looked over at my good friend and longtime partner, Norman Tandy . . . he just rolled his eyes.

"Susan," I said, "Susan, calm down. How much do hairdryers cost?"

"Sniff . . . 17 dollars."

At this point, I'm amazed, and on the verge of bursting out laughing, "If it will make you feel any better, I'll buy you another one."

Naturally, any time someone gets so upset over a hairdryer, something else is really wrong. So, I started talking to Susan, trying to help her come to terms with whatever was really bothering her. In the process, I lost my mental focus.

I looked at my screen, and wheat had dropped 2 cents below my mental stop. That's $100 times 40—4000 bucks. I immediately called and sold the position, losing $4000 more than I had mentally allowed. A $4017 hair dryer, and I didn't even get to pick out the color.

I couldn't help but laugh about it then, and I still laugh about it now. The point is that there are all kinds of ways to lose money that you never think about. To paraphrase the song, "Fifty Ways to Leave Your Lover," there must be 50 ways to lose your money.

The single biggest way traders lose money, however, is by not following the rules, by somehow thinking that "this one time" there is an exception. It's a mistake that everyone makes, but one that is controllable. If you understand the rules, and more importantly, *why they exist,* it's a mistake that is possible to avoid 99% of the time.

TRADING RULES AND THE REASONS BEHIND THEM

Many people make the mistake of thinking that market behavior is truly predictable. Nonsense. Trading in the markets is an odds game, and the object is to always keep the odds in your favor. Like any other odds game, in order to win, you've got to know the rules and stick to them. Unlike other games, however, the single biggest reason rules are necessary is to keep a check on your emotions. Assuming you have the knowledge you need to take a position with confidence, the hard part is executing the trade correctly. That's what the rules are for.

There are so many factors affecting market behavior that, with just a little mental energy, you can twist and distort them, even if only slightly, and rationalize yourself into taking unwarranted risks or closing a position too early or too late.

Just recently, on an S&P futures trade, I went short 10 minutes after the opening with a stop set 5 ticks above the day's high. In the next 30 minutes, the market went down about 10 ticks from where I sold them and then looked like it might rally. I did not have a clear buyback signal on the trade at all, but, *emotionally,* I didn't want the small profit to turn into a loss, and I had my assistant buy them back at a 10-tick profit ($250 per contract).

Just 15 minutes later, the market broke down two full handles (a *handle* on the S&P futures is 1 full point, which is 20 ticks or $500 per contract). If I had followed the rules, I would have made five times more profit than I did. My thinking process was something like, "This market looks like it is going to rally, so I better bail out and take the profit while I have the chance." But that was really just a rationalization which was shielding my fear of being wrong in the trade. The market did, in fact, rally just a little bit, but it never even approached my stop—the point where the market would *prove* I was wrong.

The purpose of rules is to make market executions as *objective* and consistent as humanly possible. Without them, you'll end up imposing your wishes on your trading decisions and, nine times out of ten, your wishes will fly in the face of market action. The purpose of this chapter is to outline the major trading rules and the reasons behind them. I'll also discuss a few ways to lose money that you don't hear people talk about very much.

THE RULES DEFINED

Rule Number 1: Trade with a plan and stick to it.

Before you make any trade, it is absolutely essential that you know your objective and how you intend to reach it. This means not only identifying the risk/reward, but also defining all possible courses the market *might* take and then defining your response. In other words, you have to know, before you ever enter the trade, all the possible outcomes. Confusion is your biggest enemy during a trade; it will cause you anguish and emotional turmoil as the trade progresses. But confusion, by definition, comes from ignorance, from not understanding what is going on or how to respond to it.

The main thing you have to ask yourself in forming your plan is where, timewise, your interest is in making the trade. That is, you have to decide if you are taking the position as a day-trade (open and close the position within the day), a short-term trade (held for days to weeks), an intermediate term speculation (held weeks to months), or a long-term investment (held months to years).

This decision determines which trend you focus your concentration on and therefore where you set your stops (see Rule Number 3). Once you decide, then identify all possible scenarios in terms of the price movement and determine what your response to each scenario will be. Specifically, identify where you will place your stops, price objectives to take profits or to increase the size of the position, and so on.

There are sometimes sources of confusion you can't control—another of the 50 ways to lose your money. For example, one day, while trading at Interstate, I was long 40 or so stocks, in lots of 2000 or more. I owned calls on the indexes. I had futures positions. I was trading very, very intensely. Then suddenly . . . everything went black.

No, some goon didn't come in and knock me on the head. The power went out. We had a backup system, but it failed too. Somehow, the phones were connected to the electrical system, so even they didn't work.

Now, I'm dealing with several exchanges, several different brokers, and I don't know what the hell is happening on the market. I ran out into the hallway and down the stairs, fumbling in my pocket, trying to find quarters for the payphone. I didn't even have the numbers to the pits I was trading in, because I had direct lines to them in my office.

So there I was, out in the middle of the street at a pay phone, closing my positions in a panic. Can you imagine calling directory assistance and asking for the number of the S&P futures pit in Chicago? It's funny now, but it was awful then. And, as Murphy's Law would have it, the markets had moved against me. Now that's a kind of confusion you can't control, but you may want to make sure your system has double back-up.

Rule Number 2: Trade with the trend. "The trend is your friend!"

This is probably the most well-known rule of all. But as simple as it seems, it is easier to violate than you might think. Remember, there are three trends—the short-term, the intermediate term, and the long-term. Each trend is moving all the time and may be going in a direction opposing the other two. The short-term trend changes more rapidly and more often than the intermediate trend, and the intermediate trend changes more rapidly and more often than the long-term trend.

Know which trend you are involved in and its correlation with the other two. Identify, using the 1-2-3 change of trend criterion, the point at which the trend has reversed. If the market hits that price—get out! Also watch for 2B patterns and other technical indicators that can give you an earlier indication of a probable trend reversal.

Rule Number 3: Use stop loss orders whenever practical.

Before opening a trade, you should know the point at which the market proves you are wrong. One of the hardest things for many traders is to close the trade when the market hits that point. One way to avoid this problem is to trade with stop loss orders. A stop order is one which converts to a market order when the price stated in the stop order is reached.

If you are trading in size, you must use *mental* stops. If you put huge stop orders in, then you can be sure the locals will hit them if they can.

So, once you open a position, you should place a second order to close the position at a stop. The exact way to do this depends on what trend you are involved in. As a general rule, stop orders are valid until the close on the day you place them. But you can place a stop order with the addendum "good 'til cancel," or GTC, which means that the order is good until you cancel it.

In fact, you really have to watch both yourself and your broker when you place *any* order. My good friend, John Malley, who is a trader, tells me about people who call up and say things like, "Sell me 500 IBM at the market." So John replies, "Mmm . . . sell me, that means you're a buyer, you want me to sell to you 500 IBM?" And, of course, the customer impatiently replies, "No, no, no, I'm a seller!"

But John is right. When you "buy puts," you're short. When you sell them, you're long. "Get me 10 December S&P's at the market," doesn't mean anything. Words have definite meaning, especially when you're placing an order in the markets, so make sure you get it right, and make sure your broker understands you.

Rule Number 4: When in doubt, get out!

Another way of stating this rule is that when you are evaluating your positions, every long position you hold should be a buy *today,* and every short position you hold should be a sell *today.* It also means that you should never enter a position without confidence.

It is only natural to experience a little bit of fear or anxiety when your money is on the line, and by no means should you close a position every time you feel an inkling of doubt. But if changing conditions start to pile the odds against you and you are plagued with nagging doubt and uncertainty, then close the position.

This rule also has a second meaning. There is a fine line between fear and justifiable doubt. It may sound harsh, but if, because of fear, every position you take fills you with doubt and uncertainty, then get out of the markets! You have no business trading if you can't trade with confidence, at least most of the time. Chronic fear and doubt will take a dreadful toll on you physically, emotionally, and probably financially. It's nothing to be ashamed of; it's just a personality trait that is not conducive to being successful in the markets.

The single best way to avoid doubt during a trade is to have all the possible information you can on your side. Sometimes, though, even that is not enough.

I was told a story about a very wealthy man who dealt with a takeover analyst and usually did very well by him. The analyst had been talking about several stocks as a buy: Northwest Airlines and Cessna among them, both potential takeover stocks at the time. One day, the rich man got a call from the analyst, who said, "I just got the scoop, this thing is on. Buy *the plane*."

The rich man proceeded to go out and buy 400,000 shares of Northwest Airlines at $60 per share. That's $24 *million* worth of stock. The next day, the stock went to $59, then to $58. The rich man called the analyst.

"What's going on here, I thought the deal was on?"

The analyst was very busy, "Yep, yep, it's still a go . . . real busy . . . gotta move," and he hangs up.

Within the next two days, the stock went to $55, and the rich man called again. This time the analyst wasn't so busy.

The rich man asks, "When is this thing going to happen?"

"Day after tomorrow."

"At what price?" confusion in the rich man's voice.

"*Above* the market."

"I don't get it then," says the dumfounded rich man, "the stock's down five bucks, at $55."

The analyst is surprised: "What do you mean, $55, *Cessna* is at $24!"

"Cessna! . . . CESSNA!"

"Yeah, Cessna! I told you to buy the *plane*," says the analyst in shock.

And the rich said, "But Northwest flies, too!"

The rich man blew out his position, losing 2 million dollars. All along, his doubts were justified. One more story to verify the rule, "When in doubt, get out!"

Rule Number 5: Be patient. Never overtrade.

Frankie Joe used to say that there were usually three or four excellent trading opportunities per year in any given market, including individual stocks. Frankie was a speculator; he traded primarily in the intermediate term. But the essence of his point applies to every trend. You can flip a coin and say, "heads long, tails short," and trade one hundred times a day if you want to. But if you do, the only way you're going to win is through sheer luck.

The way to make money is to watch the markets you are interested in and wait until as many factors as possible are in your favor before taking a position. For example, in day-trading the S&P futures, there is usually a maximum of two or three good trading opportunities each day. Sometimes there are none.

Each market index, each stock, and each commodity has its own unique pace, rhythm, and trading characteristics. Don't trade until you feel familiar with the price action of your market(s) and then wait for opportunities that promise large profits if you are right and small losses if you are wrong. Observe, watch patiently, and when all the factors come into play in your favor, act without hesitation.

Another aspect of this rule is that, if you are trading just on your own account, it is prudent to limit yourself to under ten stocks if you are active in the stock market, or to under five commodities if you are trading in the futures. The biggest reason for this is a simple matter of focus.

How many phone numbers do you know off the top of your head? Maybe as many as eight or ten. Well, if it's that hard to remember phone numbers, imagine trying to maintain the intensity required to stay on top of more than ten or so trades at once. Awareness of your positions and what they are doing is key to performing well. For most of us, thinking about five things at once is plenty of challenge.

Rule Number 6: Let your profits run; cut your losses short.

Of all the trading rules, this is the most important, most commonly stated, and the most commonly violated rule of them all.

The market is like a courtroom where you are the accused — innocent until proven guilty. That is, when you initiate a trade, you have to assume that you are right until the market proves you wrong. It proves you wrong when the price hits your stop or your mentally chosen exit point, which is as absolute as a Supreme Court ruling — no appeal is possible, your freedom to act is gone, you must close out the position.

When you are right, you have to "Let freedom reign!" When you trade on a one to three risk/reward criterion, then as a general rule you should either lose one or win at least three, as I described in an earlier chapter. The exceptions are covered by Rule Number 7.

In a sense, Rule Number 6 is a restatement of all the rules covered so far. If you have a plan, then you know when to take profits, when to double up on a position, and when to close out. If you trade with the trend, then your loss limits are objectively definable by the change of trend criterion. If you trade with stops, you will automatically cut your losses short. If you trade with confidence, you are unlikely to take profits too early. If you don't overtrade, you will both minimize losses and stand a better chance of catching the winners and riding them out. If you really understand "Let your profits run; cut your losses short," then you've rolled at least four rules into one — good mental economics.

Rule Number 7: Never let a profit run into a loss. (Or always take a free position if you can.)

This is a tough one because you have to define "profit" in your own trading terms. To generalize the rule, consider it in terms of the 1 to 3 risk/reward context. If you are up 2 to 1, then Rule 6 says to let your profits run. But if the price trend reverses and you end up getting stopped out, then you've violated Rule 7! What are you supposed to do?

What I recommend is that any time you are up two to one on a trade, raise your stop, even if just mentally, slightly above cost and take the free position! In a sense, this gives you a zero risk/reward relationship. You have everything to gain and nothing to lose. If the trade continues going your way and reaches the 1 to 3 objective, then close out one-half or one-third of the position and raise your stop to lock in a two to one profit on the rest of the position. If the trade still continues to go your way, then you can move your stop to lock in higher and higher levels of profits. And if you are playing the long term, depending on the exact nature of the market, you might even want to expand the size of your position at strategically selected points.

Rule Number 8: Buy weakness and sell strength. Be just as willing to sell as you are to buy.

This rule is primarily applicable to speculating and investing, and to a smaller degree in short-term trading. It is a corollary to Rule 2, trading with the trend. If you are speculating on the intermediate trend, the way to maximize profit potential is to sell during minor rallies and buy during minor sell-offs. If you are investing in the long-term trend, you should sell during intermediate rallies in bear markets and buy during intermediate sell-offs in bull markets.

The same reasoning holds true for adding to a profitable position in either the intermediate or long-term trend. Ideally, of course, you want to try to sell near minor rally highs and buy near minor sell-off lows when speculating in bear and bull markets, respectively; and sell near intermediate highs and buy near intermediate lows when speculating in bear markets and investing in bull markets, respectively. The 2B criterion is excellent for employing this strategy in many cases.

Many market participants are either predominantly bulls or bears and have a tendency to always be long or always be short. In fact, most market participants avoid playing the short side like a plague. This is a big mistake that defies the nature of market action. If "the trend is your friend," then playing both sides of the market is the best way to maintain a successful and lasting personal relationship. Any adept long-side player has, at least implicitly, the knowledge to play the short side—all he has to do is use converse reasoning. And when playing the short side, profits can accrue more quickly because downside movements occur faster than upside movements.

Rule Number 9: Be an investor in the early stages of bull markets. Be a speculator in the latter stages of bull markets and in bear markets.

An investor is a person looking for a long-term return and/or an income flow from the placement of capital in the market. The investor's concern is primarily with earnings, dividends, and equity appreciation.

A speculator, on the other hand, is primarily concerned with price movement and how to profit from it. Looked at from a risk/reward standpoint, the best time to be an investor is at the early stages of bull markets because, from every fundamental dimension, the chances for growth are the best.

As the market ages, entering the third, fourth, and latter legs, your emphasis on price levels should become more predominant, and the prudent market player will turn to speculation. The reason for this is that, as I discussed in Chapter 10, the progression of a bull market induced by credit expansion is such that, at some point, value appreciation ends and price inflation begins as businesses compete with more dollars for scarce resources.

In bear markets, it is always prudent to speculate. By definition, it is really impossible to be an "investor" if you are playing the short side. Long-term selling in bear markets is a means of profiting from investment liquidation; it is not investing per se. That aside, the best way to play bear markets is by moving in and out of the market, playing the short side during primary legs and the long side during secondary corrections. Bear markets are generally shorter than bull markets, and the primary swings in bear markets move similarly in extent, but shorter in duration than in bull markets.

If you manage your money carefully, you can make similar percentage profits in bear markets in shorter time with no more, and perhaps even less, risk than on the upside in bull markets. By the nature of the business cycle, you'll never see a "Black Monday" on the upside, so in that sense, bear markets are safer.

Rule Number 10: Never average a loss—don't add to a losing position.

"Averaging down" is nothing more than a rationalization either to avoid admitting being wrong or to hope to recover losses against all odds. It is called "averaging down" because it is a process of adding to a losing position such that the net percentage loss on the entire position is less than it would be if the losses were calculated on the basis of the price on the opening trade. The rationalization takes the form of "This stock (bond, future, whatever) is going up (down). I'm losing money now, but if I add to the position, then I'm getting a bargain and I'll end up making lots of money!"

Rule 10 is really just a corollary of Rule 6—cut your losses short. But averaging down is such a common error that it deserves its own "don't" rule to remind you that it *is* an error.

There are cases, however, that may at first appear like averaging down, but really aren't. For example, if you are looking for an intermediate shorting opportunity in a bear market, I've already said that the best time to go short is into a minor rally. Assuming that the stock market has been down four days in a row at what looks like the beginning of a primary leg in a bear market, a good way to short is to sell the market on the first up day. If the market is up two days, then the odds of its being up a third day are relatively low, so you could increase the size of the position on the second up day. If it is up a third day, then the odds of its being up a fourth are less than 5%, so you could short again. But if the market is up four days in a row, then there is a strong possibility that the intermediate trend is in fact going up, and it's time to close the position.

The difference between this strategy and averaging a loss is that you have a plan and a point at which you admit that you are wrong. Part of the plan would include an evaluation of the extent of each daily move as well as the number of days. From the outset, you would consider not only the number of days, but you would also have established an exit point in terms of the price level that would prove you wrong. Averaging down is without limits, and closing the position becomes a subjective, emotional decision.

Rule Number 11: Never buy just because the price is low. Never sell just because the price is high.

Unlike shopping at a grocery store for fruit, there is no such thing as a "bargain" when it comes to trading. Either a trade is good or it isn't; the price of the instrument has almost nothing to do with it. The only times price comes into play are if you simply can't afford a position because of margin requirements, or if there are, by comparison, other trades available with greater leverage and equal or better risk/reward ratios.

Avoid thinking in terms like, "This thing is at historical lows, it just can't go any lower!" or "This thing just can't go any higher, I've got to sell it!" The fact is, unless you see some sign of a change of trend, the chances are that the trend will continue. When a market is at historical highs or lows, but there is no sign of a change of trend, my advice is to leave it alone and wait for signs of a change of trend. Trade with the trend and be patient.

Rule Number 12: Trade only in liquid markets.

A lot of people who live in the Northeast right now might tell you that they live in a $500,000 house. But what they really mean is that they either *paid* $500,000 for their house, or had it appraised at $500,000 a couple of years ago when they got a second mortgage. In truth, right now the market is glutted with homes offered for $500,000 and there are no buyers to speak of—the market is almost totally illiquid. That $500,000 figure may work on a financial statement for the time being, but it has nothing to do with market value.

The same thing can happen to you if you trade in illiquid or "thin" markets. Prices can change very rapidly, moving right through your stops so fast that you lose perhaps twice as much as you planned on. So avoid thin, illiquid markets. Trade the front month in the commodities and currencies, and the active, high-volume stocks and options.

Rule Number 13: Never initiate a position in a fast market.

This is a rule for upstairs traders—people who rely on electronic information systems for the latest price quote. A fast market is one in which transactions are occurring so fast on the floor of the exchange that the people recording the transactions can't keep up with the pace of the price changes. It is a formal declaration made on the floor as a warning to participants who trade by watching the latest print on a screen.

In other words, in a fast market, what you see on the screen is not necessarily what you get. It can be sorely tempting to buy a breakout or sell a break into a fast market. You watch prices skyrocketing or plunging, and those dollar signs start appearing in your head.

One new trader in my office who didn't believe this rule sold the S&P futures into a fast market break. His fill was 16 ticks ($400 per contract) below where he placed his market order. Even then, according to the screen, he was up 16 ticks on the trade when he placed the buyback order. His fill was 10 ticks *above* where he sold them—a $250 per contract loss on the trade. And if this wasn't lesson enough, he made the same mistake on the following day and got burned again. I don't think he'll ever trade a fast market again. Your trade is only as good as the information you base it on. In a fast market, the information is totally unreliable, so DON'T TRADE!

Rule Number 14: Don't trade on the basis of "tips." In other words, "trade with the trend, not your friend." Also, no matter how strongly you feel about a stock or other market, don't offer unsolicited tips or advice.

Just in terms of odds, when you consider the hundreds of thousands of people involved in the markets, what do you think the chances are that one of your acquaintances knows something that the rest of the world doesn't? If he or she really *does* know something, then the chances are that it is "inside" information, and trading on inside information is illegal.

But 999 times out of 1000, the so-called "tip" is just someone else's opinion. Henry Clasing, in his book *The Secrets of a Professional Futures Trader,* points out that consistent winners tell virtually no one the details of their activities in the marketplace, while consistent losers "tell virtually anyone who will listen the details of their market activities, to the point of campaigning for their point of view."[1] Psychologically, people who are eager to give out tips are probably seeking recognition and admiration. For sure, they aren't doing you a favor. So, if you get a tip, my advice is to say "Thanks, but no thanks."

I took a tip . . . once. When Jim Bruckie, the former head of compliance at the CBOE whom I had dealt with before when we had some trouble at Ragnar, came to Interstate, we had a small reception for him. I was leaving, literally one step from being out of the door, when I heard a familiar voice, "Hey Vic, Vic, wait a minute!"

I turned and a friend of mine came rushing up to me. He said in a hushed tone, "Vic, *Dataforce.*" I said, "Huh?" And my friend replied, "Vic, trust me, put this one away for the kids." He told me that Artie Wagnar, who ran the OTC desk at Lehman Brothers, had given him the tip. Artie was then like a god in the OTC business; his record was phenomenal.

So, just out of curiousity, I looked up the stock. It was at $7/8$ and traded over the counter. In those days, I was trading so well that I looked at this stock as a kind of "perpetual option." How much lower could it go than $7/8$?

How about 0? That's where it went. I bought almost 350,000 shares of that stock, that "perpetual option," and it fell to absolutely nothing. To make matters worse, when it was at 3–7 cents, I bought another 350,000 shares, thinking this time it *must* move up. It didn't . . . zero. When the price quit printing, I tried to look up the company, and I couldn't even find it. Not a phone number, no address, it just vanished.

One little step would have saved me from ever hearing my friend's tip. Some tip. As my best friend, Norm, says, "Put enough money into the 'bank this one for the kids' tips, and the kids'll grow up in an orphanage." He also offers the following sage advice when you smell a tip coming: "Say 'excuse me, I have to go to the bathroom.' And then avoid the tipster for the rest of the night."

Just as you shouldn't listen to tips, you shouldn't offer them. It may be an admirable thing to want to help your friends out, but if you have a friend who trades, exchange ideas and discuss trading tactics *in general*. If you really want to be a good friend, then don't make recommendations; your friend has a mind—let him or her use it.

The main point of this rule is that there is never a good substitute for your own judgment. If you don't have enough confidence to trade based on your own judgment, then don't trade. Follow the trend, not your friend.

Rule Number 15: Always analyze your mistakes.

A losing trade isn't necessarily a mistake, and a mistake isn't necessarily a losing trade. You can make a good trade and lose money, or you can make a mistake and still make money. If you follow the rules and lose, then just let it go; you don't need to analyze it. Say to yourself, "Oh well," and move on to the next trade. But if, for example, you close out a position too early and then watch your would-be profits keep coming in, think about what you have done.

The most important reason to analyze your mistakes is that mistakes and failures are always the best teachers; they reinforce the fact that you should always follow the rules. If you can truly and honestly identify the reasons you make a mistake, then your chances of making it again are much less.

Most often, mistakes are rooted not in ignorance, but fear: fear of being wrong, fear of feeling humiliated, and so forth. To trade well, you have to conquer fear; and to conquer fear, you first have to admit having it, which means admitting your mistakes and analyzing them. I'll go into this in much more detail in the final part of the book.

Rule Number 16: Beware of "Takeunders."

I got a call one day from a friend of mine who was on the board of a major company.

"Victor," he said, "XYZ just agreed to merge with ABC. You gotta buy XYZ, it's a sure bet."

"Fred," I said, "is this legal, you telling me this?"

"Absolutely! We don't have anything to do with either company, and they've already made the announcement; it just hasn't made the wires yet."

So I looked at the price of XYZ, which was at $6 per share, and I bought a small position. Two weeks later, the companies merged . . . ABC bought out XYZ at the agreed-upon price, $4.50 per share! I lost on the trade and dubbed it "a takeunder."

I guess this was the second time I traded on a tip, and it was the last. It was *the only time* I ever got a tip that came true. There was a takeover, but it was actually a takeunder. Since then, I've always shied away from alleged "takeover stocks."

Rule Number 17: Never trade if your success depends on a good execution.

When Norm was managing Merrill Lynch's international options trading desk, he kept a list of excuses they got for poor or untimely executions. One day, he put in an order, and after 10 minutes he still didn't have a fill. He called the floor: "Hey, what's goin' on here, 10 minutes and no fill!" The floor broker, without a moment's pause said, "You see, I was on the market maker's left side, shouting, and I thought he heard me. Finally, I went up and nudged him, and said, 'Did you get that?' He said, 'Get what? Don't you know I'm deaf in my left ear?' "

Yeah, sure.

One of the biggest losses of my life occurred because of a clerk's error. It was in the 1982–1983 era, when the S&P futures and the NYFE futures were traded heavily (the NYFE contract was the New York equivalent of the S&P contract). I was long 350 S&Ps and short 500 NYFEs in an arbitrage play. I was looking to get out. I called Paul, my Chicago floor broker, on my direct line and asked him for a market.

"40–45, size bids and offers," said Paul.

I hung up the phone and immediately bought the 500 NYFEs back to cover my short, so I was then naked on a 350-car (a *car* is one contract) long S&P futures position. Then I tried to sell my S&Ps, which, according to Paul's quote, were 40 bid. When I got to my broker in the S&P pit, I found that the market wasn't 40–45, but 20–25! As it turns out, Paul read the wrong hand signal!

If the market had in fact been 40–45, I would have been in a profitable position. Had I known it was actually 20–25, I would have never bought those NYFE contracts back — 4 ticks was a lot in the days before programs.

Instead, I was just barely up, and I decided to play the S&P position for a while. Then some bad news broke out about a tax bill, and the S&Ps dropped 2 to 3 points before I could liquidate the entire position, and I lost hundreds of thousands of dollars on the trade.

Now this is an extreme case, but the point is that you will be handicapped by bad executions sometimes, and you never know when. Make a habit of double checking and verifying quotes when you can. If something looks or feels fishy, question it. Never mind that they are busy on the floor. Their job is to give you good information, the best possible executions, and timely reports.

I don't mean to knock floor brokers. If you ever get a chance to visit the floor of an exchange on a busy day, you should. It really gets hectic sometimes, and brokers are human; they make mistakes. All I'm saying is don't get caught in the trap of thinking these people are infallible machines. Protect your interests, shop for the best and most reliable firms, and double-check whenever possible.

As another example, I recently developed a day-trading system for the S&P futures. On paper, it looked great, and I turned it over to Douglas, my trading associate, to put it to the actual test. In principle, the system worked pretty well. But what I didn't count on was losing three ticks on the entry, and three ticks on the exit. Who would have dreamed that the market was so thin that trading a few lots on a test run could move the market 3 ticks! But it did, so we had to adjust the system to allow for the volatility of the executions.

Rule Number 18: Always keep your own records of trades.

It is sometimes tempting, especially when just trading on your own account, to pick up the phone, place your order, and not write everything down because your brokerage firm does it for you. But brokerage firms make mistakes.

With each order, write down the date, the time, the instrument, whether it was a buy or a sell, the opening fill, and the closing fill. Compare your records regularly with the reports from your broker. If you don't keep records, you have no way to verify the accuracy of your broker's reports.

Rule Number 19: Know and follow the Rules!

For every trading rule, there are probably five known ways to break it, and no doubt, traders will find a few more ways as time goes on. I've listed eighteen rules, so by that reasoning, there are at least ninety ways to break them. And, each time you break a rule, that's one more way to lose money.

THE 85% RULE

No one is 100% all the time. All kinds of things can distract you. A fight with your spouse or loved one. A call from a friend like the one I mentioned in the beginning of the chapter. There are all kinds of distractions.

For example, May 4, 1984, I got invited to go to Chicago to make a speech. I was on the platform with Steve Walsh, managing director of Walsh Greenwood, and a market maker named Gary Knight. As an aside, during the QA session, a member stood up and said, "I want to address the market maker. All the rules on the exchange favor the market makers who own seats."

Without hesitation, Gary said, "Yes."

"I don't think it's fair!" said the guy in the audience.

"Buy a seat," said Gary, "they're currently going for $250,000."

Remember, the rules favor the floor traders; that's how they make their living.

Anyway, there I was on the podium. I was a bear at the time, and I had hit a nice home run in January. The market had rallied and was drawing a line. I was looking for another opportunity to go short, and I had been waiting for the break for a couple of months. As luck would have it, the market broke the day I left. Frankie Joe won a trading competition by being short . . . I was on a damn plane. Distractions.

The point is that, if you want to make a living in the market, you have to be as close to 100% mentally, physically, and emotionally as possible. And in my estimate, if you can average being at the 85% level, you will do well.

So when you trade, be prepared to lose money in ways you never dreamed of. At some point, when you're right on top of the market, when you're poised and ready to hit that home run, you'll have a fight with your spouse, a family member will die, *something* will happen that you never expected.

Shoot for 100%, but be satisfied with 85%; that's the reality of it.

Conclusion to Part I:
Putting It All Together

There you have it, from the ground up. What I've presented so far is the essential knowledge that has helped make me money throughout my career. I gave you a brief history of my career, and then showed you the knowledge I picked up along the way.

The common thread to everything I've presented so far is that it is what I consider to be basic, essential information and principles. I think if you apply these basic ideas and develop your own unique style of market participation, the information will work for you, too.

If you think in essentials, and integrate your approach to trading with principles that stand the test of time, you'll be able to adapt to ever changing market conditions. As opposed to changing your hat on short-term strategies that change as the market changes, a principled approach will keep on working.

If you define your business philosophy and stick to it, you'll achieve focus in your work; you'll avoid getting off track. More specifically, if you preserve capital and shoot for consistent profits instead of the big hit, you'll avoid blowing out like so many traders do.

If you study Dow Theory, you'll gain more insight into the markets—all markets—than you will by studying any other theory of market behavior that I know of. You'll learn that market movements are largely a psychological phenomenon, unpredictable in absolute terms, but highly predictable in terms of probabilities.

If you understand trends, what they are and when they change, you'll be equipped with knowledge that will save you countless hours of study. You'll be able to avoid moving in and out of markets arbitrarily and, instead, trade with the trend.

If you understand technical analysis, its merits and its pitfalls, you'll be able to use it as a powerful tool to aid your market-timing decisions. If you keep your technical observations to a few essential ones, you'll keep your mind free of the extraneous clutter that paralyzes many market technicians.

If you understand some simple basics of economics, including how money and credit affect the business cycle, you'll be able to predict the effects of government interference in the marketplace and make money with the knowledge.

If you learn to manage your money, limiting involvement according to the associated risk, you'll be able to stay at the table, year after year.

And if you follow the rules, you'll achieve consistency in reaching your trading goals—the hallmark of every good trader with staying power.

But as I have said before, knowledge alone is not enough. I've taught 38 people most of the ideas I have presented so far, yet all but five of them lost money. But it wasn't the knowledge that was at fault. It was the people, specifically their inability to consistently put the knowledge into practice. All of the people I trained were *capable* of making money, all of them could *recognize* when they violated a rule or deviated in their thinking from the principles I taught them. But they just kept on making the same mistakes over and over again.

I puzzled over why this happened; I studied psychology and read over 200 books. And the answers I came up with are presented Part II.

Part II

THE COMMITMENT
TO MAKE IT HAPPEN:
EMOTIONAL DISCIPLINE

*Learning is, after all, not whether we lose the game, but how we lose and
how we've changed because of it and what we take away from it that we
never had before to apply to other games. Losing, in a curious way, is winning.*

—*Richard Bach*

When you picked up this book, it was most likely with the hope that it will help
you make money in the financial markets—a potentially noble goal. Actually,
the purpose of the book is to help you become a total success, not just to make
money, for there is a difference between successful living and attaining
financial goals. In all my years on Wall Street, I have seen too many individuals
destroy their lives while growing rich (or attempting to) to address only the
financial part of success in this book. The following fable illustrates my point.

The Trader's Dream: A Fable

Once there was a rich and famous trader. His whole adult life had been devoted
to becoming one of the best traders in the world and making a lot of money.
And he had attained his goal, for now he had more money than he could ever
spend. When he spoke, the financial world listened. But the trader was troubled.
When he woke up in the morning, his limbs felt like lead no matter how much
he slept. At work, he lacked his former energy—his efforts seemed pointless. Inside, he felt a deep void, a cavern that neither riches nor fame could fill. For the
first time in his life, he felt helpless and out of control.

One day, feeling laden and tired, he dragged himself to work, but when he sat at his desk, he simply couldn't bring himself to switch on his Quotron machine. Numbly, he opened the window thinking some fresh air might help. But the air was damp and stale. Without even bothering to close the window, he slumped onto his couch wondering, "What's wrong with me? I have everything I have ever worked for. I should be happy." Bewildered, unable to think, he drifted off . . . asleep.

He was falling into a deep black hole without dimension, feeling the emptiness sucking him down, when suddenly he felt an uprush of cool air, and he began to float in mid space. In the distance, he spotted a white dot of light, and he began to struggle through the black void toward it. On his approach, he watched as the dot grew larger and larger, until it was no longer a dot, but a brightly lit hallway leading to a large mahogany door. The trader moved faster, feeling compelled to reach the door, sensing that something important was behind it. Finally, sweating in spite of the cool air, he landed in the hallway, and feeling his feet on firm ground, he began to walk toward the door.

The sounds of his footsteps echoed in the hallway, which was bathed in a blinding white light with no apparent source. Only the door was clearly visible, and with each step it grew larger and larger. As he drew nearer, he saw a brass plaque on the door, but he was still too far away to read it. He quickened his step until finally the inscription on the plaque became readable. He stopped and read:

IF YOU ARE SEARCHING FOR THE PROBLEM, COME ON IN.
IF YOU ARE LOOKING FOR SOLUTIONS, LOOK WITHIN.

When he finally stood before the door, it towered above him at least three times his six-foot height. When he turned the latch and pushed, the huge door moved easily, but dust fell from the space where the door met the jamb. Tentatively, he stepped in.

He was in his first office, a converted warehouse space with no windows and meager light. But where his old grey army surplus desk had been was his huge new cherrywood desk with unfamiliar stacks of files and ledgers on it. Behind the desk was a long table upon which was a single keyboard hooked to a huge screen showing the image of his own face. At the keyboard was an old man with a long white beard cloaked in flowing white robes. Vaguely, the trader thought of Father Time. The cloaked figure turned and spoke as much with his piercing eyes as with the rich voice that disowned the aged face, "What took you so long? I've been expecting you."

"But I don't even know what this is, or why I am here," quavered the trader.

"Sure you do; you came here to learn about success," smiled the aged one.

"But I *know* about success," said the trader defensively, "I *am* a success!"

"Perhaps. But by what standard?"

And without waiting for an answer, the robed man turned around and started punching buttons on the keyboard, paging through the events of the trader's life.

The trader watched as episode after episode of his past appeared before him on the screen. He saw things that he had long forgotten, and things that he had known of, but never seen. As he watched, he, the man who had prided himself on his emotional control, found himself crying and laughing at strange and unexpected times. He cried as he watched himself sell his guitar in college because he had decided playing it was a frivolous pursuit. He laughed watching the anger on his face on the day he lost $300,000 in a bad trade. He cried when he saw his former wife give birth to their child while he had been working. He laughed when he saw her graceful movements and joyous expression as she played tennis with the man who had become her lover and later her new husband. And as he continued to laugh and cry with the changing images, he began to see how shallow he had become and the richness of the things he had denied himself. Then the screen went blank, and the old man turned to him.

"Do you still think," he said with ageless fire in his eyes, "that you know so much about success? You have done so much—achieved fame and fortune—but where are *you* in the equation? What do you want? What do you dream of?" He paused thoughtfully, patting the stack of ledgers, then continued, "Some dream and never do. Others do and never dream. But then there are those very few who dream, and do what they dream."

Shaking his head slowly, the trader whispered, "Who are you?" But as he said it, the old man drifted away in a misty haze and he awoke repeating aloud, "Who are you?"

A cool breeze blew through the open window as an early cold front purged the city of its damp, stale air. The trader watched as the grey clouds were pushed away by the clear autumn air. Soon, the leaves would turn and fall, driven by the promise of new life in spring. He arose from the couch and began to walk toward the door to his office. And as he walked, he heard the echoes of his own footsteps in the hallway . . . and he began to dream.

I think the meaning of this fable is clear: To be rich and famous is not synonymous with success. For everyone and in any endeavor, success isn't achieved through the attainment of any particular goal—it is a state of living. As one market professional put it, "A successful life is a progression of successful years, which is a progression of successful months, which is a progression of successful weeks, days, hours, minutes, and moments. Success is the achievement of a goal or set of goals. Therefore, to be successful, you must have goals not only for the long term, but for the moment; and each goal should be related to the other, unified by a single purpose—happiness and fulfillment in life."[1]

There is nothing new or revelatory in the idea that goals are required for success. Pick up any book about how to achieve success, any biography about a successful person, and you will find that goals and success are inextricably linked. In the absence of clearly set goals, it is impossible to focus, impossible to plan, and impossible to acquire and maintain the energy needed in the pursuit of excellence. But goals alone don't provide the formula for success. The trader in the fable, after achieving his lifelong ambitions, felt empty and unmotivated— he lost the will to execute.

I think that all of us have shared some semblance of the trader's experience. In variant forms and to different degrees, all people experience conflict between their emotional state and their conscious convictions. When the conflict becomes so great that it is impossible to function effectively, we make mistakes . . . sometimes huge mistakes. One of the toughest challenges in human life is to attain a state of integrity; a state in which reason and emotions combine on a common front, providing us with knowledge, method, and motivation to succeed. Reaching this state involves integrating knowledge of the external world with your unique inner experience. The central problem is how to establish goals that are not only viable, but also feel real and drive you toward achievement— realistic goals that are experienced emotionally as important and life serving.

For all animals there is one fundamental alternative: life or death. Each species has its distinctive method of survival, but human beings stand apart; the tiger hunts and the deer roams in search of safe pasture, but man thinks.[2] He is the only known creature that must *choose* to live through the conscious, active exercise of his mind. For any animal, success means sustaining life by living according to its distinctive nature. For man, this means living as a rational animal. He must use logic and reason to identify reality, define the requirements for survival, and learn how to achieve his needs. Then he must act to realize them.

Success requires a complete dedication to reality, to identifying and living the truth, not because it is the "Truth" as passed from Heaven with a capital "T," but because only the real, the actual, the true, has power in human life.

Translating the truth into action is the fountainhead of meaningful success. In philosophical terms, this is the source and power of the virtue of honesty. Honesty is the practice of continuously striving for knowledge, including self-knowledge, and basing your actions on nothing else; it implies a recognition that anything attained through self-deception or the deception of others is unearned and will have destructive consequences. Honesty isn't living according to the dictate, "Thou shalt not bear false witness," for fear of punishment; it is a requirement for survival as a thinking, rational human being.

In the fable, the trader, while honest in his intentions, did not practice personal honesty, and so brought himself to a state of near paralysis. Instead of constantly striving to grow by examining and evaluating both his inward and outward states, he made his goal to be rich and famous, and in so doing became shallow. By measuring his self-worth in terms of money and influence, he diminished his capacity to enjoy the process of living. He created what the noted psychologist Karen Horney calls "an idealized image of himself," which he could support only by living according to a rigid set of "shoulds" that had little or no relation to the values which could bring him happiness.[3] His "shoulds" of hard work, productivity, and pride, which could have been life-serving values, served instead his idealized image of himself and gave him a feeling of detachment from life; values that could have helped produce a sense of self-esteem produced instead a feeling of self-alienation. Because the trader failed to strive for self-knowledge—because he lacked deep personal honesty—his values and virtues became a destructive agent in his life.

Thus far, nothing that I've said about success applies exclusively to a career in the financial markets, so why do I bring it up? The answer is that far too many people enter the markets in a quest for money and fame that is doomed to frustration. The trader in the fable represents an element in most of us which says, "If I just had enough money, then I could do anything I wanted and everyone would adore me . . . I would be free . . . I would be happy!"

My personal experience and my observations of others have taught me that to react to this element in ourselves can be devastating. Money can bring out the best in people, but it often brings out the worst; and the reason is lack of self-understanding. Many, too many financially successful people end up in the cardiac ICU from stress-induced heart disease. Some find calm each day at the end of a bottle, using their money to gradually dissolve the abilities that produced it. Others, who have made and lost fortunes several times over with seeming calm, take their own lives. Then there is another whole category of people who enter the world of the financial markets with vigor, intelligence, and enthusiasm, but leave with their heads bowed and their confidence destroyed, unable to perform under pressure.

A compulsive desire to be rich may indeed drive you to learn about the markets and make money, but only at tremendous personal cost. A driving desire for fame usually has at its root a fundamental lack of self-confidence and self-respect, and any fame achieved on that basis will be empty and meaningless. The extent to which you are motivated solely by the desire for money and fame is the extent that you will fail as a person, and usually as a businessperson as well.

The reasons for this are complex, and I will discuss them in detail in this section. My sole purpose is to provide knowledge that will enhance your ability to see yourself as you truly are and enable you to start the process of change required for success. What it all revolves around is the nature and source of emotional discipline—the will to execute knowledge.

13

The Spock Syndrome: Reason and Emotions at War

INTRODUCTION

My late friend, Frankie Joe, called this business a war. But the field of war is the inner self, and the nature of the battle varies with the person.

I've seen traders sit quietly, motionless, appearing in control while their minds are in such a twisted rage that they are incapable of closing a bad position that is going against them. I've seen a man with arms like pencils heave a 15-pound time clock against a solid, two-inch thick wooden wall with so much force that it shook two entire rooms. I've heard cursing that surprises even me, and I'm no neophyte to foul language. I've seen people curled up in their seats holding their stomachs in physical pain from stress. I've been before the screen myself: palms sweating, blood pounding, face flushed, and adrenaline pouring through my veins as if I were in physical danger when all that faced me were numbers on an electronic screen. What is the inner enemy that makes this business such a battle? What are the forces within us that can bring out irrationality and even violence in the face of something as logical as numbers?

Answering these questions and learning how to conquer the inner enemy is probably the single most important element of succeeding, not only as a trader or speculator, but as a person. Throughout my career, I've worked with many different men and women. A few of them were consistently profitable, real pros, but most of them ended up losing money and are no longer in the business. For example, out of the 38 people I trained in the 1980s, only 5 made money and went on to pursue their own careers as traders. I taught each of them the knowledge and method needed to survive and profit in the financial markets. All of them had free access to any information in my office, including talking to me at any time, and yet most of them blew out in less than six months. In watching them and evaluating their actions, I began to see the crucial difference between those who succeed and those who fail not only in trading, but in any endeavor.

The difference is neither intelligence nor knowledge, but the *will to execute* knowledge. Acquiring the requisite knowledge to trade, or to do most things, is relatively easy. For example, consider the area of weight loss. You can walk into any bookstore and find countless books on the subject by experts who outline proven and healthy weight loss techniques. Yet, only 12 in 100 people who start a weight loss program actually lose weight, and only 2 of those 12 maintain the loss for more than one year. That's a 2% success rate—worse than the 5% success rate for commodity trading!

Whether it's trading, losing weight, or pursuing any other goal, the most difficult part isn't in knowing what to do or how; it is in making the decision to *do it* and stick to it. Any time we make a decision, we choose one out of at least two (usually many) alternatives. When following through is difficult, it is because our minds are still in a state of conflict regarding which course to take. What is the source and nature of this conflict? Why is it that even when we *know* what we *should* do, it often seems impossible to do it?

I think the answer to these questions is brilliantly personified in the character of Mr. Spock on the old T.V. series, *Star Trek.* Half Vulcan and half human, Spock is a being at odds with his nature. The ancient Vulcan heritage, the story says, is one of savagery, barbarism, and violence. Only through the imposition of a rigid philosophical discipline totally dedicated to logic and reason were the Vulcans able to tame their barbarism and replace it with a dispassionate dedication to expanding knowledge through total focus on mental pursuits. So rigid is their dedication to logic that "pure" Vulcans are supposedly incapable of experiencing feelings and emotions. But Spock, because he is biologically part human, and because of his mother's emotional influence during his childhood, experiences emotion in spite of himself. The most compelling stories are those that depict him as a man torn between rationality and emotion, where he is forced to deal with his emotional reactions in making life and death decisions.

I think the reason Spock is such a fascinating character to so many people is that he dramatizes and makes larger-than-life a central conflict of human existence. In conversation, you will often hear statements like "My head tells me to stop, but my heart tells me to go for it," which imply a dualism in the nature of human beings: the rational side on the one hand and the emotional side on the other. Most people believe that these two aspects of human nature are separate, unrelated, and often in opposition to each other. The acceptance of this dichotomy between emotion and reason—the belief that they are necessarily unrelated and even conflicting—is at the root of most human conflict, both internal and interpersonal.

If, like Mr. Spock, we are by nature a house divided, if we have two separate and competing aspects, then upon which side do we rely? Perhaps even more important, how can it be possible to lead an integrated, fulfilled life without suffering constant inner turmoil and frustration?

I think it is *not possible* if you accept the premise that emotions and reason are mutually incompatible. As long as you believe the soul is destined to permanently duel with itself, it will. I call this self-imposed affliction of an embattled self the Spock Syndrome. It is the enemy that makes this business a war, and so much of life a painful struggle. But as with most wars, the way to end the violence permanently is not necessarily to fight, but to uproot and replace the false ideas that give rise to the conflict. In this case, that means challenging the premise that emotions and reason are separate and unrelated aspects of human nature, which means focusing on the nature and purpose of emotions in human life, with particular emphasis on the role of anger and fear.

Most conflict arises from misdirected anger and fear. Like the Vulcans, we have a savage and barbaric ancestry in which fear and anger played an essential, life-serving role. But in the context of modern civilization, fear and anger have very little productive use. Moreover, they can be life-threatening, self-destructive. So why do we still experience them, and how can we make sure they work for us, instead of against us? The first step in answering these questions is to understand the source of anger and fear, and to do that, we must turn to our biological heritage.

FROM PREDATOR TO TRADER: THE EVOLUTION OF HUMAN EMOTIONS

Picture Org the cave man, his club at his side, dozing lazily under a tree and digesting a lunch of wild bananas when suddenly, SNAP!, a twig breaks not 30 feet away under the weight of a large beast. Instantly, Org is on his feet, muscles tensed, his club balanced in his hand ready to strike, and his eyes peering in the direction of the noise. He sniffs the air . . . a boar, a dangerous beast, but also excellent meat, and it is upwind.

Stalking the animal, with his blood pounding and all his senses heightened, he inches toward the sound and smell. There is a rustle in the brush 10 feet away, then, an ominous stillness. Org raises his club, he has an impulse to run, but he remains, motionless, poised to strike.

With a terrorizing howl, the boar explodes from the bush with tusks hung low, ready to rip up through the flesh of his enemy. With an equally chilling scream, Org jumps sideways and swings his club a moment too late, landing only a partially damaging blow to the boar's back. There is a searing pain in his thigh, and he looks to see his flesh opened and bleeding. The boar turns, hesitates, and charges again. Org, enraged by his injury, swings his club with superhuman strength, and, timing the blow perfectly, shatters the skull of the boar, killing it instantly. After tending to his wound, he drags the boar to his cave, where it will be a source of meat for himself and his mate for a week.

Now consider John Trader sitting in his private trading room before his CRT screen, waiting for the bond futures exchange to open on the CBOT (Chicago Board of Trade). Yesterday, on news that the Japanese Central Bank was raising interest rates, he opened a new trade by selling 200 bond futures contracts at the end of the trading day. His reasoning is straightforward and logical. The bond market has been bullish for months and is showing technical signs of a top.

The Japanese are among the largest holders of U.S. bonds, and it is reaching the point where the interest charge on borrowed money to buy bonds is higher than the yield. The dollar is already declining in value relative to the yen. The Fed can't raise rates to protect the value of the dollar because of an already slumping economy. In fact, there are rumors that the Fed may *lower* rates. Foreign investors, the holders of 20% of long-term U.S. government securities, are going to dump bonds . . . he knows it. This is an opportunity that comes once in several years!

But he also knows that he might be wrong. So he has set a mental stop 5 ticks above yesterday's highs, which amounts to 10 ticks[1] above the price where he sold them. He is willing to risk $62,500 in the trade . . . no more.

The bond pit opens. His heart beats a little faster. The opening price is even with yesterday's closing price! He had expected it to gap down! Something is wrong. After 10 minutes, prices are 2 ticks above yesterday's opening. He picks up the intercom phone and calls his assistant.

"Bill, call the bond pit, see what's going on."

"Got it, John." Click.

He puts down the phone and lights a cigarette, his eyes on the bar chart. "I've got to be right," he tells himself, "I *know* it's going to turn around, it *has* to." His assistant comes on the intercom.

"Lots of activity, but nothing unusual to report; nobody is selling any unusual size."

In the next hour, the price keeps ticking up, approaching his mental stop. He is down 7 ticks, 8, . . . 9 . . . and then suddenly, as swiftly as an animal on the attack, the price jumps up 5 more ticks, right through his mental stop.

"NOOOOOOO!" John's scream is heard down the hallway. Then there is an ominous silence. After a minute, the silence is broken by the sound of Bill picking up the intercom.

"John, should I buy 'em back?"

"No, they're going to sell off . . . hold on."

John's voice is calm . . . way too calm. He has to actively keep his voice down to stop his head from exploding. His heart is pounding; he can almost feel the adrenaline shooting into his bloodstream. He lights another cigarette. Another uptick . . . he is now down 15 ticks on 200 contracts—$93,750.

For the next few hours, the price is basically unchanged: first up a tick, then down a tick. John's hopes rise with each down tick and fall with each up tick.

Then, suddenly, out of nowhere, the price starts to move up again, gradually but surely. With his ashtray full and sweat rolling from his forehead, John watches with a perverse fascination, his mind automatically tallying the losses: $100,000, $106,250, $112,500, $118,750. The intercom clicks again; it is his assistant.

"John?"

"GOD DAMMIT, NO!!! IT HAS TO GO DOWN!"

He slams the phone down, pounds his fist on his desk, and yells at the screen, "Come on you filthy b____! Come on you filthy, lousy, rotten b____!" Suddenly, it is all too much.

"Bill!! Buy the whole goddam lot back . . . NOW!"

And he storms out of the room and heads for Michael I's on Trinity Place to drown his anger with Dewar's.

The next morning, bonds gap down and sell off dramatically for five straight hours. The word on the floor is that the Japanese are dumping bonds in size. Bill, the assistant, is watching the screen, slumped and despondent. John isn't there; he is sleeping off his hangover.

Org, the predator. John, the trader. Both *Homo sapiens,* brothers deriving their nature from the same process of evolution occurring over millions of years. The similarities between Org and John outweigh the differences; the differences are a matter of degree. Both are equipped with a highly developed intelligence. Both have imagination (as evidenced by cave drawings). Both experience emotions. The greatest difference is that John has much more intellectual capacity and far more knowledge.

And yet, who behaved more in accordance with his nature and surroundings? Obviously, Org did. His anger and fear served him, helped him protect himself and acquire food. John, on the other hand, while experiencing a predominantly similar emotional response, acted self-destructively.

According to psychiatrist Dr. Willard Gaylin, anger and fear are provided by Darwinian evolution to enhance survival in times of emergency or stress, but some of what we inherited is no longer useful. In his words:

> Anger and fear are essential emotional resources for coping with danger shared by a broad range of animal species. When our culture conformed more closely to our animal derivations, these emotions served us well. We could attack the beast that threatened us with a force alerted and mobilized by our rage, and augmented by our intelligence. But now danger is more likely to fall out of an envelope than to jump out of a bush . . . Millions of years of evolution may have been made obsolete by a mere ten thousand years of civilization.[2]

Gaylin by no means contends that anger and fear have *no* place in modern life, but he implies that we are responsible to direct them properly. Otherwise, they can contribute to our demise. Anger and fear are emotional reactions which occur in anticipation of danger and prepare animals mentally and physically for the response of fight or flight—a basic survival tool. But unlike other animals, modern man is not limited to fight or flight in his range of responses. Faced with circumstances that threaten us in any way, we can most often eliminate the threat by correcting the threatening circumstances:

> [W]e can change the very nature of our reality. We are in that sense coauthors with nature of our future, not merely passive subjects of it.[3]

On the other hand, our broad range of alternatives combined with our ability to imagine and project coming events can actually help bring about that which we dread. Unlike other animals, our emotions are not automatic responses to what happens in reality, but are a result of our *interpretation* of what occurs. The man who believes that wind is caused by the spirits of the dead seeking a resting place will respond much differently to a violent storm than will the trained meteorologist. Depending on the accuracy of our beliefs and our judgments about what occurs in reality, emotions can either serve us or harm us; they can act as a protector or a destroyer.

EMOTIONS AS BENEFACTOR

"An emotion," to use psychologist Nathaniel Branden's definition, "is the psychosomatic form in which man experiences his estimate of the beneficial or harmful relationship of some aspect of reality to himself."[4] The fact that emotions are "psychosomatic" means that emotions are a physical response arising from a mental process. The mental process is one of evaluation, which means that we make a judgment as to whether something is "beneficial or harmful," for us or against us.

For example, upon seeing a loaded, silver-plated revolver, a child with no awareness of what a gun is or what it can do would probably be attracted to the shiny appearance and the moving parts. But had the same child previously seen his parents murdered by a gun at the hands of a burglar, he would almost certainly have feared the sight of the revolver and avoided it. In the first case, the revolver is pretty and interesting, a new discovery. In the second case, the revolver is dangerous and harmful, a thing that kills.

In the same way, how we react emotionally to any thing or event depends on how we subconsciously evaluate it in the context of our current knowledge. The judgment and the response is super-rapid, far faster than our conscious mind can grasp during its occurrence. We have to pause, reflect, and introspect to recognize the source of our emotions, if indeed we can figure them out at all. Where do we look? Ayn Rand has answered this better than anyone else that I know of:

> Man has no choice about his capacity to feel that something is good for him or evil, but *what* he will love or hate, desire or fear, depends on his standard of value. If he chooses irrational values, he switches his emotional mechanism from the role of his guardian to the role of his destroyer. The irrational is the impossible; it is that which contradicts the facts of reality; facts cannot be altered by a wish, but they *can* destroy the wisher. If a man desires and pursues contradictions—if he wants to have his cake and eat it, too—he disintegrates his consciousness; he turns his inner life into a civil war of blind forces engaged in dark, incoherent, pointless, meaningless conflicts. . . . [5]

To understand our emotions, we must understand their source: our values. "A value is that which one acts to gain and or keep."[6] Our values are a vast array of things, ideas, and principles that we consider necessary or desirable, and they exist in our subconscious minds in an ordered hierarchy whether we like it or not.

The hierarchy is a structure that our mind gives our values—our desires, goals, and beliefs—in order of the relative importance we ascribe to them according to a standard of what is good or bad, for us or against us. Ideally, if our standard of evaluation is consistent with our nature as rational beings, then every value, every belief and goal that we maintain, is noncontradictory, consistent, and life-serving. We choose our values, consciously or subconsciously, and the choices we make provide the programming for our inherited emotional mainframe.[7] And like a computer, the content of the programming is what determines the value of the output.

We are beings of *volitional* consciousness. In order to survive, human beings must *choose* to think; to identify reality and integrate the material available to the senses. This is the meaning of free will. We have free will in the sense that we can choose to provide or change the programming of our subconscious computer, but we cannot change the nature of its functioning.

Our emotions are one part of that functioning. Our biological evolution provides us with a mechanism designed for a super-rapid response to complex events, but the values and beliefs we have accepted into our subconscious minds determine what form the emotional response will take. Therefore, the validity of our values, in terms of their efficacy in reality, determines the validity of our emotions. In addition, the fact that we can conceptualize and project events, whether real or imaginary, into the future extends and expands the role of emotions beyond that of its "design" for lesser animals. Again in Ayn Rand's words:

> Just as the pleasure–pain mechanism of man's body is an automatic indicator of his body's welfare or injury, a barometer of its basic alternative, life or death—so the emotional mechanism of man's consciousness is geared to perform the same basic function, as a barometer that registers the same alternative by means of two basic emotions: joy or suffering. . . . [E]motions are estimates of that which furthers man's values or threatens them . . . lightning calculators giving him the sum of his profit or loss.

> But while the standard of value operating the physical pleasure-pain mechanism of man's body is automatic and innate, determined by the nature of his body—the standard of value operating his emotional mechanism is *not*. Since man has no innate ideas, he can have no innate value judgments.[8]

This is a far different view than that of Mr. Spock and the Vulcans. Whereas Spock chose to deny the existence and validity of emotions because he thought them irrational and negative, Rand defines the direct logical connection of emotions to values, and values to reason. She maintains that the accuracy and validity of values determine the power and integrity of emotions. In Rand's view, an emotional conflict is rooted in a conflict of values, and it is within our power to change values if they are wrong through the exercise of reason.

So we are not doomed to inner conflict by our nature and heritage. But to avoid inner conflict, we must choose and maintain values that are consistently life-serving, and the only way to discover what these values are is through the application of reason.

Given consistent, accurately defined values, emotions can assume their protective role as the pleasure–pain mechanism of the soul, providing instantaneous and valid reactions to complex events that require immediate attention. This is the source of what people refer to as "intuition," or "a gut feeling." Even more important, they can then provide the reward—that wonderful complex of mental and physical responses that we call a state of joy—for actions resulting in life-serving achievement at work, at play, and in human relationships. With a healthy emotional framework in place, we can not only strive for achievement, but also *enjoy* the process of living; and the enjoyment provides the resource for a constant refueling of our motivation.

EMOTIONS AS THE VILLAIN

Unfortunately, achieving emotional consistency is probably the most difficult challenge that faces us. Human beings are fallible; we make mistakes, our parents made mistakes, and so on down the line. Every belief we hold and every choice we make affects the programming of our subconscious mind and therefore our emotional responses. The impact of new choices and information cascades through the entire emotional framework as the mind runs a self-check, trying to reconcile the new information with the old.

The more fundamental the new information, in terms of its placement in the hierarchy of one's values, the more dramatic and sweeping the impact it will have on our emotional responses. Reality forces us to suffer the consequences of our actions existentially—a good trade makes money, a bad trade costs money. The structure and content of our conscious and subconscious values determine how we *experience* the consequences emotionally—how we *feel* about what we do. When we experience joy, we are motivated to live, to continue to move forward with desire. When we feel suffering, we are struck by a state of depression and fear, and we tend to pull away from what we think has caused the pain.

So what happens if we attempt to integrate false or conflicting beliefs into the hierarchy of our values? What happens if we make a bad choice or fail to choose at all when we should? If emotions are determined by values and beliefs, then holding false beliefs or conflicting values will result in misleading or "mixed" emotions and may provide the motivation to act self-destructively.

If, for example, a person believes fundamentally that people are born evil and should spend their lives in atonement for their natures and in preparation for the afterlife, then it is unlikely that he or she will be able to gain significant pleasure from producing and acquiring material wealth. If a person has a subconsciously held belief that he or she is undeserving of happiness, then it is very likely that in the face of what should be a joyous event, guilt will take its place. If a nation of people believe that they are of a superior Aryan descent, empowered by God to dictate the fate of lesser peoples, then they will feel indifferent to the deaths of innocent people ordered by their leadership. It is possible, perhaps even common, judging by the number of people who engage in therapy, to experience pain, fear, or guilt in the face of positive achievement, and excited anticipation and joy in an act of self-destruction or the destruction of others.

Very few of us, if any, lead lives that are either totally self-serving (in a positive sense) or totally self-destructive. Instead, we hold *mixed* and contradictory values and premises; some beliefs are life-serving, others are life-negating. Take John Trader in the example above. He valued knowledge and applied it correctly (albeit his timing was off). He went into his position with confidence and admitted to himself at the outset the possibility that he was wrong. We can assume that he had previously been successful because he could afford to trade 200 contracts. If the trade had gone his way, he undoubtedly would have been elated and enjoyed both being right and making some money. All very healthy. But when the trade went against him, he felt attacked, threatened, fearful. He let his fear and false pride[9] overcome and override his otherwise good judgment. He *let his wish become a claim on reality* while *knowing* that he was violating his rules.

The reasons that John Trader, or anyone in the real world, acts in defiance of knowledge are very complex and will be discussed in detail in the next chapter. But if I had to reduce the reason to a single sentence it would be: He was trying to avoid the pain of being wrong. It wasn't the money loss that threatened him so deeply—a good trader accepts losing money on some trades as part of the business. What brought about the overwhelming fear that made him behave irrationally was the possibility of suffering the pain of being wrong. He acted to avoid pain, and therein was his problem.

Look at his last action in the story—flight. He literally ran out of the office and spent the rest of the day altering his mental state with alcohol, trying at that point to transform the pain. Look at the results: He lost more money than he should have, missed a better trading opportunity the next day, and suffered a head-wrenching hangover, all because he valued the avoidance of pain connected to being wrong. His emotions led him on a path of self-destruction.

Sometimes, even when you think you are doing your best, you can be acting self-destructively. For example, when you day-trade the S&P futures from upstairs, you are going to get a lot of poor executions. It works like this. I call the floor clerk and ask for a market.

Floor clerk:	"345 25–30."
Victor:	"Buy me 30 at the market."
Floor clerk:	"You bought 30 at 35."
Victor:	"At 35! What's the market?"
Floor clerk:	"25–30."

I put a market order in when the market is 25–30, get none at 30, get filled at 35, and the market is still 25–30. Someone has just stolen $25 from me 30 times, and there is nothing I can do about it: $750 is gone. These are the kinds of activities that brought the FBI to the floor of the Chicago futures exchange. It makes me furious.

In 1986 and early 1987, I was trading the S&Ps as many as 30 times a day and was getting a lot of executions like I just described. Even though I was making money, the injustice of it all kept me angry, and I developed high blood pressure. Being health conscious, I had to consider the alternatives:

1. Don't day-trade the S&Ps.
2. Expect to be cheated when you do trade them.
3. Continue getting angry and risk your health to make some money.

Being health conscious, I chose a combination of one and two. I quit trading the S&Ps so intensely, and when I did trade, I resigned myself to getting robbed. My blood pressure went down.

This kind of scenario is what Gaylin was referring to when he postulated that modern civilization has made fear and anger somewhat obsolete. Returning to John Trader, all of his emotional reactions were designed by nature to protect him, to prepare him to respond to danger either by fight or flight. John faced a real, tangible threat with the possibility of losing money, and some fear response would be quite understandable in that regard. But his anger was totally out of proportion with what actually occurred. He could, in fact, neither fight nor flee, at least not in the physical sense. He tried to flee, but look what it got him. The only way to flee was to execute his stop. And what is there to fight? If you want to live a life of frustration, just try to fight the markets.

What if John *had* executed his stop, where would that have put him? In much better shape. He would have suffered some pain, but he would also have saved money and been in a position to step back with confidence, knowing that he had followed his rules. Then he could have reconsidered what was happening. He might have concluded that he was doing too good a job of anticipating the market and decided to wait for a new selling opportunity. But he didn't. He let his contradictions beat him; he let his emotions change roles from protector to destroyer.

THE SOURCE OF CONSISTENCY: EMOTIONAL DISCIPLINE

I have yet to meet a totally consistent, integrated person, and I'm not going to hold my breath while waiting. To expect that people can grow up in this difficult world with all the crazy philosophies that exist, inherit the pressure of their family's errors, reap the contradictions of a troubled educational system, try to make a living, put their entire value system in perfect integrated order, and simultaneously change their emotional responses to fit their value structure is simply stretching the bounds of probability. So what *can* we do? All we can do is strive for integrity—for consistency in thought, action, and emotion—and do it in such a way that life is experienced as a predominantly joyous process.

To trade well you have to:

1. Establish goals.
2. Acquire knowledge of the markets.
3. Define rules of trading that work.
4. Execute in strict adherence to the rules.

The first three steps are relatively easy, but executing them can be terribly difficult. With perfect knowledge of ourselves and the markets, execution would be easy. The same is true for everything we pursue in life. But given that our knowledge is incomplete and that mistakes are inevitable, to act to the *best* of our knowledge without succumbing to the temptation to break the rules because of the unavoidable fears and anxieties that pop up is both mentally and physically difficult. As with any skill, gaining mastery over irrational impulses requires training and discipline, in this case, *emotional* discipline.

Discipline is training to act in accordance with a set of rules or principles. As I've already discussed, emotions are inherent in our biological nature and dependent on our values and beliefs. Strictly speaking, emotions cannot be trained directly, and the concept of discipline in the emotional realm applies not to the emotions themselves, but to how we deal with them, how we respond to emotions in both thought and action.

Emotional discipline is an active and ongoing process of accepting emotions, attempting to identify their source in our values, and evaluating their validity in relationship to the event at hand in order to establish an integrated and consistent relationship between our goals and actions. With consistent practice, exercising emotional discipline becomes almost habitual, allowing you to deal with your emotions without being overcome by them.

By accepting emotions, by understanding that emotions simply exist and you cannot fight them, you free your mind to look at them not as a villain, but as an integral aspect of yourself that provides invaluable information about the content of your subconscious. Then, by redirecting the energy formerly used in a futile fight with your emotions, you can introspect to find their source and establish why you reacted as you did to the event at hand. Through this process, and by projecting the disastrous consequences of acting according to the impulsive desires born in your emotional state, you reinforce the belief that alternatives exist, that you have a choice whether to behave rationally or irrationally, that you are in control.

Nature provides us with an enhanced state of energy and awareness when we are in an excited emotional state. Why not *use* that energy and awareness instead of fighting it? Practiced consistently, emotional discipline helps build a sense of confidence and control over your actions. It allows you to channel formerly wasted energy into the life-serving goal of self-understanding. Emotional discipline is the tool that lets you harness your heightened state and *choose* the best course of action rather than be *controlled* by reaction—it provides you with *the will to execute* your knowledge.

Having the will to execute means having the capability or power to carry through on a plan of action designed to achieve a specific goal. It means having the ability to *decide*. The word *decide* comes from Latin roots that mean "to cut off." When you really make a *decision*, your mind has concluded that no other alternative is either desirable or possible. When you achieve this state of mind, carrying through your plan becomes less a matter of choice and more a matter of necessity. The plan itself becomes a value, and if integrated into your subconscious, can actually be supported by your emotions. In this way, practicing emotional discipline not only enhances your ability to act, but also reduces the level and frequency of emotional conflict—it becomes a source of consistency in thought, actions, and feelings.

CONCLUSION

Mr. Spock personifies a central problem that we all share: the conflict of emotion and reason. But in his method of handling the conflict, he violates the supreme rule of Vulcan philosophy: he is illogical. He ignores the fact that emotions are an integral part of our biological make-up that cannot be ignored without creating a constant state of war in our minds. He fails to realize that we are beings that must define our values according to a *chosen* standard: life as a rational being.

Our emotions are determined by the values we choose, consciously or subconsciously. To ensure that emotions are life-serving, we have an inescapable responsibility to provide order and integrity to our emotional responses through the practice of emotional discipline. Otherwise, our emotions and reason will remain in a state of permanent conflict.

As a trader, speculator, or investor, you put your judgment and emotions on the front line every time you take a position. By definition, you take a risk, and with risk comes some degree of fear and a whole complex of other emotions. If, like Spock, you attempt to ignore or fight your emotions, then you will create a state of inner turmoil that will take a toll both mentally and physically. Mentally, a mind burdened with emotional conflict is debilitated in direct proportion to the degree of the conflict. Physically, the stress induced by emotional responses can result in high blood pressure, loss of sleep, exhaustion of energy, and worse.

By practicing the active and ongoing process of emotional discipline, you can take control over your mind and become decisive, while simultaneously reducing the intensity and frequency of emotional conflicts. This is crucial not only to trading, but to a positive approach to life. It is the only method I know of that engenders consistency and the constant nurturing and/or growth of self-esteem.

But because most of us have accepted mixed and contradictory values and beliefs, many of which are hidden in our subconscious, practicing emotional discipline is never easy. In particular, sorting out the roots of our emotional reactions is an enormously difficult task. It requires looking inward to identify and understand the relationship of our values and beliefs to reality and discarding beliefs that are contradictory. Further, simply discarding wrong beliefs and adopting new beliefs is no guarantee that our emotional reactions will change. To change emotional responses takes constant self-awareness, time, fundamental personal honesty, and the willingness to suffer the pain of letting something go that we *feel* is dear to us.

In this chapter, I have identified a central problem not only in trading, but in life: the Spock Syndrome; and I've outlined a broad approach to resolving the problem: emotional discipline. In the next chapter, I will discuss the meaning and source of success and break down the problem of emotional conflict in much more concrete terms. Specifically, I will address the nature of motivation and commitment, how they relate to achieving success, and what stops us from achieving them. The objective is to break down the problem of emotional conflict into defined and understandable areas that lend themselves to the application of a formula for change.

14

Success Is
What You Make It

THE PREREQUISITES OF SUCCESS

The nature of this business requires a set of personal attributes without which I doubt anyone can build a consistently successful career as a trader, speculator, or investor.

First is a soundly based self-confidence, a realization that your mind can learn the truth and apply it with positive results in every realm of life.

Second is self-motivation and commitment, the ability and willingness to put the time and energy into learning what to trade and how to trade it.

Third is intellectual independence, the ability to stand on your own judgment based on the facts as you see them in the face of countervailing opinion.

Fourth is a fundamental personal honesty, a total commitment to identifying and dealing with the truth about yourself, the markets, and your decisions.

And finally is a sincere love of what you do, the recognition that the greatest reward comes from the process of the work itself, not the money or fame that may come with it.

These attributes are fundamentally important in every area of life, but the rapid pace and volatility of the financial world make them even more critical. Without self-confidence, you will live in constant fear of making a wrong decision, and sooner or later the fear will paralyze your ability to think and make decisions. Without self-motivation and commitment, the self-motivated and committed competition will eat you alive. Without intellectual independence, you will be swept away by the changing tides of opinion into the whirlpool of financial ruin. Without fundamental personal honesty, your wishes will become claims on reality, and you will find yourself making choices based not on the facts, but on your wishes and hopes. And without love of what you do, your work will become stale and uninteresting; you will lose your motivation and drive to continue.

All of these attributes are attainable, but only through a complete commitment to understanding yourself and your relationship to reality, which means understanding what you want out of life, why you want it, and how to get it. Self-understanding is the compass that will guide you on the road of successful living and the beacon that will provide direction during the inevitable times when your course is darkened and confused by frustration and pain. But it will guide and direct you only if you are striving to move forward.

In the introduction to this section the old advisor says, "Some dream and never do. Others do and never dream. But then there are those very few who dream, and do what they dream." Look at people who are happy and successful. They *love* what they do first and foremost. Watching them, you get the impression that they would work without pay, that making money is just the gravy. For them, each day is a new challenge approached with vigor and enthusiasm. Their actions at home, at work, and in recreation are integrated into their life by a hierarchy of goals set for the hour, the day, and for a lifetime. They take *action* based on their passion for living and accept failure, pain, and setbacks as part of the process of moving forward, not as insurmountable obstacles. They transform their dreams into reality.

On the other hand, look at people with emptiness in their eyes, devoid of energy, plodding through each day with an embittered reluctance. They live their lives unfulfilled, either dreaming without doing until in the end even their dreams die, or doing without dreaming in mechanical, unrewarding repetition. These people have never grasped, *realized* in the strictest sense of the term, that their values and goals *are them;* that in spending energy in pursuits unrelated to a well-defined and -understood self-interest, they are their own persecutor and victim, trapped in a web of their own making as prey to insecurities and fears born of self-doubt.

We have a choice: We can decide to take control over our lives and succeed, or we can give in to fear and pain and let other people and events control us. The right choice is obvious, and making it begins with one simple commitment: CARPE DIEM!! Latin for "Seize the Day!!" This means *commit* yourself to the fact that each moment in life is precious, is yours, and is to be experienced with as much awareness and passion as you are capable of. It means recognize that, at any moment and in any situation, you can begin the process of change required to be and feel successful. It means grasp on to life and take hold with a devoted grip that clings to unlimited possibility. Seize the day. Dream, but dream with the conviction that you can harness the power within you and turn your dreams into reality.

THE MEANING OF SUCCESS

In a fundamental sense, success doesn't arise from ability or achievment in any one particular field. You can be a business success but a personal failure, similar to Howard Hughes, and experience your misery in style. You can also be poor but happy, and enjoy the "simple" things in life. But given the opportunity, wouldn't most people prefer both financial attainment and personal fulfillment? I believe virtually everyone would.

I believe that, with the right motivation and commitment, every human being living in a free country *has* the opportunity to achieve both personal fulfillment and financial attainment.

It is strange. In a country abounding with financial opportunity there exists a love-hate relationship with money. Some people view money as something that enslaves them, thinking, in effect, "If I weren't trapped by the pursuit of the almightly dollar, then I could do what I want and be fulfilled in life." Other people view money as an end in itself and spend their lives acquiring it without ever learning to enjoy it. One's view of money is intimately related to any concept of success. We all know the old adage which says, "Money can't buy happiness," and it is quite true, but money maintains its allure nonetheless. Why? What *can* money buy?

The essential answer to this question is really quite simple: Money is a tool that allows men and women either to exchange the product of their labor for the products and services of others, or to save the results of their efforts for the future. *Money is a means with which to transform personal energy into matter; a vehicle to turn dreams into reality.*

We live in a time when it is almost always possible to make a career out of doing what we love. The beauty and appeal of money is that it makes so many other material ends attainable in the process. In this sense, the importance of money is an intensely personal issue that depends on striking a balance between the answers to two important questions. First, "What do I love to do?" and second, "What do I want materially?" If the answers to these questions are irreconcilable, then only one course is possible: change the answers! Otherwise, you are dooming yourself to a life of frustration. It is just such conflicts, and the way to eliminate them, that I will be discussing in detail in the rest of this book.

I think it is possible for anyone in any endeavor to achieve a sense of total personal fulfillment *and* a satisfying level of financial success, and that is my idea of being a success. Success is a state of living—a condition of being alive. Success is change; it is a *dynamic* process of goal-directed action resulting in a constant progression of personal growth, achievement, and happiness.

Reality doesn't hand out success to a select few on a silver platter. Success is self-created, not given. Life is a process. More specifically, it is a process "of self-sustaining and self-generated action."[1] This is true for all living organisms, from the most primitive form of plant life, to amoebas, to human beings. Life is a process of action, and to fail in this action is to die. In this sense, there is only one *fundamental* alternative and one measure of ultimate success or failure: life or death. Each action of a living being is either self-enhancing or self-destructive. Human action is no exception, but it has one huge distinction: Each of us has to identify and define, in the unique aloneness of our own mind, the difference between life-serving and life-destroying goals and actions. We must *evaluate* the alternatives available by using the distinctive faculty given to us by nature—our rational, conceptual form of conscious awareness.[2] It is the use of the mind, what and how you think, feel, and act, that determines success or failure in life. Therefore, to take control of your life and achieve success, you have to grasp how your mind works and how to use it to achieve your objectives.

THE SUPERCOMPUTER OF THE MIND

The direct stimulus for every action we take comes from our subconscious mind, not our conscious mind. When I pick up my coffee and take a sip, I essentially tell my conscious mind, "Drink coffee now," and from there my subconscious mind takes over, putting into operation countless skills that I learned in early childhood and have practiced throughout my life.

This same process applies not only to physical actions, but also to mental actions, including thought and emotions. When I look at my charts every morning, most of the thinking and analysis that I do isn't on the verbal, conscious level. I take in the data and in effect say to my subconscious, "Look at this and see what you come up with." When I look I almost immediately know my opinions and conclusions about the market, and I could state them, but those opinions and conclusions are formed subconsciously. It is like knowing that $2 + 2 = 4$: I don't have to consciously learn the fundamentals of addition every time I'm faced with the problem; the knowledge is already integrated in my subconscious mind.

The mind is like a vast and powerful computer, and as with all computers, the quality of the output depends on the quality of the input and the nature of the programming. The input consists of past knowledge and experience plus the daily events of your life. The output depends on how you process the information, on how you have trained or failed to train your mind to function. At any given moment, you don't have complete control over the thinking process; it is substantially automatic.

Right now, your motivation—the beliefs, values, and associations that drive your actions—are already in place in your subconscious mind. You may feel in control of your actions, but actually your range of volitional control is quite limited.

Your subconscious mind is like the processor and memory bank of a computer, preprogrammed by past learning and experience. The only power you have over it is the keyboard of present conscious awareness and thought. If you are not satisfied with the output, then you have to change either the input, the content and structure of the programming, or, and in most cases, both.

The power of the subconscious mind is an enormous resource that, if tapped correctly, will drive you to achievement. Have you ever noticed how effortlessly sports fans learn and remember names, statistics, playing schedules, game strategies, and so forth? Do you know why? Because the subconscious mind puts a flag on the daily input which says in effect, "This is important; save for immediate recall!" Just by reading the sports page over a cup of coffee in the morning and watching games while drinking a few beers, dedicated sports fans are able to absorb and integrate new and fairly complex data every day with ease. Most of them don't study intensely. Reading the sports page doesn't feel like *work*. They simply read or watch the game in a relaxed, but focused awareness, and the subconscious mind takes over from there. How far could you go, how successful would you be, if your mind worked that well in every area of your life?

If you are not a sports fan, there is bound to be some area in your life which you find fun and exciting in a similar way. Maybe you are one of the fortunate few who feel that way about work or your personal relationships. But for now let's assume the most likely case, which is that the area you find fun and exciting is some recreational activity like bridge, golf, or dancing. Whatever it is, when you do it, how do you feel about it? Doesn't the activity sometimes seem almost effortless, even energizing? Don't you find that you perform best when you don't consciously think about what you are doing, but instead just relax and let your subconscious mind take over? Don't you wish you could function like that most, if not all, of the time?

You've probably had a similar experience to the following one, too. Assume you love to play golf. One day, you go out to play and everything just "clicks." You are playing the best round of your life. Every shot you hit is perfect and you are one-putting almost every green. You feel sensational, but your awareness of the feeling comes in small flashes that don't interrupt your focus.

The other players keep murmuring that you are playing "out of your mind" or that you are "unconscious." Then, after eight holes, the whole experience hits your conscious awareness and you think to yourself: "Wow, I'm really hitting great. If I can keep this up, I'll play the best round of my life! And who knows, I might even be able to turn pro!" Well, guess what happens next?

Yep, you lose your focus and your game starts falling apart. Now you start getting angry and talking to yourself: "How can this be happening to me? Dammit, I'm going to blow the best round in my life! OK. Keep your head down. Slow down the backswing. Relax," and so forth, but your game keeps getting worse. By the time you reach the last hole, you have messed up so badly that what should have been the best scoring round of your life is just average. You feel miserable, like you had personal greatness in your hands and just let it slip out. And do you know what? You're right!

Personal greatness, achievement, and success are a direct result of the supercomputer of the mind functioning according to its design. When we are "on" during any physical or mental activity our conscious awareness and subconscious mental processing are in a state of integrated, harmonious interaction. Armed with accurate knowledge of the what and how to perform, the subconscious mind takes the immediate input of conscious awareness and provides rapid and accurate output in the form of physical and mental activity. The output is accurate because the programming is good and the input is valid. The input is valid because our conscious awareness is totally focused only on the data in reality relevant to the objective.

When you were "on" in the golf game, for example, you had already provided your subconscious with the programming it needed by taking lessons, learning the rules, reading good books by successful professionals, watching professional players and emulating the key elements of their style, and hitting hundreds of balls on the practice range.

Your conscious awareness was totally occupied with gathering information needed by your subconscious to perform the specific shot at hand such as the lie of the ball, its distance from the pin, the direction of the wind, and so forth. It was totally unencumbered by the fear of mishitting, or the potential excitement of hitting another excellent shot. Your focus was directed by the ultimate goal of shooting the lowest possible score by hitting each ball to the best of your ability; the direction of your conscious, outward mental focus triggered and held the focus of your subconscious mental processes. As soon as your conscious focus shifted from concentrating on each shot to illusions of being a pro, another subprogram of the subconscious kicked in and sabotaged your game. But for a while, you were a total success at golf. Your supercomputer provided you with goal-serving *motivation*.

I believe it is possible to harness and control the power of our supercomputers and be "on" most of the time in everything we do, and I believe that almost anyone can do it. The key to harnessing this power is understanding the nature and source of personal motivation and how to change it.

DISCOVERING AND USING MOTIVATION

When you are "on" during any activity, you are in the most positive and highly *motivated* state you can attain. Let me explain what I mean by that. To be motivated means to be full of a reason or cause that makes you act in a certain way or that *determines volition*. Volition is the act of willing or choosing. If volition is determined when you are motivated, you are beyond choice: The choice is made, and your mind is set on its path. You are in a state of total concentration and focus; your mind is totally *committed* to the task at hand.

This is not a state of mind you can just choose at will. You can tell yourself all day, "I'm going to lose weight, I'm going to lose weight," but without the right motivation, your subconscious mind will just keep saying back, "Nope, nope," and you'll be left feeling frustrated and self-recriminating. Instead of growing, you will stagnate, at best. Instead of achieving, you will fail.

In life, as in any particular endeavor, the process of growth and achievement has four key elements:

1. Goals: You have to know what end results you are after and commit yourself to achieving those results.

2. Actions: You have to develop a plan according to your goals and *execute* the plan through decisive actions.

3. Awareness: You have to observe the results of your actions and evaluate their degree of success or failure, not only in material terms, but also in personal, emotional terms.

4. Change: If you fail, you have to reassess both your goals and your actions, identify the flaws, and be willing to try something new.

Each one of these four factors is crucial to success, but setting goals is the foundation for the whole process. Goal setting in itself may seem easy. Anyone can pull out a piece of paper and write down a list of things that he or she wants. But writing a few sentences won't *establish* goals. Goals have no power until you experience them as *real;* until you experience them not as something you merely desire, but as something you *need* to sustain life—like food.

If you can program your supercomputer to experience a goal as a fundamental need, then it will do everything it can to drive you toward it, and the rest of the steps will follow much more easily. This state of mind is called *commitment,* and it is the source of consistency and the wellspring of emotional discipline.

If you are like most people, you recognize that making a commitment is necessary to achieve anything, but you feel simultaneously that it is a trap. You may associate it with denial of the things that make you comfortable, with rigidity and absolute discipline, with a lack of freedom and spontaneity. These associations are garbage that need to be thrown in the rubbish heap where they belong.

The word *commit* comes from the Latin word *committere* which means "to bring together." In this context, commitment means to bring together your conscious and subconscious mind (including emotions) in the pursuit of your goals. Acquiring commitment is the key step that will make your goals viable, that will give them power, that will give you the ability to execute the plans you lay out.

Notice that I said "acquiring" commitment, not "making" a commitment. I use this term because if your mind isn't oriented correctly, then it is often *impossible* to "make a commitment." Following through in the achievement of a goal isn't a matter of steely "will power," or denial of "temptation"; it is a matter of finding a way to change the content and associations in your mind so that true and consistent motivation exists.

When most people say that human beings have free will, they mean that at any time and in every issue a person has the power to choose and control his actions. For example, I can reach out and pick up this glass of water in front of me or not, I can close my current short position right now or not, I can lose weight and keep it off or not. I don't think it is that simple at all.

Going back to the computer model of the brain, what you do—the output of your mind—depends on the input, what you perceive, and how you process the information, on how you look at reality with your conscious mind and have trained or failed to train your subconscious mind to function. Free will *does not mean* that you can do anything you want, when and how you want to; it means that you can choose to change the programming in your mind.

Free will comes down to one fundamental choice: to think, or not to think. This doesn't mean that in every issue and in every waking moment you must consciously and logically dissect your thoughts and actions—your conscious mind works too slowly for that. What it means is devoting yourself to knowledge and awareness of the nature and source of your motivations and to correcting them when necessary.

It means introspecting—using your conscious awareness to access, identify, and evaluate the content of your subconscious mind. So let's look into the nature of the subconscious mind and see where motivations come from.

Emotions determine motivation. Specifically, we are driven by two fundamental forces at the emotional level: the desire to attain pleasure and the need to avoid pain. Think about it. When we want something, is it the thing itself that we really seek? No. It is what we think attaining the goal will bring, the change we think it will cause in our mental and physical state of being, that makes us want it. For example, most people who desire to lose weight don't care so much about the actual fat cells; they want to change the way they *feel* about themselves. What they really want is to feel in control of their lives, to feel healthy and live longer, to feel more attractive to others, to feel more energetic and excited by life, and so on.

As another example, almost all of us want a positive relationship with the opposite sex, but what we really want is to feel seen and understood, to enjoy the positive feelings of warmth and sharing, to feel the security of having a friend and confidant who will always be there, to experience the ecstasy of sex, and so on.

All of these wants imply a desire to change our current state. Specifically, they imply a desire to move from a state of dissatisfaction to satisfaction, or from satisfaction to more satisfaction; from pain to pleasure, or from pleasure to more pleasure. The potential feeling of pleasure is the real goal and the immediate source of desire. This desire alone, however, may not be enough to establish motivation. We may have conflicting desires which arise from the need to avoid pain.

Dieting and acquiring or maintaining healthy relationships are, like trading, examples of areas in which most people *want* and have the knowledge to succeed, but fail in the attempt more often than not. Most often, the reason for failure is not because the person *cannot* do it, but because he or she *will* not do it; the true motivation does not exist.

Someone on a diet, munching his lettuce and carrots with lemon juice, sees that juicy, 16-ounce steak delivered to the next table and says, "What the hell! I've had enough of this suffering!" Or, the guy who has met a woman he is strongly attracted to and has even obtained her phone number never calls because he thinks, "What if she doesn't like me?" or, "I'll probably just be disappointed again."

In the case of breaking the diet, the process of dieting is experienced as painful, as a process of moving away from enjoyable things instead of moving toward *more* enjoyable things. Achieving the goal of weight loss doesn't really mean pleasure in the person's mind, but pain!

The guy who doesn't make the follow-up call acts almost totally on the desire to avoid pain: the pain of rejection, the pain of disappointment, the pain of being wrong, the pain of losing his "freedom," and so on. Again, the process of acting to attain the goal is associated with pain in the mind, not pleasure. There is a pleasure/pain paradox that the subconscious mind can't deal with effectively: to move towards a goal is painful; to remain the same is to stay dissatisfied. Given the alternative, the subconscious will usually let the need to avoid pain predominate over the desire to attain pleasure, so the person falters in the pursuit of goals and fails.

In watching people day-trade, I have seen this process at work many times and in many people, myself included. A profitable trading record can and often does have more losing trades than winning trades. But if this is the case, then obviously the profits from good trades have to be larger than the losses from the more frequent losers. The most common error traders make is taking profits too early and letting losses run too far. The reason they do this is that they are not *motivated* by the rules. They understand them, but they don't *realize* them.

If you have made a trade based on a 1 to 3 risk/reward ratio, then you ought to either lose 1 or win at least 3. Often, however, a trader sees a profit of 2 to 1 and can't stand the pain of watching it dip back to even. His subconscious mind projects pain and sends a flood of misleading output, and in his fear and confusion, the trader sells his position when the market starts going against him, realizes maybe a 1.5 to 1 profit, and then screams at himself when the market rallies back to where he could have realized 3 to 1 or better.

On the flip side, when the market immediately goes against him and hits his exit point, instead of taking the lick and getting out, he starts hoping that it will turn around and he'll get lucky. Then the market keeps going down, and what should have been a loss of 1 turns into a loss of 1.5, 2, or even more. His need to avoid the pain of losing and of being wrong drives him to deny rules he knows to be right. It is the same paradox in a different form: To execute the rules is painful, but not executing them increases his state of dissatisfaction and depletes his trading capital!

I think you will find upon self-examination that some form of the pleasure/pain paradox is at work any time you are having trouble moving toward the achievement of a goal. Assuming you have the right knowledge, the problem of not being able to execute emanates from conflicting motivations arising from what your subconscious experiences as opposing needs, and in general, the motivation arising from the need to avoid pain almost always predominates.

Ironically, when this happens, the pain of frustration and dissatisfaction is always the result. In an effort to avoid pain of one kind, the subconscious mind creates pain of another kind that leads to further feelings of frustration and dissatisfaction. If left unchecked, this process creates a downward spiral that erodes self-esteem, stifles achievement, and arrests personal growth; it leads to a destiny of failure.

To establish positive, noncontradictory motivation, the subconscious mind must experience the process of pursuing a goal as pleasurable and not pursuing it as painful. If you can create this state of mind, then the choice to act toward achieving goals is essentially made; there is no alternative possible. The essence of being able to make a decision and stick to it is the ability to achieve commitment—a state of mind in which knowledge, motivation, and execution are totally directed toward the same goal. In this state of integrity, your mind will drive *you* towards achievment and a destiny of success.

CONCLUSION

Success is a dynamic process of goal-oriented action resulting in a constant progression of personal growth, achievement, and happiness. The key ingredient of being successful is the ability to commit yourself to achieving your goals, which means joining together your conscious and subconcious minds to work for the same ends. Most people have trouble committing themselves because they have conflicting motivations, which arise from conflicting emotions, which arise from conflicting values and beliefs. With this understanding, the formula for positive change seems clear:

1. Identify limiting and destructive values and beliefs and eliminate them.
2. Adopt new and life-serving values and beliefs.
3. Eliminate the subconscious associations which create limiting emotional responses and replace them with new, empowering associations.

Like most formulas, the statement is easy but the application is quite complex. In the next chapter, I will discuss how to translate the formula into positive, life-serving action.

15

Changing So It Sticks

If you don't know where you are going, you'll probably end up somewhere else.
    —David Campbell

To be a successful trader, you have to obtain the mindset that following the rules is pleasurable and breaking the rules is painful. But, even when you follow the rules, you'll still lose money sometimes, and losing money is almost always a little bit painful. You have to understand that the pain is normal, natural, like the occasional nick you get when shaving. You have to be able to accept, on an *emotional level*, that the pain is unimportant, that it will pass. You have to realize, in the strictest sense of the term, that success is a process of change, and pain is part of the process.

If success, as a trader *and* a human being, is a process of change driven by the desire to change our current mental and physical state, then the essential element of being a success is mastering the art of managing both our mental and physical environments. But as I have already said, given adequate knowledge, the problem of changing our physical environment—of taking effective action—depends on having the right motivation, or will, to act upon knowledge.

Since we know that the lack of will to execute is a result of limiting associations, values, and beliefs, doesn't it makes sense that the way to begin the process of change is to examine the content of our minds and isolate those limits? I think it does.

Specifically, the way to change is to unlock the content of the subconscious mind; to find limiting associations, values, and beliefs; and to replace them with new ones which move us on the path of our choosing. Remember, the objective is to achieve a mental state in which the pursuit of goals is pleasurable and not pursuing them is painful.

We have three basic tools we can use to achieve this end: the physical body, the conscious mind, and the automatic workings of the subconscious mind. These three tools are already working all the time, and they behave interactively, each

221

either supporting or undermining the operation of the others. What I want to do is explain the basic principles of how to take personal control of them and get them working jointly for you instead of against you.

USING YOUR BODY

Maintaining any state requires energy and effort, but just as a poorly designed machine consumes more energy than an efficiently designed one, so being depressed, frustrated, or miserable takes more energy than feeling good about yourself and life. Being unhappy and dissatisfied is extra work; it wastes energy and it depletes desire; it negatively *affects your physical body.*

Picture someone who is depressed. What are the physical characteristics that let you know how he or she feels? Probably slow movements, listless gestures, slumped posture, quiet and monotonous speech, and shallow breathing intermingled with heavy sighs. How about someone who is happy and excited? Probably quick movements, animated and expressive gestures, increased volume and inflection in speech, erect posture, faster and deeper breathing, and so forth. How about anger, elation, suffering, rejection, love, and so on? All of these emotional states have characteristic physical actions associated with them as well.

Everything we feel is manifested in our body, and this makes sense, for as I mentioned earlier, emotions are both a mental and a physical response to value judgments made in the subconscious mind. But doesn't it make just as much sense that a change in your physical body would affect you emotionally? Absolutely. For example, motivation specialist Anthony Robbins does the following exercise on one of his audiotape programs.[1] Try it and see what happens:

> Stand up straight and erect, shoulders square, and look up at the ceiling. Put a big smile on your face, no matter how stupid it feels. Now, try your best to feel depressed without changing any aspect of your posture or your smile. Keep trying.

Did you end up laughing? The point is that to feel depressed, tired, miserable, or inept you have to relinquish control of your body to the subconscious mind to keep feeling that way. A large part of being motivated is moving like you are motivated. A large part of feeling good is moving and walking and acting like you are feeling good. A large part of feeling full of energy is how much energy you actually have, which means what you eat, how much you exercise, how you use and treat your physical body.

You can use your body to interrupt the associations in your mind that stop you from taking positive action. Anthony Robbins has made a science out of how to do this, as well as with many other ways to create change, so I will refer you to his tapes and books for further study. But to begin the process of change, recognize that you have it in your power to change your mental state, at least to a significant degree, simply by changing how you move, how you carry yourself, exercising, and putting good, nutritious food into your body.

When you watch professional athletes, you will notice that they almost all have some kind of ritual before they participate. For baseball players, it may be the way a player taps his feet with the bat, then grabs a handful of dust and rubs the bat, and then "digs in" at the batters box. For tennis players, it may be the particular way and number of times they bounce the ball before serving or hop around just before receiving serve. Football players are notorious for their almost superstitious rituals in preparing for the game. What these rituals all have in common is that they are repetitive, physical actions that force the subconscious mind into a state of focus on the coming task. These players use their bodies, through rituals, to manage their subconscious processes.

When I was working at the Interstate offices, we had rituals too. One trader wore a cowboy hat and cap pistols on his belt, and when a trade went against him, he would "draw" and shoot at the screen. I often wore an old leather bomber's cap, which I still have, and would playfully "bomb" the market when I wanted it to go down or when the action went against me. While these activities may sound childish, they were an important means of relieving the pent-up tensions and stress associated with trading. They allowed us to rechannel energy that could have turned to anger, and more importantly, they made the process more fun, *even when we lost money!*

We all have physical rituals whether we are aware of them or not. One of mine is the way I post my charts every morning. I could easily put the data I log on a computer and let it print out the charts and calculations for me, but the actual physical act of writing the numbers and drawing the lines triggers focus in my mind.

Not all rituals are positive, however. Because I used to work in New York City, one that first comes to mind is people ceaselessly honking their horns (especially cab drivers) in locked-up or slow-moving traffic. It is so pointless; all it does is feed the already unhealthy tension that causes the honking in the first place.

What are your rituals? You do have them. Ask yourself what purpose they serve in your life. Why do you do them? Do they energize you, or deplete you? Do they make you focus, or distract you from your intended purpose? Do they move you toward pleasure and away from pain, or the reverse?

Be aware of how you use your physical body—your rituals. When you catch yourself shouting at a trading screen, slumping with depression after a loss, angrily honking the horn in traffic, or anything else that reinforces a state that makes you feel less than successful, try instead taking a deep breath and asking yourself questions like those above.

But most important, do something different that makes you feel better. Sit upright, breath deeply, walk differently, talk with more energy, play a piece of music that you like; use your body as you would if you felt the way you want to feel, and you will interrupt the negative associations that are controlling your actions. If you succeed in changing your feeling, then relish in the change; feel the pleasure of it and the pleasure of being in control. If you do this enough times, you will establish a new association in your mind and a new ritual that you can call upon to change your emotional state when you need to. The nice thing is, you can effect *immediate* change this way.

It may seem ingenuine or false to change the way you feel simply by changing your physical state. After all, isn't it what we feel that makes us what we are, and isn't mechanically changing the way you feel a form of personal dishonesty? My answer to this is to ask you to consider which is more false or ingenuine: screaming at traffic you have no control over, or feeling more relaxed by taking a deep breath, changing your posture, and asking yourself a few questions? Which is more real: Waking up depressed for no apparent reason and giving in to the feeling, or snapping yourself to attention, clapping your hands, and energizing yourself for the coming day?

What you feel *is* a huge part of what you are, but you can *choose* to feel how you want to feel in large part just by making some physical changes. In addition, learning to manage your state by changing the way you use your body is only one aspect of making permanent change. When combined with what I'm going to talk about in the next couple of sections, using your body accelerates the process of change and helps install new associations of your choosing into your subconscious mind.

This is especially true in trading. You just won't see the opportunities, you won't react well, you won't feel confident if you are depressed or low. There isn't a routine of trading that will carry you through those rough times. You've got to be sharp, focused, and attentive to do the job well. When you're not, try to energize yourself with physical movements. I often use a deck of cards to keep up my intensity. I sit there watching the screen while shuffling, doing one-handed cuts, and so forth to help keep me focused. I've been told that you can tell when I have a position on by how many times per minute I shuffle my cards.

One aspect of using your body I particularly want to emphasize is exercise. Study after study has shown how exercise reduces stress, increases energy and mental stamina, and generally boosts self-esteem. Trading, because of the inherent uncertainty in dealing with the markets, is very stressful. I can personally testify to the benefits of exercise, and I know from the times that I have let my exercising regimen lapse that all the studies are correct.

When you are tired and stressed, sometimes the last thing you feel like doing is exercising. But there is almost always that moment when you know that all you have to do is stand up, get your work-out clothes, and head outside or to the fitness center and *do it*. In my personal experience, when I grasp that moment of hesitation and go do it, I'm always glad I did. Something else about exercise: The worst time *not* to do it is when you feel down. What you need to do when you feel down is interrupt the patterns that make you feel down, and exercise is one of the best ways to do it. It's tough sometimes, but it pays off.

I've known people who treat their exercise time just like an important business appointment. They block it out on their calendar like a meeting or business luncheon, and only extraordinary circumstances can make them cancel it—like a death in the family. Think about it. Isn't your health, your energy, your *life* just as important as any other business appointment or social engagement? Exercise is an investment in how you feel now and how you will feel in the future, plus it will pay off financially for you in business by giving you more energy, greater ability to concentrate, and enhanced self-confidence. That's my pep talk, for me and for you.

Using and managing your physical body is the quickest way to change your state, but it is not enough to affect permanent change. You can use your body to help interrupt old patterns and install new associations, but to really get those new associations ingrained into your subconscious, you have to install the beliefs and values to back them up. To do this, you have to turn to your most powerful asset: the conscious mind.

USING YOUR CONSCIOUS MIND

Although I spoke first about changing your state by using your body, implicit in the discussion was the use and exercise of the conscious mind. What I mean is that before you can make a change of any kind, you have to be aware of a problem with yourself, focus on it, evaluate the consequences of your present actions, and project the effects of alternative courses to determine what action you are going to take.

Awareness, focus, evaluation, and projection are the tools available to us that we have to learn to use in order to become successful. They are tools that are already at work, but that may be working against us due to poor personal management. If they are working against us, then it is because they are being issued conflicting orders by the subconscious mind due to the contradictory and limiting associations, values, and beliefs we hold.

Ironically, the only way we can gain knowledge of these limitations is by using the very faculties which they debilitate, namely awareness, focus, evaluation, and projection.

In the early eighties, when I was training traders out of my office, I told them that to trade well they had to learn to do three things: observe, focus, think. What I was trying to get across to them is the mental state you have to be in to trade successfully. Assuming that you have the fundamental knowledge required to make a trading decision, the next step is to observe market behavior; to watch and take in the current data such as economic and political news, market price movements, the interaction of prices in related markets, and so forth in the same way you would if you were reading the sports page, playing bridge, or doing something else that you find interesting and easy to learn.

If you can achieve a state of focus, a state where your conscious awareness is directed toward the markets and away from other of life's problems, then what happens next is you will get a "feel" for the direction of price movements and you will "hear" an inner command coming from your subconscious saying, "Sell the S&P Index futures now."

This is the point to intervene with your conscious mind and evaluate the conclusion of your subconscious before actually making the trade. You evaluate by verifying whether the trade meets the requirements set by your trading rules. You ask yourself: "Is there a minimum 1 to 3 risk/reward ratio? Is this trade in the direction of the trend you want to be involved in? Have prices tested a previous important high and failed?" and so forth.

In other words, you use all the applicable rules you know to test the validity of the judgment delivered by your subconscious mind. If the facts verify the judgment, then you make the trade. If not, you don't. If you go through this process consistently, you will trade well and gain more and more confidence in the "inner voice" of your subconscious mind; the process of evaluation becomes more and more automatic, and you approach the point where you can almost fully "trust your instincts."

Unfortunately, when I was training traders, I wasn't able to articulate the nature of this process as clearly as I have just done, because it was my *implicit* mode of operation; that is, I practiced the method, but I wasn't fully, verbally aware of what I was doing. Many people who are good at something don't know why they are good at it. They may say, "I trust my instincts," or "I just let go and it happens." I am willing to bet, however, that the process I just described is active, in varying degrees and with minor variations, in everyone who excels at anything.

"Observe, focus, think," is just another way of expressing that you have to integrate the faculties of awareness, focus, evaluation, and projection to make good decisions and take effective action. If you understand how these faculties work, then you can learn to manage and direct every aspect of your life. So let me discuss these faculties in more detail and outline the principles of how to apply them to identifying and changing limiting associations, values, and beliefs.

DISCOVERING AWARENESS

What exactly is awareness? Philosophers have been debating the answer to this question for 2000 years, but we're going to operate with a very simple answer: Awareness is the ability or faculty of perceiving that which exists. What we perceive, what bombards our senses, is the raw data of reality. What we do with it, how our mind makes sense of it, depends on what we know and believe.

For example, if you show a stock chart to someone who knows virtually nothing about graphs and the financial markets, what are they *aware* of? Basically, they would see a confusing collection of lines, numbers, and so on, and at most they would see the price plot as some sort of wavy pattern. My point in using this example is to demonstrate that your range of awareness is *contextual*. In order to be aware of anything, you have to understand the nature of what you are dealing with. That is why knowledge is so important—it expands the range of awareness available to you. Remember that your subconscious mind can only make sense of that which it is programmed to make sense of, so it simply won't take in very much extraneous information—it just doesn't know what to do with it!

The biggest block to awareness, however, is not lack of knowledge but rather the inadvertent misprogramming of our minds. If we instruct our subconscious mind *not* to take in certain kinds of data, then it won't, and it will be impossible to be fully aware of what is occurring. But you can use the faculty of awareness to realize that you are missing something, that there is a problem, just by remembering a few things that you already know.

When you aren't getting the results that you want in life, something is wrong— there is a contradiction somewhere in your mind blocking you. Probably the biggest blocks to achieving goals are the limitations to awareness that we inadvertently place in our minds through the acceptance of negative associations and beliefs. Conversely, positive associations and beliefs enable awareness.

If you keep missing important things and the only symptom that makes you aware of missing them is some form of failure, then take that as a starting point. Recognizing and owning not only your successes, but also your failures, is the first and absolutely essential step to enabling yourself to be consistently successful. Recognizing mistakes and failures and learning to own them is a *positive* thing.

What I mean by "owning" your successes and failures is recognizing that *every* result you achieve is a result of a choice you made. You, and only you, are responsible for the results you get. Supertrader trainer Dr. Van K. Tharp explains it this way:

> The best thing an investor [or anyone] can do, when things go wrong, is to determine how he or she produced those results. Now, I don't mean that you should blame yourself for your mistakes either. I mean that at some point in time, for any situation, you made a choice that produced those results. Determine what that choice point was and give yourself other options to take when you encounter a similar choice point in the future. Change the decision at similar choice points in the future and you will change the results you get. And by imagining doing so now, you can make it easy to select those alternatives in the future.[2]

It is extremely tempting to blame our mistakes, failures, and pain on other people and events. But if you continually remind yourself that they are yours and are a result of your actions, then you enable yourself to become aware of what caused them. Mistakes, failures, and pain are a part of life, and we all want to avoid them. But we can't avoid them by denial. If we can instead choose to own them, then they lose their power over us. They become OK, acceptable, normal, even a positive opportunity to learn, grow, and achieve.

In *Reminiscence of a Stock Operator,* Jesse Livermore wrote, "I don't mind making mistakes, what I don't like is being wrong." The way I interpret this is that making an error is okay, but what isn't okay is making an error, not admitting it, and continuing to do it. I once gave a lecture at Lehigh University and asked the audience of 200 students how many of them liked to admit their mistakes. Only one student raised his hand! I promptly offered him a job as a trader, and I meant it.

So dedicate a portion of your mind to be a watchdog over your behavior. Listen to the "little voices" in your head and to the actual words you say to yourself and *key in to those which try to blame bad results and pain on outside forces.* What you are doing in these moments is trying to change reality to meet the content of your mind, rather than fixing the content of your mind to accurately perceive reality. This process is called rationalization, the most dangerous and confusing method of avoiding pain. Rationalization is dangerous and confusing because it is always shrouded by a semblance of logic.

In some aspects of life, rationalization can go on for a long time before you have to deal with its effects. On Wall Street, rationalization can be instant death. If you don't own your failures, if you try to blame your failures on external events, then you'll end up not learning from your prior mistakes, and you'll likely end up blowing out.

It is amazing how ingenious and resourceful we can be in finding reasons outside ourselves for mistakes and failure, and they often have a semblance of truth. People who have had a series of failed relationships, for example, may find themselves keeping a controlled distance from a new person they are attracted to. They may say to themselves, "I'm fooling myself. I can't move from one relationship into another. I'm not ready for another relationship. I want to date, and to re-establish my sense of self." While there may be merit to this, it is also possible that the real motivation is simply the fear of failing again.

In any case, we must be careful and lock in to those fleeting moments when the truth is within our grasp. If you can seize those critical moments of denial and recognize them for what they are, then you can apply focus, evaluation, and projection to eliminate them.

FINDING YOUR FOCUS

Focus is the method of directing awareness, the means with which we simultaneously narrow down and open up the field of conscious awareness. For example, traders who have a general knowledge of how the markets work should trade in only two to five markets (preferably related) at one time. By narrowing down the number of markets under consideration, they expand the amount of information they can take in about those specific markets.

The conscious mind can only take in so much at one time. In order to take in and understand the constant barrage of sensory data open to awareness, the mind selectively isolates the material available to the senses and integrates it into the context of prior learning and memory. We take in what we think and feel is important, and our values and beliefs act as the filters that direct our focus.

Values and beliefs determine the direction of our focus, which in turn determines how we perceive ourselves and our relationship to the physical world and to other people. If, through vigilant self-awareness, we can identify where our focus is, then we can isolate the values and beliefs that determine the direction of our lives and take control of that direction.

For example, when I examine where I acquired my ability to focus on the markets, I realize that I was very fortunate in my early childhood to have adopted a very empowering belief about learning and achievement. At some point, and I don't quite know how or why, I decided that the only way to achieve anything was to learn as much as possible about what I wanted to do by reading, practicing consistently, and modeling myself after people who were successful.

I did this first with baseball, then with gymnastics, next with cards, and finally with trading and speculating in the financial markets. To put my belief into a single sentence:

With enough knowledge and practice, I can master anything I set my mind to.

There is also another very important association that I adopted very early about the whole process of learning and practicing to achieve my goals:

This is fun!

I wasn't aware of it at the time, but these associations set me up for success. They are deeply rooted in my mind, and they serve me better now than they did when I was learning to play baseball, because I know so much more about how to learn and grow now than I did then.

The belief that learning is important directs my focus to acquiring as much knowledge as possible such that I have a broad context for awareness. When I was learning baseball, for example, once I read about the fundamentals of the game, I could watch professional players and take in how they applied the fundamentals. That in turn widened my context of awareness and knowledge because the pros became a standard of evaluation with which to judge my own performance. I could picture in my mind how the pros looked and try to emulate their style in practice until I perfected my swing and my fielding skills.

In the present day, the belief that learning and practice are both important and get results enables me to focus on the pursuit of my goals with confidence, vigor, and enthusiasm. It makes me feel positive and energetic about doing what many people consider "hard work." My study of the markets *is* hard work, but that carries no negative connotation in my mind. Work is a source of pleasure for me. Like playing a baseball game, it is *fun*. Viewing what I do as fun enables me to open up my mind and take in *all* the data without fear. My subconscious mind has no reason to block my awareness of what is occurring because, in essence, I feel that in the long run I'll be a winner just by participating in the manner that I do.

By contrast, I adopted another association in childhood which severely limited me and became something I had to overcome and still have to be cautious about. While I was excelling in baseball, gymnastics, and at cards, I was a very poor student in high school. I never studied, and did the minimum just to get by. My grades were mostly C's and I failed foreign language. School to me seemed nothing more than an encumbrance to doing the things I loved, a necessary evil to be put up with because I had no choice. In effect, the association I made was:

School is painful, boring, drudgery that takes me away from doing the things I love.

I can't tell you how many times I have wished that I had applied the same vigour and enthusiasm in school that I applied to other things. I had to hire a writer to help me with this book not only because I didn't have adequate time, but also because I never developed adequate writing skills in school.

Fortunately, I have always loved to read, and that has been a great help, but I still find myself feeling intimidated at the prospect of learning some new things. For example, I rely totally on Douglas, my computer wiz and associate trader, to take care of all the computers in the office and to teach me how to use them. When we installed a new market quote system, I looked at it and said, "Man, am I glad I have Douglas around, I could *never* figure out how to operate this thing on my own."

Can you see how the limiting belief about formal education tends to arrest my focus when it comes to learning about computers? In moments such as when I made that statement, I don't think of learning as fun, but as drudgery. Consequently, I take care of the problem by calling for Douglas whenever I don't understand how to operate the system or when something goes wrong. I *know* that I could learn about computers—they can't be any more complicated than the markets are—but in general, my focus just isn't there. Fortunately, I really don't need to learn, because I can always have a Douglas around, but if I had to learn, I would have to challenge statements like the one I made.

Think of the power of the statement "I could *never* figure out how to operate this thing on my own." It is statements like this that limit our ability to focus. The subconscious mind may be a powerful resource, but it is also gullible—it believes whatever we tell it to believe. When you say to yourself, "I will *never* figure this out," or "I *can't* do this," or "I'm kidding myself, this is *impossible*," or "People just don't *do* things this way," your subconscious mind dumbly says, "OK, got it!" and starts reinforcing the limit that you are already feeling.

This type of limitation can be brought under control very quickly just by being aware of the things you say to yourself and changing what you say; by making a practiced and conscientious effort to rephrase what you say in a way that forces your subconscious into *positive* action. You have to use the subconscious mind's gullibility in your favor to manage your focus.

For example, instead of saying "I will *never* figure this out," you might say, "This is difficult—how can I approach this differently to make it easier?" Instead of saying, "I *can't* do this," you might say, "When I felt this frustrated before, how did I get out of it?" Instead of saying, "I'm kidding myself, this is *impossible*," you might say, "Why does this seem impossible, what am I missing?" Instead of saying, "People just don't *do* things this way," you might say, "I wonder why no one has ever done it this way before," or even, "I might be on to something here, I don't think anyone has ever tried it this way before!"

The way we speak to ourselves directs our focus. What we say to ourselves and how we say it makes the difference between a positive and a negative approach to life. In addition, I think it makes a tremendous difference in the quality and quantity of results that the subconscious mind puts out.

If you are aware of how you talk to yourself, what you ask yourself, and what you demand of yourself, you can shift the focus of your mind away from negative associations and toward positive associations simply by consciously changing the tone and focus of the statements you make to yourself, the questions you ask yourself, and the demands you place on yourself.

THE POWER OF QUESTIONS

Did you notice how when I rephrased the statements most of them came out as questions? This is not accidental. Questions are the best possible way to shift the focus of your awareness.

Each and every one of us has an enormous store of knowledge in our heads, much, much more than we consciously realize. By asking ourselves questions, we direct the subconscious to find a solution to a genuine problem instead of trying to accept self-imposed limitations. Often, the answers are right there, all you have to do is ask! But you have to ask *positive* questions, genuinely and sincerely, while fully expecting to get an answer.

An excellent example of the power of questions in my own experience is one I mentioned in the introduction to Part I. When I missed the October lows in 1974, I asked myself, "What do I need to learn so this won't happen again?" This question led to a whole chain of questions, such as "What exactly *is* a trend? How long does it normally last? How high or low does it normally go?" During the process of answering these questions, the concept of using statistical distributions of historical price movements as a means of assessing risk "occurred" to me, like the classic cartoon lightbulb.

How different would my life be, not to mention my net worth, if I had asked instead, "Sperandeo, how could you have been so stupid to have missed that move?! Just look at all the money-making potential you missed!" Obviously, there is no way to tell just what or where I would be, but I might never have developed my unique statistical approach to risk analysis, probably the achievement I am most proud of in my life.

So be aware of how you speak to yourself, and learn to change recriminating and reproachful conversations with yourself into questions that direct your focus toward positive change. Beware of questions like "How can this possibly be happening to me? How can I be so unlucky? How can I be so stupid? Why is the world so unfair? Why can't I be rich, too? How can anyone treat me so badly?" When you ask questions like this, your subconscious may well provide answers that have nothing to do with reality, like "Because you are undeserving. Because you were born to lose. Because you are an ignorant, worthless person. Because life is always unfair, except to the lucky. Because only the lucky are rich, and remember, you were born to lose. Because, as I already told you, you are ignorant, worthless, and undeserving."

When you ask yourself these kinds of questions, it is like asking a man if he still beats his wife, even though you never had evidence that he did. The questions are loaded; they imply acceptance of a negative belief that needs to be challenged, not reinforced.

I've spent a lot of time talking about questions not just because they are so useful for changing the direction of your focus, but also because they are an essential element of evaluation, and evaluation is the way we can get to the root of the limiting values and associations that hold us back from achievement.

THE IMPORTANCE OF EVALUATION

I think, before I proceed, that a review of the way the mind works is in order. Our actions are not so much decided upon as they are driven by the programming of the subconscious mind, by the beliefs and values that we hold whether we are aware of them or not. Specifically, we are motivated to act by two primary emotional forces at the subconscious level: the desire for pleasure and the need to avoid pain. These emotions, in turn, are determined by associations formed in the subconscious mind according to the values and beliefs we have accepted, whether consciously or not.

Until now, I have been using the terms "value" and "belief" as if they were virtually the same thing. They are not. Values are that which we seek, what we act to gain or keep. In order to value something, you first have to *evaluate* it, to place importance according to some standard of value or worth. Beliefs are the standards for evaluation; they determine the way we respond to that which we value. Values are the objects of action. Beliefs are the standards that allow us to experience values in a particular way.

For example, suppose two people both value money; that is, both want to make a lot of money. One person has a healthy view toward money, seeing it as a means to many desirable ends. The other person, however, holds the subconscious belief that "money is the root of all evil." If both people make a lot of money, the first would be more likely to enjoy it, spending it for a nice house, that dream vacation, and so on. The second person, however, may find it impossible to truly enjoy his wealth. He may feel a vague uneasiness when spending it, or may be inexplicably guilt-ridden when booking that dream vacation.

Your overall ethical structure—your values *and* your beliefs—determine character; it determines what you do. Beliefs determine personality; they determine how you do things and how you experience them. Understanding our values and beliefs and the distinctions between them is so important that I need to discuss each of them in more detail.

VALUES AND CHARACTER

Other than your unique physical characteristics, what makes you truly individual are your character and personality. Your character is set by *what* you value, what you strive for. Your personality is set by *how* you do it. As we have already established, what you do depends on what you value. How you do something depends on the unique set of rules or standards that you operate by—your beliefs. Let me talk first about values.

There are two basic types of values: *means* values and *ends* values. Do you remember the definition of economics that I gave in Part I? It is the study of the *means* applied for the attainment of *ends* chosen. Means values are the things that carry us forward in life, such as money, career, personal relationships, health, and cars. Ends values are states of emotional pleasure we want to attain, such as love, success, happiness, contentment, comfort, security, and excitement. It is primarily ends values that we are concerned with in this context; it is ends values that are the drivers in life.

Every ends value we hold has a negative emotional counterpart; let's call it a *disvalue*. Disvalues are states of emotional pain that we act to avoid, such as rejection, failure, frustration, anguish, anger, humiliation, and depression. We are motivated by the desire for pleasure and/or the need to avoid pain, and it is our ends values and disvalues that are the motivators.

One way to identify what your ends values and disvalues are is to ask yourself the following two simple questions:

What is the most important thing in my _____?

What are the things in my _____ that I would do almost anything to avoid?

Fill in the blanks first with "life" and later with particulars such as career, relationships, or any other aspect of your life you want to consider. When you write down the answers, do so rapidly, never letting your pen or pencil stop until you run out of answers. For example, you might come up with something like:

The most important thing in my life is _____.

love	security
success	fulfillment
passion	contentment
adventure and excitement	compassion
ecstasy	having a full head of hair

The things in life that I would do almost anything to avoid are _____.

rejection	physical danger
failure	anger
humiliation	depression
embarrassment	being bald

When you do this exercise, be careful not to glorify yourself in the process, which is something I will talk about in the next chapter. Try to dig deep inside and answer these questions truthfully. After you answer them, place both the values and the disvalues in their order of importance to you. This will give you insight into the hierarchy, or order of importance, of your values. Now examine both lists carefully, looking for consistencies, contradictions, limiting values, and positive ones. You will probably be amazed at the results.

For example, if love is at the top of your values list and rejection is at the top of your disvalues list, then how likely is it that you will find love? Do you think it is possible to find love without facing some rejection? Certainly not, and remember, the need to avoid pain will usually override the desire to attain pleasure, and the opposite of desire is fear.

If you analyze your lists, you should be able to determine why you do many of the things you do. For example, if success is at the top of your list and love is second or third, then it shouldn't be surprising if you are the type that stays late at the office even at the expense of incurring the wrath of your spouse or close companion. If at the top of your disvalues list is embarrassment, then it shouldn't surprise you that you are often afraid to speak out or try new things in social settings. What your values and disvalues are determines your *character*. How you act to obtain them, your behavior, determines your personality.

If you are like most people, your character is something that has been defined, not in a planned and organized way, but rather through a process of osmosis. You have absorbed values and disvalues throughout your life from the outside in as a result of your upbringing, environment, education, social contacts, and all the choices you have made along the way. Your values may be disorganized, confused, and even contradictory.

Or you may have well-organized and structured values, but find yourself operating according to a mixed set of disvalues. Either way, if you want to take control of your life, then it is essential to understand the structure of your character so you can start making the changes that you want to make.

So I urge you to sit down and go through the exercise I described above and engage in the adventure of self-discovery in as many areas of your life as you can. You may be surprised just how unknown the frontier of your own mind is to you.

BELIEFS AND PERSONALITY

Most people have similar ends values and disvalues, but each of us experiences them differently. This is because of the differences, both major and subtle, in our beliefs. Beliefs take two forms: broad generalizations about life, people, and things; and rules we use to measure the worth of our own and others' actions.

The broad generalizations, often called *global* beliefs, reflect our view of the world, other people, and ourselves. Consequently, global belief statements usually take the form of the verb "to be," such as "Life *is* _____ , people *are* _____ , I *am* _____ ."

Rules are more particular, and determine in our minds things and events which must happen in order to experience results in a particular way. They usually take the form of "If, then" statements, such as "If I make a million dollars, then I'll be happy. If you love me, then you will spend every free moment of your life with me. If I make a mistake, then I'll learn something from it." All of us have our own unique set of global beliefs and rules, and it is this unique set that gives each of us a distinctive personality.

Consider, for example, the beliefs that give rise to one of the attributes I listed in the last chapter as a prerequisite for success: self-confidence. Feeling self-confident comes from recognizing your personal worth and efficacy. How you feel about yourself depends not so much on what you actually do, but how you judge what you do, and how you judge what you do depends on your standards for judgment—your beliefs about what it takes to be a worthwhile person.

For example, suppose a talented and profitable young trader holds the following set of beliefs for judging his success or failure:

> If I am a good trader, I will be right on 90% of my trades.
>
> If I am a good trader, I have to make more money than any other trader in the world.
>
> If I am a good trader, I should be able to trade any market better than anyone else in the world.

Ambitious fellow! But he is dooming himself to frustration and personal insecurity. These are impossible standards that would allow no one to establish a steadfast self-confidence.

To gain self-confidence, you have to establish standards that make self-confidence possible. That may sound circular, but it's really not. For example, my standard of being successful as a businessman is to cover overhead and make a profit each month. Suppose instead that I set my standard at netting $1 million each month. It would be hard to be self-confident under those circumstances.

A standard is different from a goal. A goal is something you strive for; a standard is the reference point you use to judge your actions. I would love to net one million dollars a month, and I think it is possible (although it actually isn't one of my goals), but to set that as my standard for success and self-worth is totally unrealistic. On the one hand, I believe that to be successful you have to demand more of yourself than anyone else could possibly expect—the higher you set your goals the more you will attain. But on the other hand, I think it pays to be easy on yourself in terms of the standards you set for evaluating your self-worth.

Limiting beliefs are at the core of most failure, including the inability to experience life as a joyous process. Here are some classic examples of limiting global beliefs:

> I am not intelligent enough.
> I am not confident enough.
> I am too young.
> I am too old.

I am too ignorant.
I am undeserving.
I will never be wealthy.
I can't change what I am.

Life is a bitch.
Life is absurd.
Life "is a tale told by an idiot, full of sound and fury, signifying nothing."[3]
Life is out of my control.

People are cruel.
People are stupid.
People are lazy.
People are by nature evil.
People will use you for what they can get and then dump you.

If you hold these kinds of beliefs, or anything similar to them, then how do you suppose that you can achieve the values you seek?

If you value love, for example, but hold the belief that people will use you for what they can get and then dump you, then it is likely that anytime you feel the stirrings of love, you will also feel cautious, suspicious, and fearful of being used.

If you hold the core belief that you are not intelligent enough, then no matter how much you study, you will never achieve any significant level of intellectual independence. In the face of countervailing opinion, you will always fear that someone more intelligent knows more than you—you will feel unsuited to make independent choices.

If you believe that life is a fool's tale meaning nothing, then, like Macbeth, you will drive yourself toward your own destruction.

Your beliefs are the ultimate self-fulfilling prophecy. Remember that your subconscious is gullible—it believes what you tell it to believe. If you believe you don't deserve to be rich, your mind won't let you be rich. If you believe you don't deserve love, it won't let you achieve love. If you believe that you aren't intelligent, it will make you stupid.

So you have to get rid of limiting beliefs in order to succeed in life. The first step toward changing limiting beliefs is gaining an awareness of what they are, and awareness comes first from recognizing their symptoms as manifested in your actions. The symptoms are very similar to the ones I discussed regarding values, namely the recurrent inability to follow through on the achievement of your goals and the negative nature of the questions and statements you make to yourself. This isn't surprising since values and beliefs are so intimately connected.

The statements we make to ourselves and the questions we ask of ourselves are both a cause and a consequence of our beliefs. When you say something to yourself like "I am so stupid!" you are both stating and reinforcing a belief, however briefly you may think it is true. You may not mean this self-reproach in a fundamental sense, but if you say it often enough, especially in a highly emotional state, then your mind is very likely to start believing it.

An excellent way to help gain awareness of both your limiting global beliefs and your limiting rules is once again to put pen to paper and ask yourself some questions:

What are the limiting global beliefs that are stopping me from achieving what I want in my _____?

Use the same procedure that was described for listing your values. First, fill in the blank with "life," and write as many answers as you can as fast as you can. Then get more particular by answering the question for whatever area of your life you want to consider, such as career and relationships.

The second step of this process is to access the rules that you live by. If you cannot immediately identify the major global beliefs that are limiting you, this second step may lead you toward answers. Start with the values you listed in the hierarchical order you gave them. For each value, ask yourself what has to happen in order for you to achieve it. Your answers will probably take either the "if, then" form or the form, "To be _____, I must _____." For example, if success is at the top of your list, you might come up with something like this:

What must happen in order for me to feel successful?
To be a success, I must _____
make one million dollars a year.
have an attractive spouse and two children.
have a body like Arnold Schwarzenegger (or Kim Basinger) and have at most 13% body fat.
feel totally happy 100% of the time.
never have a conflict with anyone.
never feel angry or frustrated.
be the best at everything I do.

Depending on your unique circumstances, some of these rules may be quite reasonable, but most of them are totally unrealistic. What if instead you believed that to feel successful, all you had to do is wake up and do your best every day? *No one* can feel totally happy all the time. *Everyone* is going to feel angry and frustrated. Not everyone can look like Arnold Schwarzenegger or Kim Basinger.

My point, once again, is that we often sabotage any chance of gaining the states we seek in life because we make the rules impossible to win by.

In doing these exercises, you will often find yourself listing attainments expressed in terms of *means* values such as quantities of money and so forth. It is possible that your values, your core beliefs, and even your rules may all be consistent and positive, but that you hold negative or conflicting beliefs about the means values that make the ends values you seek possible. To get to these negative beliefs, it is helpful to use the following sentence completion technique:

Having *(means value)* means _____.

When you answer this question, first list all the benefits you see yourself deriving from attaining whatever value you are seeking. For example:

Having a lot of money means _____
> I would be completely free.
> I would have more time to spend with my loved ones.
> I wouldn't have to worry about my bills.
> I could pay off all my bills.
> I could get the clothes, house, and car that I've always wanted.
>
> I could help out the people in need that I care about.
>
> I wouldn't be dependent on the welfare of my company for my livelihood.

Next, list all of the things that you were taught or believe that might limit the attainment of the means value. For example:

> Money is the root of all evil.
> Money can't buy happiness.
> To be rich you have to exploit the poor.
> Rich people are snobs.
> It is easier for a camel to pass through the eye of a needle than for a rich man to enter the kingdom of heaven.
> Making money means I would lose my spirituality.
> Making money means I would have to take on too much responsibility.

If you dig into your mind, you will be amazed at all the knowledge you have in your head that can stop you from feeling how you want to feel and being what and where you want to be in life. You can look at these limiting "truisms" in your mind and say, "That really doesn't make sense to me." You can remind yourself that all rich people aren't snobs, and there is no compulsion for you to be one if you become wealthy. In short, you can mentally cancel out the validity of these beliefs.

I'm telling you, right now, you have the intelligence and the ability to succeed; you just have to get rid of the limits you place on yourself. So examine your beliefs and rules and identify the ones that are limiting and impossible.

Thus far, my main focus has been on identifying limiting beliefs, but in order to change, you have to get rid of those beliefs and replace them with positive, empowering beliefs. Let me just list a few positive global beliefs to set the tone for the beliefs and rules you might adopt in your own way and your own phrasing:

Positive Global Beliefs:
> Life is full of unlimited possibility.
> Every problem is a new challenge and an opportunity to grow.
> I am fortunate to be healthy and alive.
> I am capable of controlling my own destiny.

People are a source of knowledge, inspiration, and joy.
There is always a way to achieve what I'm committed to.

When it comes to defining new rules that you want to adopt, remember to rig the game of life so it's easy to win. The rules that allow you to feel passion, love, happiness, success, and so forth don't have to be difficult or impossible.

We all need challenge in life, yes, but there is more than enough challenge in striving for a constant progression of goal achievement without setting ourselves up to "dream the impossible dream," and "fight the unbeatable foe." Life is too short, too precious, and too full of potential to waste time by setting ourselves up to experience life as futile.

Once you have spent some significant time doing these exercises, you will have a grasp on the values and beliefs that limit you, and you should have a pretty well-defined idea of the positive values and beliefs that you would like to replace them with. The problem now is *how* to go about making the replacement. Once again we are faced with the problem that knowledge alone is not enough; we need a method of execution. This is where the importance of projection comes into play.

HARNESSING THE POWER OF THE SUBCONSCIOUS

There are significant events in all of our lives that, when recalled, recreate pleasure or pain that feels nearly as vital as when the event actually occurred. For example, perhaps you had a major triumph in your career, and when you recall it, you find yourself smiling and feeling proud. Or perhaps you had a failed relationship, and when you recall the conflicts that you went through, your stomach tightens, your muscles tense, and you relive the pain and loss that you felt.

We have also all experienced the pleasure or pain of projecting some event into the future. You may picture yourself basking in the Bahamian sun, piña colada in hand, feeling the gentle breeze as the waves softly swoosh against the shore. On thinking about this, you may actually feel the sense of total relaxation that you would experience, and smile at the prospect. Or you may be driving along and imagine someone running out in front of you and feel the total dread and horror of accidentally killing someone with your car.

Feelings of pleasure and pain are not limited to the present; we have the ability to recall them from the past, and project them into the future.

Since the subconscious provides motivation according to two primary emotional forces—the need to avoid pain and the desire to attain pleasure—it makes sense that to eliminate a limiting association, we need to convince the subconscious that it will cause pain, lots of pain.

Conversely, to install a new, positive value or belief, you have to convince the subconscious that it will lead to enormous amounts of pleasure.

The way to do this on the conscious level is to link up the negative and limiting values and beliefs with pain in the past, present, and future; and to link the positive, life-serving values and beliefs with lots of pleasure in the present and the future.

Anthony Robbins has devised a method he calls the "Dickens Pattern," named after the method of change used on Scrooge by the ghostly visitors in Charles Dickens' story, *A Christmas Carol*. If you will recall, what the ghosts did was to take Scrooge on a journey through past, present, and future, demonstrating along the way the sources of pleasure and pain in Scrooge's life. It is noteworthy that the most effective impetus to change for Scrooge was the pain that his present course would cause in the future.

Basically, the Dickens Pattern is as follows:

1. Pick two limiting beliefs that you want to change. Close your eyes and think back in time about all the pain that this belief has caused you. Feel the weight, the burden that you feel as a result of holding the belief. Think about all the consequences of having this belief. Think of all the things you have missed out on, the love, the material things, the fun. What have these beliefs cost you financially, in your career, in your relationships with people? Really focus on the pain and loss you have experienced just as if it was happening to you all over again. Go back as far as you can remember and relive all the painful experiences you can that were caused by the limiting belief.

2. With your eyes still closed, think about the pain that these limiting beliefs are causing you in the present, including all the pain that is in your mind because of the past. How do you feel about yourself right now? Do the beliefs enervate you or drain you? Do they make you feel in control of your life, or helpless? How do they affect you socially? What opportunities have you missed to enjoy other people? How do they affect you physically, emotionally, spiritually? Feel the pain.

3. Move ahead into the future, projecting the pain that the belief will cause in your life in one year. Drag all the painful baggage of the past with you and *feel* the burden. What is this pain going to cost in your career? What will it cost you in your relationships? What will it cost in terms of your self-image and self-confidence? Really feel the pain on an emotional level; use your body; breathe as you would breathe; hold yourself the way you would if you were feeling the pain. Live the pain. Focus on it. Now repeat the process, only this time project yourself five years ahead. Imagine how the failures in your life are going to multiply, and feel the weight of these piled-up failures. What do you say to yourself, how do you feel about yourself? Are you stronger or weaker? More in control, or more out of control? Picture what you will look like as a result of holding on to this limiting belief. Do you look older? Do you look more energetic or less energetic? More attractive or less attractive? What are the costs to you in every area of your life? What has it cost your loved ones? Its been *five* long years. Let the pain that you were feeling compound, let your body slump with the pain. Project the cost to you in every area of your life. Now repeat the process for 10 years, and 20 years.

Note: This process is very painful if you carry through and do it right. When Terry, my writer, did it, he felt an impulse to quit after projecting into only one year. But if you feel the pain strongly enough, your mind will force you to change . . . NOW! Do whatever it takes to make the pain of the future feel real.

4. Come back to the present, shake out your body, and take some deep, energizing breaths. Now, pick out the new, positive belief that you want to install in place of the limiting belief. Use your body to totally energize yourself. Your mind is ready for change . . . get yourself totally excited, energized. Turn your new belief into a phrase that makes you think, "If I had these beliefs right now, it would totally change my life."

5. Close your eyes. Think about the immediate changes that would occur if you changed your belief right now. Imagine how much more confidence and in control you would feel. Feel the confidence and control, and use your body to reinforce the feelings. Breathe as you would breathe if you had the belief right now. Move five years ahead. Carry with you all the achievements you've gained as a result of making the change. How do you feel? More in control or helpless? Do you have lots of energy, or are you tired? Are you more attractive, or less attractive? Do you have more to offer yourself and others, or less? What about your confidence level? Are you generally more excited about life, or less? What about financially? Did you try some things that you would never have tried, make some commitments you would never have made? How has this change cascaded into the other areas of your life? Are your relationships more powerful, more exciting? Feel the changes, live the changes. What do you say to yourself after living this way for five years? Now go ahead another five years and repeat the process. That's a decade of positive change! How much better are you? Feel how much your life has been enhanced. Now go ahead 20 years, two decades of positive change that expands your life!

6. Look at both destinies and decide which destiny you are committed to having. Come back to today, and feel the excitement and unlimited possibilities that creating your new future will bring.

7. Sit down, and write down how each new belief you install is going to enhance your life.

What this process does is establish new associations in your subconscious mind. It links pursuing positive change with pleasure, and not pursuing positive change with pain.

You can use this method to change virtually any limiting belief you have. Its degree of effectiveness is dependent on your ability to go through the exercise and make both the pain and the pleasure feel absolutely real. I have outlined this procedure with the hope that you will try it and be titillated by its potential. I strongly urge you to experiment with it, and to do more research by studying the work of Anthony Robbins and others to further the development of your ability to change and take control of your life.

ANCHORING

Every day, in every moment, your subconscious mind is at work forming associations that link things, events, and people to pleasure and pain. What I have been talking about throughout this chapter is how to gain control over these processes so that you can direct your life. There is one particular process that I am just learning about that is particularly powerful and compelling. It is called anchoring.

Anchoring is the subconscious mental process that links a sensory stimulus to an emotional state or set of states. What does this mean? Whenever you are in a relatively intense emotional state, whether positive or negative, any significant, repetitive external stimulus becomes associated with the emotion or set of emotions you are experiencing. If the association is strong enough, then a recurrence of the external stimulus can actually trigger the emotional state.

The external stimulus can work through any one or any combination of the five senses. For example, how do you feel when you see a flashing red light in the rear-view mirror of your car? Most people feel dread, regardless of whether they were actually doing something wrong, because at some point in their life they got a ticket.

Another example is the feelings and memories that certain songs evoke in our minds. If you and your "steady" in high school had "your song," for example, when you hear that song you will almost always think of your old steady and the good or bad times that you shared when that song was playing. Your spouse or close companion may have a particular way of touching you or a tone of voice which evokes feelings of closeness and warmth. The smell of baking bread may make you feel hungry, even if you have eaten less than an hour before. You get the idea.

I spoke earlier of physical rituals. Well, guess what? Physical rituals are triggers for anchors established in the subconscious. It is possible to actually install anchors to trigger any state you desire. If you want to feel focused at work, you can develop and install a trigger/anchor association that lets you call upon that state when you need it. Once again, I refer to Anthony Robbins to describe the methodology:

> Basically, there are two simple steps. First you must put yourself, or the person you're anchoring, into the specific state you wish to anchor. Then you must consistently provide a specific, unique stimulus as the person experiences the peak of that state. For example, when someone is laughing, he is in a specific congruent state—his whole body is involved at that moment. If you squeeze his ear with a specific and unique pressure and simultaneously make a certain sound several times, you can come back later, provide the stimulus (the squeeze and the sound), and the person will go back to laughing again.[4]

The four key elements of creating and using anchoring successfully are:[5]

1. *The intensity of the state*—for an anchor to be strong and enduring, you need to achieve an intense emotional state; the whole body and mind should be involved. The strength of the anchor is in direct proportion to the intensity of the emotional experience.

2. *The timing of establishment*—the anchor trigger (whether established with sight, sound, touch, smell, or combination) should be induced at the peak of the emotional experience.

3. *The uniqueness of the stimulus*—the stimulus must be something unusual. If you habitually rub your chin, that would make a bad trigger, because you would inadvertantly induce the state and your mind wouldn't know what to do with it. The trigger would soon be diluted and the anchor would wear off. The best anchor triggers are a combination sensory stimuli such as both a unique sound and a touch.

4. *Replication of the stimulus*—the stimulus must be repeatable. For example, if the anchor is the phrase "I love you" said in a certain tone, then both the words and the tone must be replicated to successfully trigger the same response.

When you go through the anchoring process, you usually have to repeat it several times before it takes hold. After you have gone through the process several times, test it. One young fellow I know was having trouble smiling at pretty young ladies when he caught their eye. He didn't feel intimidated, he just couldn't smile. Then he learned about anchoring.

One day, a very nice and vivacious-looking young lady smiled at him, and he found himself smiling back. Because he had just learned about anchoring, he recognized an opportunity. While he was feeling exactly the way he wanted to and doing exactly what he wanted to, he touched his left ear on the jawline right above the lobe. Now, at any time, he can touch his ear in the same way and smile a warm and friendly smile, and his report is that he elicits many more smiles from attractive ladies than ever before in his life.

I suggest that as a supplementary method of change, anchoring can be very powerful. It is so powerful because it works directly on the subconscious. You can use it to harness any emotional state you need to help you accomplish the task at hand. You can use it to achieve focus on your work, to energize yourself when you are tired, to feel excited and powerful when you are feeling down, to feel confident and enthusiastic before you give a speech.

Why does it work? I really don't know. In the story of Dumbo the elephant, the infant elephant with huge ears convinces himself that he can fly as long as he holds a "magic" feather. The feather of course isn't magic; it's a psychological crutch. Perhaps anchoring is just another magic feather. But so what? It works!

CONCLUSION

All I've done up to now is scratch the surface of the central problem and the solution to attaining the ability to consistently act in accordance with your knowledge. I've identified the central problem: the conflict of emotion and reason. I've discussed the supercomputer model of the human mind and shown that the key to success is establishing goals backed by consistent and viable motivation and commitment.

In this chapter, I've touched briefly on some techniques you can use to attain that motivation and commitment. All of these ideas come from spending a large portion of my adult life reading, learning, and figuring out why people (myself included) do the things they do and how they can change. But it is far beyond the scope and intent of this book to provide much more than this kind of broad outline. There is a lot more detailed information out there beyond what I have offered, and I urge you to pursue it. I think the bibliography I've provided is a good starting point.

One thing I have learned about myself and other people is that anyone can change, but only if he or she *desires* to change. I have an acquaintance who calls me regularly to discuss her current personal problems. Her life is an endless loop of making the same mistakes in different forms over and over again. I feel for her because she has so much potential. But as I have observed her and the many other people around me, I have seen a common element: something that approaches love of misery.

It is a phenomenon that I first found unbelievable, until I discovered a psychologist named Karen Horney, who in her books explains how people get trapped into endless loops of self-destruction and yet find the drive to continue making the same mistakes, often with incredible vigor, passion, and enthusiasm.

The process revolves around an intricately organized system of false pride. It is so predominant that it exists to some extent in virtually every person I have ever known, myself included, and I believe it deserves special attention. I will address the problem in the next chapter.

16

Conquering False Pride

Self-knowledge... is not an aim in itself, but a means of liberating the forces of spontaneous growth.
—Dr. Karen Horney

THE MOST IMPORTANT REASON
PEOPLE FAIL IN TRADING

In considering what made the difference between success and failure among traders, the most puzzling thing to me for a long time was the incredible human capacity for self-delusion. I didn't understand how or why normally good traders could be capable of making trades in obvious violation of their own rules. I didn't understand how other traders could make the same mistake time and time again without ever learning from their errors. I didn't understand what motivated people who were obviously unhappy, even miserable, to get up each day and be unhappy and miserable again without ever making an attempt to figure out what was wrong, much less change their behavior.

I knew that at the root of the explanation had to be some form of self-deception and rationalization, but the scale of it boggled my mind. I felt a little bit hopeless trying to figure it out. I was reading virtually every book I could find on psychology to try to figure out this and other problems, when I found *Neurosis and Human Growth*,[1] by Dr. Karen Horney. This book really opened my eyes to the roots of self-deception and self-delusion, so much so that I feel compelled to share the essential elements of it here. It helped me understand not only the self-delusions of others, but it opened my eyes to some of my own motivations, both positive and negative.

According to Dr. Horney, each of us is provided by nature with a unique set of "given potentialities" and we have a natural drive to realize them. In other words, we are born with a "real self" and our purpose in life is to actualize and grow into that self through a constant process of self-discovery. But because it is an imperfect world, it is possible that "under periods of inner stress . . . a person may become alienated from his real self. He will then shift the major part of his energies to the task of molding himself, by a rigid system of inner dictates, into a being of absolute perfection. For nothing short of godlike perfection can fulfill his idealized image of himself and satisfy his pride in the exalted attributes that (so he feels) he has, could have, or should have."

In a terrible irony, the artificial view becomes a tyrant, driving people to mentally reconstruct reality to fit the idealized image of themselves, their relationship to the world, and their relationship with others. The result is an ever-widening system of falsehood and evasions that take people further and further away from being able to identify and live the truth.

What I've said is so full of subtleties that I need to break down and discuss the essential elements that give rise to this gigantic illusion called the false pride system, an illusion that hinders many traders regularly. In particular, I want to cover what I consider to be the most insightful portions about a false pride system that Dr. Horney writes about in her book: the idealized self-image, the search for glory, the tyranny of the shoulds, and neurotic pride. These concepts are so active in trading and our society in general that understanding them is crucial to gaining self-awareness, which, you will recall, is the first step in any process of personal change and growth, especially for traders.

I truly believe that self-awareness is more important in the financial world than in other professions. The reason I think so is that when you trade, the judge's gavel comes down every day on the ledger sheet. A doctor can evade the truth that he or she made a mistake and tell the relatives of a deceased patient, "I did my best, but. . . ." A lawyer can drink too much the night before his final address to the jury, and when he loses, convince himself and his client that the jury was biased. But a trader has no one to convince, no one to lie to. The market is the final judge, and it issues its verdict every day. I therefore think that understanding how the false pride system works can be crucially important to a successful and lasting career as a trader, speculator, or investor.

YOUR EVIL TWIN: THE IDEALIZED SELF-IMAGE

Think of your "given potentialities" as a core self which you strive to realize and bring out throughout your life. Unfortunately, many of us often strive toward a set of false potentialities that we ascribe to ourselves as a means of protection against the pain involved in true self-discovery. We develop a sort of dual personality that places us in a state of inner conflict. On the one hand, the core self—a sense of what our lives should be—is always there, and we naturally want to realize our true potential. But on the other hand, we develop an "evil twin" that strives to make good on unrealistic and idealized potentialities and subverts the growth of the core self.

Through the use of imagination, the evil twin builds a fortress against the perception of a hostile reality. For protection, "[g]radually and unconsciously, the imagination sets to work and creates in his mind and an *idealized image* of himself.

In this process he endows himself with unlimited powers and with exalted faculties; he becomes a hero, a genius, a supreme lover, a saint, a god."

THE SEARCH FOR GLORY

According to the model of the mind that I have set forth in preceding chapters, our actions are motivated by values and beliefs programmed into the subconscious. If, as Dr. Horney postulates, people adopt an idealized image of themselves as a protection against basic anxiety,[2] then, according to the model, the logical outcome would be an attempt to actualize this idealized self-image. In Dr. Horney's words:

> . . . self-idealization inevitably grows into a more comprehensive drive which I suggest calling . . . *the search for glory*. Self-idealization always remains the nuclear part. The other elements in it, all of them always present, though in varying degrees of strength and awareness in each individual case, are the need for perfection, neurotic ambition, and the need for a vindictive triumph.

The need for perfection is one element that I think most of us can relate to. One of the hardest things to accept in life is that mistakes and pain are an inevitable and essential part of it. The question I ask is: "Why is it so hard to accept?"

The answer, I think, is that it upsets our idealized image of ourselves. If we have ascribed exalted attributes to ourselves, then we should not make mistakes, we should not suffer pain, we should be able to get along with anyone, we should be able to convince anyone and everyone of our viewpoint, and so on.

Should, should, should. The need for perfection manifests itself in a rigid set of "shoulds" and "taboos" that are derived from what we think attaining the perfect idealized-self requires. In the last chapter, I used the example of a young trader who applied totally unrealistic standards to his evaluation of success. Such a person is probably motivated by an idealized self-image.

I have a weakness as a trader, a big one, that stems at least partly from the need for perfection. I often call myself a "perfectionist" when it comes to playing the market at major turning points. Since 1971, I have only missed two down moves, and I've caught the others exactly at the turn. But when I do miss an exact turn, I have a hard time moving in and trading with the trend, and that is a big weakness. For example, I was looking for an opportunity to short the market in late July 1990. But I didn't have a short position and was taken by surprise when Saddam Hussein attacked Kuwait.

I watched the market plunge, and couldn't bring myself to go short in the middle of the down move. If I had acted, I could have made as much as 10% for my accounts, but I didn't do it . . . I was afraid of selling near the lows instead of the highs, which is what I strive for.

As another example, during 1989, I became totally infuriated with myself for not paying closer attention to some of the commodity markets and missing perfect buying or selling opportunities. Although it is true that as a trader I should have been paying closer attention, as a human being and a businessman during that period, my focus was elsewhere. Instead of just accepting that maybe my focus was a little off, I got furious with myself for not being perfect as a trader.

Both of these examples illustrate how an underlying need for perfection can affect our lives. The need for perfection is such a radical force, that I reserve a more complete discussion of it for the section entitled, "The Tyranny of the Shoulds."

Neurotic ambition—the compulsive drive for external success—is one aspect of the search for glory that is especially pervasive on Wall Street. This is not really surprising, because such ambition is fed by a competitive environment, and Wall Street is very competitive.

The source of neurotic ambition is an attempt to prove and realize exalted attributes. A person lacking real self-confidence seeks high ranking on a comparative scale in an attempt to achieve what psychologist Nathaniel Branden calls, *pseudo self-esteem*. Neurotically ambitious people, believing themselves to be innate geniuses or potentially omnipotent, must produce results in the external world that prove this claim. Such people are driven to be "the best" and to be recognized as such in order to actualize their idealized selves.

But because the ideal striven for is by its very nature imaginary and impossible, the quest is inherently futile. Therefore, people seeking to actualize the idealized self can never stop in their striving. To stop is to admit the falsehood of their view of themselves and of the world. For that reason, one of the hallmarks of neurotic ambition is often genuine talent and ability that is compulsive and driven in nature, and that never results in a sense of personal fulfillment. A man like Ivan Boeskey is a perfect example. It was neurotic ambition, not simply money, that made him resort to buying his success rather than earning it.

There is often a fine line between neurotic ambition and a genuine need and desire to succeed and make money. The difference is manifest in the motivation of the person and the emotional results attained when external goals are actually achieved. For the neurotically ambitious person, life is not experienced as a process, but as a path toward an unreachable future. Activity is the only outlet: "[W]hen they do attain more money, more distinction, more power, they also come to feel the whole impact of the futility of their chase. They do not secure any more peace of mind, inner security, or joy of living. They started out on the chase for the phantom of glory, but their inner distress is still as great as ever."

When I said that neurotic ambition is pervasive on Wall Street, I didn't mean that most people are compulsive neurotics driven only by the desire for external success. However, I do believe that there is a strong element of neurotic ambition in many, many people involved in the financial world, especially among traders.

Anytime we think in terms like, "If I were rich, then I'd be happy," neurotic ambition is at the root. Hidden beneath such statements are false and idealized beliefs about what we would be and what we would do if we had a lot of money. "Burnout" is another symptom of neurotic ambition, especially among formerly successful traders. The inherent futility of achievements driven by the search for glory eventually just wears people out. It is important to understand if and how much we are driven by neurotic ambition; it sabotages the ability to enjoy the *process* of living.

The worst element of the search for glory, in terms of the damage and human suffering it causes, is the need for vindictive triumph. Again, it is an element which is not dominant in most people I have observed, but it is there to some degree in almost everyone. Dr. Horney describes it like this:

> [The need for vindictive triumph] may be closely linked up with the drive for actual achievement and success but, if so, its chief aim is to put others to shame or defeat them through one's very success; or to attain the power, by rising to prominence, to inflict suffering upon them—mostly of a humiliating kind. On the other hand, the drive for excelling may be relegated to fantasy, and the need for a vindictive triumph then manifests itself mainly in often irresistible, mostly unconscious impulses to frustrate, outwit, or defeat others in personal relations. I call this drive "vindictive" because the motivating force stems from impulses to take revenge for humiliations suffered in childhood—impulses which are reinforced during the later neurotic development.

A perfect example of the need for vindictive triumph was concretized in the character of Gordon Gecko in the movie, *Wall Street,* written by Oliver Stone. Gecko rose to a position of wealth and power primarily out of the need for vindictive triumph. His measure of success and failure wasn't even as mundane as how much money he made. Rather, he measured success by his ability to manipulate the markets and to hurt and control people of his choosing in the process. Under the guise of taking an overly (and neurotically) ambitious young trader under his wing, Gecko actively used him to destroy and displace people who represented a challenge to his idealized view of himself.

Before I proceed, I want to state for the record that the movie *Wall Street* made me angry because it painted a false picture of the way Wall Street works. It implied that most people who rise to the top, especially during takeovers, are cold, ruthless, and vindictive. There is an element of the Gordon Gecko type on Wall Street, but it is not predominant and, in general, the people who rise to the top do so on the basis of ability, not parasitism. I heard on a TV program that Oliver Stone's father was a stock broker. I find it interesting that an author should so compellingly berate his father's profession. Maybe vindictive triumph was at the root of his motivation, but who knows?

Nevertheless, Gecko did concretize the vindictive element in many people that gives rise to "political" manipulation and "back stabbing" within many corporate structures. He also concretizes that element in many of us that desires to hurt back when we feel hurt by someone or something.

This need for vindictive triumph is inherently destructive, both to the individual with the need and to the people he deals with. It can be blatant. For example, I worked with a trader whose favorite book was *The Prince,* by Machiavelli; he literally slept with it at his bedside. I watched him cultivate a co-worker's friendship and trust, only to use it to get the co-worker fired. When I challenged him about the ethics of his actions he would say, "If you want to get ahead in this world, you've got to operate this way."

I by no means think that the search for glory is *dominant* in everyone; I do not believe that the world is full of hopeless neurotics. What I do believe is that the elements of the search for glory operate to some degree in almost everyone and are the cause of many unnecessary mistakes, failures, and pains; especially among traders. But they are most often deeply hidden from awareness and mixed with healthy motivations based on positive values. It is important, therefore, to be able to identify motivations born in the search for glory.

COMPULSION AND IMAGINATION

Motivations arising from the search for glory have two characteristics that distinguish them from healthy motivation: their compulsive nature and what Dr. Horney calls their "imaginative character."

Actions are compulsive if the motivation for them arises out of the need to avoid a falsely perceived pain. In Dr. Horney's words:

> When we call a drive compulsive we mean the opposite of spontaneous wishes or strivings. The latter are an expression of the real self; the former are determined by the inner necessities of the neurotic structure. The individual must abide by them regardless of his real wishes, feelings, or interests lest he incur anxiety, feel torn by conflicts, be overwhelmed by guilt feelings, feel rejected by others, etc. In other words, the difference between spontaneous and compulsive is one between "I want" and "I must" in order to avoid some danger.

This observation fits nicely with the model of the brain I presented in Chapters 14 and 15. In spite of our conscious intent, we are often driven by inner motivations which arise from subconsciously held values and disvalues we aren't aware of. *In the search for glory, we are compelled to act in order to keep intact our idealized self-image*. Thus, a key indicator that we are driven by the search for glory is when we act compulsively, with disregard for our best interests.

The compulsive nature of the search for glory can make a person "indifferent to the truth, whether concerning himself, others, or facts." For example, in Chapter 13, when I told the story of John Trader, he said in reference to the movement of bond prices, "It has to go down." What he was really saying is, "I have to be right!" As another example, I doubt that anyone reading this book has not been in or observed an argument that degraded to the point where each person was far more concerned with "being right" than discovering the truth.

Aside from the compulsive aspect, the imaginative nature of the search for glory is worth some mention. Imagination is a wonderful gift. It allows us to project ourselves into the future and mentally rearrange elements of reality for the purposes of setting goals, making them feel viable, and for creative purposes. But when the object of our actions becomes that which is purely imaginary, imagination becomes a destructive agent.

WHEN WISHES BECOME CLAIMS

The idealized self-image and the resulting search for glory are constructs of the imagination, and only through the continued use of imagination can we sustain them. Imagination used this way becomes an agent of self-deception and rationalization. In effect, to the extent that we engage in the search for glory, we are living in fantasy land. When this fantasy land is experienced as reality by the gullible subconscious mind, then *wishes become claims on reality.*

In the last chapter, I mentioned that it is important to pay attention to the way you speak to yourself, and in particular, to the questions you ask. I advised to beware of questions like, "How can this be happening to me? How can he (she) treat me like this? Why is the world so unfair?" Consider the implications of those questions.

When you ask, "How can this be happening to me?" doesn't it imply that you *deserve* more, that somehow providence, fate, or whatever you want to call it, *owes* you something? When you ask, "How can he (she) treat me like this?" doesn't it imply that the other person should *automatically* understand you and *provide* you with what you need? Doesn't it imply that the person *ought* to cater to your needs? When you ask, "Why is the world so unfair?" aren't you saying that the actual world doesn't meet with your definition of what the world *should* be.

I think so, and I think all of these implications point directly to wishes that have become claims on reality. They indicate, at minimum, a subconscious belief that reality should conform to your needs as opposed to your needs being a response to reality, to your goals, and to the facts of your unique experience.

The distinguishing characteristic of all wishes that are claims is that people holding them feel like exceptions to the rules. They are somehow different; they belong to the rare few who understand love, justice, human nature, and on and on and on. They are the traders who understand that trading rules are necessary, but their "superior wisdom" releases them from being bound by the rules. They are the ones who react with a feeling of righteous injustice when the market goes against them.

Rather than taking responsibility for their failures and dealing directly with their problems, people whose needs are claims rely on their constellation of wishes to judge truth and falsehood, right and wrong, friend and foe. Wishes that are totally unrelated to reality become the standard for evaluation in all things.

I said in the introduction to this chapter that the human capacity for self-delusion puzzled me for a long time. Now I realize that self-delusion, while apparent to an outside observer, is so deeply embedded in wishes that are claims—in an imaginary experience driven by the search for glory—that the person caught up in it is *virtually incapable* of distinguishing between a rationalization and the truth. In Dr. Horney's words:

> Neurotic claims . . . are concerned with the world outside himself: he tries to assert the exceptional rights to which his uniqueness entitles him whenever, and in whatever ways, he can. His feeling entitled to be above necessities and laws allows him to live

in a world of fiction as if he were indeed above them. And whenever he falls palpably short of being his idealized self, his claims enable him to make factors outside himself responsible for such "failures."

You can talk to someone caught in this trap about their errors until you are blue in the face, but no matter how rational, calm, and convincing your argument may seem to you, the person simply won't *hear* you; his or her awareness and perception is filtered by a distorted version of reality.

The self-delusion isn't consciously chosen, it is the result of an elaborate and hidden subconscious system developed over a period of many, many years. It is guarded and self-righteously defended as the truth in the people's minds except in moments of despair when reality slaps them in the face. But even then, they often cling to their idealized visions thinking, in effect, "I'm not there yet, but someday, when I achieve perfection, then I'll get my just rewards."

It is a common observation that "you can't change people, they have to change themselves." It is also typical that many people don't change until their whole world comes crashing down on them, until their backs are against the wall and there is no longer anywhere to go but forward. My purpose in discussing all these things is to urge you not to let yourself get caught in the downward spiral of the search for glory. Don't wait until your back is against the wall.

Desperation doesn't have to precede change. Start *now* and look for some of the symptoms I've described. It all comes down to learning to own your problems and take responsibility for them.

Making mistakes is part of the business of trading. In those moments when reality slaps you in the face, try to ask yourself what *you* have done to make them happen; not in context of self-reproach or punishment, but in the context of the *opportunity for positive change and growth.*

THE TYRANNY OF THE SHOULDS

From what I've said so far, it is possible to conclude that both self-idealization and its result, the search for glory, would create an arrogant egomaniac, but that is because I only cursorily discussed the need for perfection. Assuming that, to some degree, people create a self-image of a supreme being, they are then subconsciously "forced" to attempt to live up to that image, however unreal:

> He holds before his soul his image of perfection and unconsciously tells himself: "Forget about the disgraceful creature you actually *are*; this is how you *should* be; and to be this idealized self is all that matters. You should be able to endure everything, to understand everything, to like everybody, to be always productive"—to mention only a few of these inner dictates. Since they are inexorable, I call them "the tyranny of the should."

Beneath the surface of the need for perfection is a fundamental sense of discontent and lack of self-esteem. The quest to become perfect is a shield that guards against awareness of this fundamental discontent. As long as people hold up this image of perfection and strive for it, they feel worthy, even superior. They are able to think of themselves as some of the rare few who are willing to make the necessary sacrifices to actualize their "true" potential. The happiness that they see in others is written off as "superficial" or "phony." Only they, and a few others like them, such as their "ideal woman" or "ideal man" (whom they have never met, but long for), understand the glory that is attainable if you work hard enough at it. But, at root, the lack of real self-esteem is there, and it will surface in various ways.

Of all the drives in the search for glory, I believe that the need for perfection is the most pervasive, and it shows itself in the tyranny of the should. In place of genuine, self-chosen values and strivings, the person driven by the need for perfection subconsciously adopts a rigid system of inner dictates that "comprise all that . . . [the person] should be able to do, to be, to feel, to know—and taboos on how and what he should not be."

Once again, there is often a fine line between this rigid system and a genuinely held hierarchy of values and disvalues which everyone needs to guide their actions. It is therefore very important to understand several of the key differences between genuine, life-serving values and beliefs and the shoulds or inner dictates associated with the need for perfection.

First, the shoulds or inner dictates are adopted with disregard for their feasibility. People come to believe that they *should* simultaneously be perfect traders, spouses, parents, musicians, and athletes. They *should* be able to solve every problem of their own, or others, on their own and in short order.

Second, the shoulds are experienced with disregard for the conditions under which they could be fulfilled. Thus, a trader may understand that he or she must master market knowledge before being able to trade effectively but will feel that reading one or two books should provide mastery. He or she will ignore the fact that becoming proficient as a trader requires a period of education and daily drilling, just like any other acquired skill. Working within this context, the trader will invariably make mistakes that could have been avoided through more practice and learning. But instead of owning up to the fact of not knowing enough, he or she will rationalize away the error and find some outside factor to blame.

Third, the inner dictates operate with "disregard for the person's own psychic condition—for what he can feel or do as he is at present." A person should *never* feel hurt, *never* feel angry, *never* lack the desire to work, and so on. "He simply issues an absolute order to himself, denying or overriding the fact of his existing vulnerabilities."

Fourth, the shoulds take on the quality of abstraction—they lack the genuine and spontaneous character of true moral ideals. What I mean by this is that the shoulds are experienced as ends in themselves instead of the means to ends.

In the last chapter, I spoke of the limiting values and beliefs people place on themselves. Do you see the connection between the tyranny of the shoulds and these limiting associations? Once again, the tyranny of the shoulds shows up in how you talk to yourself and to others.

If you say, "I *can* not," you are placing an immediate and absolute limiting value on yourself.

If you say, "I *have* to," you are displacing the motivation to act from your own ends and purposes to something outside of yourself, and the result will be that you do not experience the action as your own.

If you say, "I *must* be able to," you are setting yourself up to avoid the opportunity to learn from your mistakes — you will be too busy condemning yourself for failure to be able to look at your errors objectively and positively.

People seeking mastery attempt to identify themselves totally with their idealized image of themselves and with their inner dictates:

> [C]onsciously or subconsciously, [he tends] to be proud of his standards. He does not question their validity and tries to actualize them in one way or other. He may try to measure up to them in his actual behavior. He should be all things to all people; he should know everything better than anybody else; he should never err; he should never fail in anything he attempts to do. . . . And, in his mind, he does measure up to his supreme standards. His arrogance may be so great that he does not even consider the possibility of failure, and discards it if it occurs. His arbitrary rightness is so rigid that in his own mind he simply never errs.

Driven by their particular set of shoulds, people seeking mastery through adherence to the shoulds must evade reality on a grand scale. Such people appear to thrive on admiration, respect, and blind obedience. They may be generous and charming, especially to newcomers in their lives who offer them further sources of admiration. They may pride themselves on sexual conquests, on their circle of influential friends, on their unique material acquisitions, and so forth.

For them, there is little distinction between what they are, and what they should be. But no matter what they do, they are always faced with the potential knowledge that their shoulds are, in fact, unattainable.

Because the need for perfection is so great in such individuals, they are often driven to tangible levels of achievement and ability. I don't want to mention names, but I have known several traders of this type. Without exception, they have been good at what they do, very generous with their knowledge, and charming and interesting to talk to. But also without exception, they make themselves immune to debate and disagreement in areas important to them.

Generally, when a trade goes against them, they blame it on the "stupidity" of everyone else in the market. They make excuses like, "I'm just one step ahead of everyone else." On the rare occasion that they admit to making mistakes, *their* reason for making the mistake is the only plausible one in their minds. One of the things I notice most about them is their stubbornness not only about trading, but also about politics, economics, the nature of relationships, or whatever.

I believe this is an indication of the degree of resistance they have built into their subconscious with regard to the healthy process of learning and growing. Because their main focus is self-glorification, they are unable to challenge themselves beyond a certain level without putting the whole delusion at peril, so stubbornness is the result.

People who attach themselves to an imaginary and idealized love as the solution to their anxiety are quite different. Where people seeking mastery do their utmost to adhere to the shoulds, people seeking "love" as their total solution feel totally inadequate to the task of living up to their set of inner dictates. In effect, they think that if they attain their ideal love, it will unleash the powers within them and fill them with the power to live up to the dictates of their inner tyranny.

Without going into too much detail, these types generally attach themselves to someone, usually a person seeking mastery, with complete and unquestioned devotion. They become dependents, regardless of the value of the person they are involved with. They also make lousy traders because they lack the focus, self-confidence, and independence of judgement required to play the game and stick to the rules.

People who value "freedom" are prone to rebel against their inner dictates:

> Because of the very importance which freedom—or his version of it—has for him, he is hypersensitive to any coercion. He may rebel in a somewhat passive way. Then everything that he feels he should do, whether it concerns a piece of work or reading a book or having sexual relations with his wife, turns—in his mind—into a coercion, arouses conscious or unconscious resentment, and in consequence makes him listless. If what is to be done is done at all, it is done under the strain produced by the inner resistance.
>
> He may rebel against his shoulds in a more active way. He may try to throw them all overboard, and sometimes go to the opposite extreme by insisting upon doing only what he pleases, when he pleases. The rebellion may take violent forms, and then often is a rebellion of despair. If he can't be the ultimate of piety, chastity, sincerity, then he will be thoroughly "bad," be promiscuous, tell lies, affront others.

Regardless of what form the rebellion takes, the pursuit of this kind of "freedom" makes it virtually impossible to be a successful trader because even the mention of the word "discipline" is perceived as coercion. In addition, anyone who is rebellious in this manner will be very reluctant to form a plan.

The traders I know and have known with this kind of personality are generally erratic. They may alternate between sticking to the rules and trading well and then take a position way too large relative to their account balances and lose three weeks of profits in a single trade. It is as if when they succeed by sticking to the rules, they are compelled to sabotage the results and lose their profits in an act of defiance.

In any of its many forms, the tyranny of the shoulds is a terrible, limiting force. The strength of moral imperative drives the subject of the tyranny to sail ahead directed by a phantom: neurotic pride.

REAL PRIDE/FALSE PRIDE

Genuine pride is the feeling obtained from the attainment of values established in the process of self-actualization. Neurotic pride is the feeling attained by the *apparent* attainment of one or more of the "inner dictates."

Neurotic pride is the source of motivation that keeps people from changing, that makes them stay miserable, and that, ironically, gives them the strength to carry on. It is the result of an attempt to substitute the achievement of the "shoulds" for the attainment or maintenance of genuine values. It is a sense of specialness gained by focusing and acting on the idealized self and imagined potentials.

But the core self never goes away. It is there to remind us that a life chasing a carrot on a stick leads nowhere. If we are to get the results we want in life, we have to strive to achieve values and goals based on a positive, realistic view of ourselves and our relationship to the world. We need to learn to listen to ourselves and be able to grasp those fleeting moments when that inner self speaks out saying, "something is wrong here."

If you are unable to stay motivated in your attempts to achieve your goals; if you find yourself feeling that life owes you special treatment; if you feel unrewarded in the attainment of a goal; if you feel alienated from yourself; if you recognize some of what I've talked about in this chapter as applying to you; then it is time to challenge yourself at a very fundamental level and question your deepest motivations. If you do, you will probably find the false pride system in operation.

You can conquer false pride. The first and hardest step is realizing that it is there. Challenging false pride, casting aside the idealized self-image, acting according to genuine values instead of according to the tyranny of the shoulds is something that is emotionally painful. The beliefs and associations you have formed by living within the search for glory feel very vital and important to you, and they may be very difficult to cast off.

Two million years ago, when our ancestors faced danger, they had to be right, or they would die. By contrast, making mistakes is an unavoidable part of trading. It is the unwillingness to admit making mistakes, born of false pride, that stops most traders from succeeding. It is their underlying psychology that undermines their ability to execute according to the rules.

As a trader, and as a person, you have a choice. You can let emotions born of the search for glory determine your behavior while ignoring the facts; or you can recognize that you have to learn in order to grow, and with learning come mistakes. You are going to make mistakes—you're going to win sometimes, and you're going to lose sometimes, too. When you make a mistake, you can grow by analyzing the mistake and changing your behavior according to what you learn. This process leads to constant improvement of your skills and to a positive estimate of yourself. Practiced consistently, it will lead to self-esteem, not to mention more, and more consistent, profits from trading.

Remember that, no matter how vital the pain associated with challenging false pride and the search for glory may seem, if you don't challenge them, they will rob you of your ability to experience the intense pleasure and serenity that accompany the process of true growth and achievement. By using the knowledge in this and previous chapters, as well as many other resources available, you can conquer false pride and discover the real sense of pride that comes with "actualizing your given potentialities."

17

Finding Your Freedom

I said in the very first part of the book that freedom means a lot more to me than political liberty, that it means maintaining a financial independence so secure that nothing short of outright robbery or my own imprudence can take it away. Well, it means even more than that. It means being able to experience life with an unbridled capacity for joy, regardless of your financial condition. Freedom is just easier to find when you don't have to worry about yourself or your family surviving if disaster strikes.

When I look at my youngest daughter, Janene, a smile almost always comes to my face. She embodies a rapturous sense of life that few people ever attain, and I hope that she is able to maintain it throughout her adulthood. At age 12, she wrote a poem, and in it was a line which I believe captures the essence of the spirit required to maintain that sense of life. She wrote:

> Don't look at the bad when there are so many good things to see,
> The world doesn't have to be perfect to be loved by me.

Ayn Rand said virtually the same thing in a more sophisticated way when she wrote, "Values, not disasters, are the goal, the first concern, and the motive power of life." What Janene's poem and Rand's quote both imply is that while people and the world *are* imperfect, while pain, suffering, and disasters *do* exist, they do not have to be and *should not be* the focal point of living.

Too often, for too many people, disasters and pain are the focus of living. That doesn't mean that people dwell on their pain and suffering. Some do, but usually when people focus on pain, they do it by default. Rather than spending their time and energies on the pursuit of values, they spend it trying to avoid pain. And *that* makes pain the focal point of life.

You can't pursue a negative. By definition, if avoiding pain is the focus of life, positive action is limited. If you allow pain to become the dominant force in life, you sabotage your ability to think, to grow, to produce. You may either become trapped in a dull, apparently secure routine or engage in the search for glory, but either way, you can't experience the process of living with the passion and spontaneity that you are capable of.

Life involves risks. With every action and every choice you make, the chance of mistakes, errors, and failure is there. Perhaps I am more aware of this than others because I have made my living by taking objectively controlled risks in the markets. If you don't recognize risk, failure, and pain as part of the process in trading, then forget it—you'll either lose money or be miserable in the process of making it.

The essence of maintaining your mental well-being as a trader is taking a position in which you feel confident and sure, while always knowing that you may not be rewarded for your work, your thoughts, and your willingness to take a risk. Even more important, when you don't win, you have to be willing to pick up and do it again. *You have to be open to the pain that so often accompanies honesty and growth*.

The same is true of every aspect of living.

You know, people throw around the term "love" all the time, and I am hesitant to use it in this context. But virtually every act in life should be an act of love, the essence of which is *giving of yourself*. Let me make it very clear that I am not speaking about a selfless or sacrificial giving, not giving while expecting nothing in return (I think that is impossible) but *giving with the knowledge that you may not get anything in return and, further, being able to pick up when you are unrewarded and give again*.

I'm speaking of giving as in presenting or bestowing. To present yourself to the world; to offer it your products and services in trade; to bestow upon it your achievements, your productive capacity, your energy, your thoughts and opinions: all of these are the things that make life rich, both spiritually and materially.

By giving in this way, the returns come back manifold—both financially and in terms of the happiness you experience. It's not "give and take"; it's not "give and thou shalt receive"; it's "give and receive in trade."

You can give to yourself by using your mind—dedicating yourself to learning and growth—and get your return by having new opportunities and experience available. Through your own actions and efforts you *bestow* upon yourself new options and alternatives. You can give to yourself by taking risks in the market, and receive the financial benefits. You can give to others simply by opening yourself up and letting them see the real person, by dropping the self-protective shields designed to prevent people from hurting or rejecting you, and get your return from those special friends who make you feel seen and understood, who act as the mirrors for your soul.

Opening yourself up to the risks of life may be frightening, but the fact is, there really is no alternative. You will suffer pain one way or the other.

There is no freedom from risk. There is no freedom from fear. There is no freedom from pain. There is no freedom from the possibility of failure. *But there is freedom in the acceptance of all of these as part of life, and moreover, as the least important part of life*.

That doesn't mean that risk, fear, pain, and failure are unimportant. I spent the entire first part of the book demonstrating ways to limit risk in the markets and put as many of the odds in your favor as possible. I spent a substantial amount of this second part talking about how to manage the desire to avoid pain and use it in your favor. Yes, they are important, but it is a matter of focus—focus and integration.

Finding your freedom doesn't mean being able to do what you want, when and how you want to, with total disregard for the consequences. It doesn't mean living a life free of pain, mistakes, and failure. Nor does it mean "swallowing your emotions" and forging ahead in spite of them.

Finding your freedom means attaining the ability to give freely to yourself, to your work, and to others. It means acquiring the ability to establish true motivation, to take control of your faculties such that the need to avoid pain and the desire to attain pleasure are directed at the same end. It means striving for integrity of thought, actions, and emotions. But above all, it means learning to experience joy in *the process* of living.

I hope that this book helps you in the process of finding your freedom.

Good luck, and good trading!

Notes

Preface

1. I did manage a fund in the mid-1980s, Victory Partners, that lost money, but under conditions that were rather extraordinary. For a description of what happened, see the introduction to Part I.

2. This statement is not meant to imply that analyzing securities through examination of corporate financial statements is worthless; far from it. Any information that can be acquired which supplements the knowledge to be discussed in this book can only increase the odds of making good decisions, of being right more often than not.

Chapter 1

1. John Scarne, *Scarne On Cards* (New York: Crown Publishers, 1969).

Chapter 2

1. Ayn Rand, "Credibility and Polarization," *The Ayn Rand Letter*, vol. I (1), 3.

2. The term "false pride" is taken from the work of the psychologist Dr. Karen Horney and is discussed later in the book.

3. By growth I mean a continuing accumulation of wealth.

Chapter 3

1. William Peter Hamilton was Editor of the *Wall Street Journal* from 1908 to 1929.

Chapter 4

1. *A Proven Method of Economic Forecasting*, an unpublished study by Victor Sperandeo and Sandra Kunze, Copyright 1987 by Victor Sperandeo and Sandra Kunze.

2. Unless otherwise specified, all of the quoted information in this chapter is extracted from *The Dow Theory*, Robert Rhea (Barron's, 1932).

3. *The Wall Street Journal*, July 20, 1901.

4. For further discussion on the subjectivity of the markets, see Chapter 9.

5. To the best of my knowledge, the basis of the terms bull and bear market is that the bull kills while lifting up with his horns, while the bear kills by driving his adversary down with his paw—the bull kills up, the bear kills down.

6. Victor Sperandeo, *Statistical Characterization of Stock Market Movements*, an unpublished analysis of stock market movements from 1897 to date. All data not attributed to others are a result of this study.

7. For those interested in the details of this statistical approach to risk assessment, a complete exposition will be included in my forthcoming book for the market professional.

8. In the past, our government's policy has been to inflate the country into temporary prosperity. But as the economy grows and the effects of a ballooning money supply become factored into prices, there is a net decline in real earnings and savings. People begin to realize that inflation is nothing but a hidden tax on their future, and it becomes a prime concern to the public and therefore to politicians. Then the Fed intervenes to curtail credit availability, and the false economy of credit expansions comes crashing down like a house of cards. Now our wise government is using debt expansion instead of inflation to maintain an unsustainable level of consumption against future earnings. The net long-term result will be the same, once the camouflage is removed.

9. For example, Dow Theory never gave a clearly defined buy signal after the crash of 1987. People were so badly hurt by the swiftness of the move that many did not want to reinvest. It was only by considering fundamental economic factors that one could justify reentering the market on a long-term basis.

Chapter 5

1. When applied to the averages, all related averages must confirm the trend. If they do not, then a divergence exists—evidence of a possible change of trend.

Chapter 6

1. Robert D. Edwards and John Magee, *Technical Analysis of Stock Trends* (Massachusetts: John Magee Inc., 1966) (fifth edition), p. 5.

2. For an excellent description of the ever present "they," see G. C. Seldens, *Psychology of the Stock Market* (Vermont: Fraser Publishing Company, 1965).

3. For those of you unfamiliar with this terminology, the "bid" on a financial instrument is the price at which someone on the floor has said he will buy the instrument. The "offer" is the price at which someone has said he would sell the stock.

4. An "upstairs" trader is one who continually monitors and trades from a remote location.

5. William J. O'Neil, "Program Trading vs. Investing in a New U.S.," *Investor's Daily,* 10/17/89, p. 1.

6. A contact on the floor of the exchange helps, too!

Chapter 7

1. This information is readily available in the financial section of good bookstores. A good starting point is to buy and study a Series 7 primer, which will give you an excellent broad overview of the mechanics of the marketplace. Your broker can fill you in on the different margin requirements.

2. I say the "equivalent of" because Dow Theory deals only with the change of the primary trend and secondary corrections in the stock market averages, whereas this definition applies to all markets.

3. On the floors of the exchanges, monitors watch the activity on the floor, and each time the instrument is traded at a new price, they enter the new price, which is then transmitted to the monitor screens on the floor and through wire services around the world. In a "fast market," the activity is so rapid that the monitors cannot keep up with the changing prices, and prints do not reflect price changes with absolute accuracy.

Chapter 8

1. I feel compelled to say that someone who really knows Dow Theory very seldom waits until confirmation dates to take a position. So while Gordon chose the only objective criterion possible to compare Dow Theory to the moving averages, it is my absolute conviction that, day in and day out, Dow Theory is a much stronger predictor of market price movements than is the 200-day moving average.

2. William Gordon, *The Stock Market Indicators* (New York: Investors' Press Inc., 1968), pp. 28–39.

3. This is a philosophy which states that the only measure of truth is that which gets the desired result. In other words, the ends justify the means.

4. See *New York Stock Exchange Daily Graphs*, William O'Neil & Co., Inc., P. O. Box 24933, Los Angeles, California 90024.

5. I learned about this oscillator from Justin Mamis in his publication, *The Professional Tape Reader*, in January 1975, currently published by Stan Weinstein.

6. Gordon A. Holmes, *Capital Appreciation in the Stock Market* (New York: Parket Publishing Company Inc.), p. 32.

7. Ibid., pp. 27–40.

Chapter 9

1. A "bubble" is an artful but unsound scheme to raise money which appeals to a desire to get something for nothing. Typical examples are chain letters, pyramid schemes, and deficit financing of government expenditures.

2. The Modern Austrian School of Economics was founded by Ludwig von Mises (1881–1973), who fled Vienna for Geneva in 1934, fearing Austrian capitulation to the Nazis. He came to the United States in 1940 and lived here for the rest of his life. Nobel prize winner Frederick Hayek was one of his many pupils who has had an impact on modern economic thought. The Austrian School advocates pure and unfettered *laissez-faire* capitalism.

3. Ludwig von Mises, *Human Action* (Third revised edition, Yale University Press, 1963), p. 10. I highly recommend that anyone interested in learning more about the Austrian School read Thomas C. Taylor's *An Introduction to Austrian Economics* (Auburn, Alabama: Ludwig von Mises Institute, 1980). For further information contact The Ludwig von Mises Institute for Austrian Economics Inc., Auburn University, Auburn, Alabama 36849.

4. von Mises, p. 92.

5. *The Random House Dictionary of the English Language*, College Edition, 1969.

6. The subjective nature of value, along with the fact that *differences* in perception of value drive the trade process, seems like a simple concept but was in fact introduced and formalized by von Mises. Adam Smith and the other classical economists thought that trade must be of *equal* value.

7. Fiduciary media consist of the quantity of bank notes or money certificates issued in excess of hard currency deposits. This is artificially *created* money.

8. There has never to my knowledge, however, been a totally unregulated banking market.

9. Your checking account is a *demand deposit*, which means that at any time you can go and demand actual currency. Our currency consists of Federal Reserve notes. But think about it—a note is an IOU backed by collateral. There is nothing behind our so-called "notes." This is why John Exter, former Vice-President in Charge of Foreign Operations at the New York Federal Reserve Bank calls them "IOU Nothings"!

10. The way the reserve system works and how money is created within the Federal Reserve system are discussed in detail in the next chapter.

11. In May 1989 in China we saw a perfect example, as the guardians of communist ideology flagrantly rewrote history in spite of eyewitness accounts and videotape records of the slaughter in Beijing.

12. I am deeply indebted to the late novelist and philosopher, Ayn Rand, who expounded on these views with greater clarity and precision than anyone before or since. A partial list of her works is included in the Bibliography.

13. Throughout this book, unless otherwise stated, when I use the term "inflation" I mean an increase in the money supply, *not* rising prices. Rising prices are a *result* of an increase in the money supply relative to other goods and services on the market. In other words, inflation can lead to, but does not always cause, rising prices.

14. Ayn Rand, "Capitalism: The Unknown Ideal," *What Is Capitalism?* (Signet, First Printing), p. 17.

15. For a complete discussion of originary interest, see *Human Action*, pp. 524–537.

16. Capital goods can be either goods used in the intermediate stages of production or goods ready for consumption used for sustenance during the pursuit of longer-range and more profitable goals. Both are derived from the application of savings.

17. The concept of time-preference as the driving force behind credit is distinctly that of the Modern Austrian School of Economics and was best developed by Ludwig von Mises in his major work, *Human Action*.

18. There are exceptions to this statement. Any government program which operates on a fee for service basis, such as the Post Office, may operate at a profit and generate wealth. In addition, while you can't eat tanks, the profits generated from spin-offs of defense spending generate wealth. But overall, government consumes far more wealth than the little bit that it produces, and it produces far more inefficiently than the free market.

Chapter 10

1. Ludwig von Mises, *Human Action* (Chicago: Contemporary Books, Inc., 1966), p. 572.

2. All the information in the following story is taken from *Extraordinary Popular Delusions and Madness of Crowds*, by Charles Mackay (New York: Harmony Books, 1980), pp. 1–45.

3. The livre was France's monetary unit at the time, originally equivalent to a pound of silver. The currency had been devalued, however, through recoinage and deficit financing of government expenditures, so that the exchange ratio with the British pound sterling at the time was approximately 24 to 1.

4. Louis XIV's successor to the throne was seven years old, and the Duke of Orleans assumed the regency.

5. The concept of originary interest may at first seem a little bit obtuse. It is, however, an essential economic principle which must be understood in order to understand the business cycle. Basically, originary interest is the subjective foundation for the existence of real interest. It exists in the minds of all individuals and determines their choice whether to consume the product of their labors now or save it for later consumption.

6. A study of the current savings and loan crisis would bring these points to bear in dramatic form.

7. Virtually all banking systems in the world are now fractional reserve systems. I will discuss the nature of fractional reserve systems in detail below.

8. *The Federal Reserve System: Purposes and Functions*, fifth edition, published by the Federal Reserve Board, 1965, p. 1.

9. Ibid., p. 4.

10. Depository institutions are defined as commercial and savings banks, savings and loan associations, credit unions, U.S. agencies and branches of foreign banks, and Edge act and agreement corporations.

11. In addition to loaning reserves to lending institutions on a short-term basis, the Fed can also loan money through the discount window to individuals or corporations under certain conditions. These kinds of loans are what is meant by extended credit.

12. The adjusted monetary base is a number calculated by the Federal Reserve Bank of St. Louis consisting of the total of bank reserves plus currency, adjusted for reserve requirement changes and seasonal factors. It is designed to reflect all Fed actions which affect M1, a monetary aggregate number consisting of currency, traveler's checks, demand deposits, and other deposits with unlimited checking privileges such as NOWs and Super NOWs.

13. All data in this paragraph are taken from *Grant's Interest Rate Observer*, April 27, 1990, Vol 8, No. 8, p. 5. For further information on this publication, write to 233 Broadway, New York, NY 10279, or call (212) 608-7994.

14. Ibid., pp. 2, 5.

Chapter 11

1. Note that, in this case, condition 2 was met before the break of the trend line. There is no rule which says the 1-2-3 criterion for a change of trend has to occur.

Chapter 12

1. Henry Clasing, *The Secrets of a Professional Futures Trader* (Brightwaters, NY: Windsor Books, 1987) p. 15.

Part II Intro

1. Paraphrased from a conversation with Jim Brown, a broker and asset manager with Rotan Mosle Inc. in San Antonio, Texas.
2. I use the term "man" here in the general sense, to include both men and women. Maybe someone needs to invent a new noun and and pronoun for human beings as a species, so guys like me can write accurately without offending anyone.
3. Dr. Karen Horney, *Neurosis and Human Growth* (New York: W. W. Norton & Company, 1950).

Chapter 13

1. Bond futures prices move in $\frac{1}{32}$ increments, so a tick is $\frac{1}{32}$ of a point, or $31.25 per contract per tick.
2. W. Gaylin, *The Rage Within* (New York: Simon and Schuster, 1984), pp. 17–18.
3. Ibid., p. 23.
4. Nathaniel Branden, *The Psychology of Self-Esteem* (New York: Bantam Books, 15th edition, 1969) p. 69.
5. Ayn Rand, *The Virtue of Selfishness* (New York: New American Library, 1964), p. 28.
6. Ibid., p. 5.
7. By the subconscious, I mean that part of the mind not immediately available to conscious awareness, as opposed to the "unconscious" mind postulated by Freud and others, which has an identity unto itself.
8. Ayn Rand, op. cit., p. 27.
9. The concept of false pride will be discussed in detail in the next chapter.

Chapter 14

1. Ayn Rand, *The Ayn Rand Lexicon* (New York: Meridian, 1988) p. 254.
2. For more information on this subject see, *The Introduction to Objectivist Epistemology*.

Chapter 15

1. Anthony Robbins, *Personal Power*.
2. Dr. Van K. Tharp, "The Psychology of Trading," from *Market Wizards*, by Jack D. Scwager (New York: NYIF Corp, 1989), p. 424.
3. Shakespeare, Macbeth.
4. Anthony Robbins, *Unlimited Power* (New York: Ballantine Books, 1987), p. 321.
5. Ibid., pp. 222–223.

Chapter 16

1. Dr. Karen Horney, *Neurosis and Human Growth* (New York, W. W. Norton & Company, Inc., 1950). Unless otherwise indicated, all quotes come from this book.

2. According to Dr. Horney, basic anxiety is a deeply rooted "feeling of being isolated and helpless in a world conceived as potentially hostile."

Glossary of Terms

A

advance/decline line   A measure of market movements composed of the cumulative total of differences between advancing issues (stocks whose prices are up on the day) and declining issues (stocks whose prices are down on the day) of securities prices.

alpha   A measure of stock quality that compares the performance of an individual stock relative to the market. An Alpha value of 1 means that the stock has, on average, outperformed the market by 1% per month, so if the market moves up 10% in six months, the stock should move up 16%.

arbitrage   **1.** Buying and selling, at temporarily different prices, two securities that are exchangeable for each other, as under a merger plan. **2.** Buying a security or commodity in one market and simultaneously selling the same or a related instrument in another market in an attempt to profit from short-term price differentials.

ask   The lowest currently stated acceptable price for a specific stock or commodity on the floor of an exchange. Also called the offer.

at-the-money   An option in which the price of the underlying instrument is exactly the same as the strike price of the option. (See *in-the-money, option, out-of-the-money*.)

B

bear   Anyone who takes a pessimistic view of the forthcoming long-term trend in a market; that is, one who thinks that a market is or soon will be in a long-term downtrend.

bear market   A long-term downtrend (a downtrend lasting months to years) in any market, especially in the stock market, characterized by lower intermediate lows (those established in a time frame of weeks to months) interrupted by lower intermediate highs.

beta   A measure of a stock's volatility. A stock with a Beta of 2 should be up 20% when the market is up 10%, or down 20% if the market is down 10%.

bid   An indication by an investor, trader, or dealer of the willingness to buy a security or a commodity at a certain price; also, the highest current such indication for a specific stock or commodity at any point in time.

bid and ask   The current quote or quotation on the floor of any market exchange for a specific stock or commodity. The bid is the highest current price at which anyone is willing to pay at a given moment of time. The ask is the lowest current price anyone is willing to sell the security or commodity at a given moment in time. Also called the bid and offer.

block   A large amount of a specific stock, generally 10,000 or more shares.

blue chip   The common stock of an established industry leader, such as IBM, whose products or services are widely known and which has a solid record of performance in both good and bad economic environments.

bond yields   The income available from a bond expressed as a percentage of the purchase price.

bottom   The lowest price within a market movement that occurs before the trend changes and starts moving up.

book value   A measure of the net worth of a share of common stock. It is calculated by subtracting the intangible assets and preferred stock from the total net worth of the company, and then dividing by the number of common shares outstanding.

break   A downward price movement that goes below previous important lows and continues to carry downward. The term usually applies to dramatic downward movements after the market has been moving horizontally in a "line" for a sustained period.

breakout   An upward price movement that goes above previous important highs and continues to carry upward. The term usually refers to dramatic upward movements occurring after the market has been moving horizontally in a "line" over a sustained period.

brokerage   The same as commission the fee charged by a registered securities or commodities broker for executing a customer's order.

bull   Anyone who takes an optimistic view of the forthcoming long-term trend in a market; that is, one who thinks that a market is or soon will be in a long-term uptrend.

bull market   A long-term (months to years) price movement in any market characterized by a series of higher intermediate highs (those established within weeks to months) interrupted by higher consecutive intermediate lows.

C

call   An option contract giving the owner the right to buy a specified amount of a stock bond, commodity, etc. at a stated price within a specified time period.

capital   Accumulated money or goods used to produce income.

car   Market slang for one contract in the commodities markets. (See *contract*)

commission   The fee charged to a client by a registered broker for the execution of an order to buy or sell a stock, bond, commodity, option, etc.

commodity   Any bulk good traded on an exchange or in the cash (spot) market, such as metals, grains, meats, and so on. Often, the term commodities is used to refer to any of the futures that may include stock index futures.

consolidation   A period of trading in a security or commodity market characterized by a narrow price range over a sustained period. In technical terms, consolidation periods usually indicate periods of extended large-scale acquisition or liquidation of a financial instrument, and therefore often precede strong price movements.

contract   One unit of trading within the commodities markets; it varies in size from market to market.

correction   An intermediate market price movement (one that lasts from weeks to months) that moves contrary to the long-term trend, or primary movement (the movement that lasts from months to years). Usually, corrections retrace between one-third to two-thirds of the primary movement before reversing.

D

day trade   Any trade that is made within the same market within the same day.

delivery   The change in ownership or control of the actual commodity in exchange for cash in the settlement of a futures contract.

demand   The desire and willingness to pay or trade for a good or service within the market.

dividend   A distribution of the earnings of a corporation, usually in the form of cash, stock, or property. The board of directors declares all dividends.

discount rate   The interest rate charged to member banks that borrow directly from the nine Federal Reserve District Banks.

Dow Jones Industrial Average   The most widely used indicator of market activity, composed of an average of 30 large issues within the industrial sector of the economy.

Dow Jones Transportation Average   The most widely reported indicator of stock activity in the transportation sector of the economy, composed of an average of 20 large issues.

E

earnings   The net income available for common stock divided by the number of shares outstanding, reported quarterly by most companies (also earnings-per-share).

efficient markets theory   A view of the markets that states that a market may reflect all relevant information known about the market. Consequently, adjustment to new information is virtually instantaneous.

exchange   Organized exchanges where commodities, futures, and securities transactions are carried out by member traders and brokers.

exercise   To execute the rights granted in an options or warrant contract. For example, an owner of a call contract on common stock exercises a call by executing the right to buy 100 shares of the stock at the strike price stated in the contract.

expiration date   The date specified in an option contract on which the option becomes worthless and the owner no longer has the rights specified in the contract.

F

Federal Reserve Board   A seven-member group, appointed by the President, responsible for setting the monetary policy of the United States and for overseeing the operation of the Federal Reserve System.

Federal Reserve System (The Fed)   The central bank system of the United States, composed chiefly of the Federal Reserve Board, the Federal Open Market Committee, the nine Reserve District Banks, and member banks. Its chief responsibility is to regulate the flow of money and credit.

Federal Funds   Cash reserves of banks and certain other institutions above and beyond those needed as reserve requirements. These funds are available to other banks as loans to meet reserve requirements.

Federal Funds Rate (fed funds rate)   The interest charged by one institution lending federal funds to another. This rate is largely controlled by short-term open market operations by the Fed.

firm quote   The actual price at which a financial instrument (100 shares of stock, 5 bonds, and so on) may be bought or sold.

floor trader   A member of an exchange who enters transactions for his or her own account from the floor of the exchange; synonymous with *local*.

FOMC   (The Federal Open Market Committee) A committee within the Federal Reserve System comprised of the seven members of the Federal Reserve Board, the President of the Federal Reserve Bank of New York, and four of the eight other district bank presidents, who serve on a rotating basis. The main purpose of the committee is to make decisions regarding open market operations.

free reserves   A measure of reserves held within the entire Federal Reserve System above and beyond required reserves. It is used as an indicator of the potential credit availability within the Federal Reserve System.

fundamental analysis   A method securities analysis that employs study of the overall economy, industry conditions, and the financial condition and management of a particular company in an effort to evaluate the intrinsic value of a specific stock.

futures   Contracts standardized by an exchange for the purchase or sale of a commodity at a future date.

futures contract   A standardized, exchange-traded contract to make or take delivery of a particular type and grade of commodity at an agreed, upon place and point in the future. Futures contracts are transferable between parties.

G

glamour stock   A favored, highly traded stock, usually of an established company that has performed well and paid dividends in good times and bad.

growth stock   A relatively speculative stock, usually one of a relatively new company that is expected to grow at a fast rate. Consequently, the stocks usually sell at high price/earnings ratios while paying low dividends.

H

hedge   Investing to reduce the risk of a position in a security or commodity, normally by taking the reverse position in a related security. For example, owning 10,000 shares of XYZ at 100 may be hedged by owning 100 puts of XYZ with a strike price at 98.

high   The highest price a security or commodity reaches within a specified time period.

I

inflation   An increase in the supply of money. When the increase in the supply of money outstrips the increase in the supply of goods and services, the result is a general rise in the level of prices.

insider   Anyone who has information not available to the public that may affect the future price of a stock.

in-the-money   An option that has intrinsic value. For a call, the option is in-the-money if the current market price of the underlying instrument is above the strike price stated in the call contract. For a put, the option is in-the-money if the current market price is below the strike price stated in the put contract.

index futures   Futures contracts traded on the basis of an underlying cash index or average. Unlike commodities futures, there is no tangible asset traded for delivery other than the cash value of the futures contract at the time of expiration.

intermediate-term trend   The price trend in any market lasting from weeks to months.

investor   One who buys and holds securities for a long-term period (months to years), usually for the purpose of obtaining income or value appreciation.

J

junk bonds   A general term for bonds issued by corporations during a leveraged buyout (LBO) for the purpose of raising capital to buy a controlling position of the company's shares. The differences between junk bonds and other corporate bonds are the size of the bond issue and the purpose for which the bonds are issued. They earned the nebulous title "junk" because so many of the bond issues depreciated dramatically in market value after the issue because the market value of the underlying assets securing them depreciated. There was no other collateral.

L

leverage   The use of borrowed capital to increase the potential net return in trading or investment.

leveraged buyout   The acquisition of a controlling interest in the stock of a company by borrowing the money from the public or from private sources in which capital is raised by the issue and sale of bonds (junk bonds) secured by the assets of the company.

liabilities   Debts or legal obligations to pay owned by a person or legal entity.

line   A technical term used to describe price movements within a market that stay within a narrow range (usually within 5%) over a given time period.

long   Owning securities or commodities in anticipation of an increase in value or price.

long-term trend   Price movements tending to be generally up or generally down lasting over a period of months to years.

low   The lowest price of a security or commodity reached during a specific time period.

M

Major Market Index (MMI)   A 20-stock index designed to track and augment the Dow Jones Industrials Average of 30 stocks. The MMI is composed of 15 of the 30 stocks on the DJIA plus five other large NYSE listed stocks.

manipulation   An undefined securities violation sometimes enforced by the SEC. Manipulation is the act of influencing prices in a market by artful or skillful (and sometimes insidious) means.

margin   The amount of equity (cash) as a percentage of market value of the underlying market interest held in a margin account.

O

offer   An indication by a trader or investor of the willingness to sell a security or commodity; or, in a quote, the current lowest price anyone is willing to sell a security or commodity.

open market operations   The buying and selling of government and government agency securities by the Federal Open Market Committee for the purpose of increasing or decreasing the level of bank reserves to effect control of the money supply.

option   The right to buy (a call) or sell (a put) a specified amount of a security (stock, bonds, futures, and so on) at a specified price within a specified time period.

out-of-the-money   An option that has no intrinsic value. A call is out-of-the-money if the value of the underlying instrument is below the strike price stated in the call contract. A put is out-of-the-money if the market price of the underlying instrument is above that stated in the options contract.

overbought   A technical term used to describe the opinion that more and stronger buying has occurred in a market than is warranted by fundamental considerations.

oversold   A technical term used to describe the opinion that more and stronger selling has occurred in a market than the market fundamentals would justify.

over the counter (OTC) market   A market of stocks traded that are not listed on the major exchanges.

P

premium   The market price of an option—the price one pays for an option, which varies with market volatility, time, and the price of the underlying instrument.

price/earnings ratio (PE)   The ratio of the current price of a stock divided by the annual earnings per share.

primary   Of first importance, most important, or essential.

program trading   Any of a variety of trading strategies carried out through electronic means that are executed in a preplanned sequence, usually by computer.

put   An option that gives the owner the right to sell a specific amount of a security at a specified price within a specified time period.

Q

quote   The current bid and offer for a security on the floor of the exchange on which it is traded.

R

range The price bounds between which a market or specific security or commodity trades within a particular trading period (namely, close of the day's trading, day, month, year, and so on).

reaction A price movement against the prevailing trend. A reaction differs from a secondary correction in that it may occur within the short-term trend, intermediate term trend, or the long-term trend, whereas a secondary correction is an intermediate reaction occurring within the long-term trend.

resistance Any price level that is deemed as a significant high in trading by the market. When prices approach these levels on the way up, price movements often tend to slow down or "bounce off" them, and when they break out through these levels, they often break out sharply.

S

secondary correction In the stock market, an important intermediate price movement that moves in a contrary direction to the primary trend, usually consisting of at least a 5% change in prices over a minimum period of 14 calendar days.

short The state of having sold a security or futures contract prior to ownership. A person with a short position is liable for delivery of the item(s) sold until he or she buys back the position.

short-term trend A price trend lasting from days to weeks.

S&P futures A futures exchange located in Chicago in which futures contracts are traded based on the S&P 500 Cash Index.

speculator A market participant who buys and sells market instruments in an attempt to profit from intermediate-term (weeks to months) price changes.

stop order An order given to a broker that becomes a market order when the market price of the underlying instrument reaches or exceeds the specific price stated in the stop order.

stock option An options contract in stocks, a put or a call, standardized to 100 shares per contract.

straddle A pair of options held by the same person consisting of one call and one put on the same underlying instrument having the same strike price and expiration date.

strike price The price specified in an options contract at which the underlying instrument will be bought or sold if the option is exercised.

support Any price level deemed as a significant low in trading by the market. When prices approach these levels on the way down, price movements often tend to slow down or "bounce off" them, and when they break above these levels, they often break sharply.

T

takeover stock   Any stock that is involved in takeover negotiations, or a stock that is thought to be so involved.

technical analysis   A method of market forecasting that relies exclusively on the study of past price and volume behavior to predict future price movements.

tick   The smallest incremental price movement allowed by the rules of an exchange ($\frac{1}{8}$ for stocks, $\frac{1}{16}$ for stock options, and so on).

top   The high price in any market over a specified period (namely, intraday top, weekly top, long-term top, and so on).

V

volume   The number of shares (for stocks) or contracts (for commodities) that change ownership in a given time period.

Bibliography

Brandon, Nathaniel. *Honoring the Self.* New York: Bantam Books, 1985.

—. *The Psychology of Self-Esteem.* New York: Bantam Books, 1981.

Cunningham, Noble E., Jr. *In Pursuit of Reason: The Life of Thomas Jefferson.* Baton Rouge: Louisiana State University Press, 1987.

Edwards and Magee. *Technical Analysis of Stock Trends.* Springfield Massachusetts: John Magee, 1972.

Friedman, Milton, and Schwartz, Jacobsen. *A Monetary History of the United States 1867-1960.* Princeton, New Jersey: Princeton University Press, 1971.

Gartley, H. M. *Profits in the Stock Market.* Pomeroy, Washington: Lambert-Gann Publishing, 1981.

Gann, W. D. *Profits in Commodities.* Pomeroy, Washington: Lambert-Gann Publishing Co. Inc., 1976.

Gaylin, Willard, M.D. *The Rage Written.* New York: Simon & Schuster, 1984.

Gordon, William. *The Stock Market Indicators.* Palisades Park, New Jersey: Investors' Press Inc., 1968.

Hazlitt, Henry. *Economics in One Lesson.* New York: Arlington House Publishers, 1979.

Homer, Sidney. *A History of Interest Rates,* Second Edition. New Brunswick, New Jersey: Rutgers University Press, 1963.

Horney, Karen. *Neurosis and Human Growth.* New York: Norton & Company, 1950.

Kroll, Stanley. *The Professional Commodity Trader.* New York: Harper & Row Publishers, 1974.

Le Bon, Gustave. *The Crowd.* New York: The Viking Press, 1973.

Lefevre, Edwin. *Reminiscences of a Stock Operator.* New York: Doubleday, 1965.

Lorie and Hamilton. *The Stock Market: Theories and Evidence.* Homewood, Illinois: Richard D. Irwin Inc., 1965.

Mackay, Charles. *Extraordinary Popular Delusions and the Madness of the Crowds.* New York: Harmony Books, 1980.

McKeon, Richard. *The Basic Works Of Aristotle.* New York: Random House, 1941.

Merrill, Arthur A. *Behavior of Prices on Wall Street*. Chappaqua, New York: The Analysis Press, 1966.

Pacelli, Albert Peter. *The Speculator's Edge*. New York: John Wiley & Sons.

Rand, Ayn. *Atlas Shrugged*. New York: The New American Library (Signet), 1959.

—. *The Virtue of Selfishness*. New York: The New American Library (Signet), 1965.

—. *Capitalism—The Unknown Ideal*. New York: The New American Library, 1967.

—. *Philosophy—Who Needs It?* New York: The New American Library, 1982.

Rhea, Robert. *Dow's Theory Applied to Business and Banking*. New York: Simon & Schuster, 1938.

—. *The Dow Theory*. New York: Barron's, 1932.

Robbins, Anthony. *Unlimited Power*. New York: Ballantine Books, 1987.

Seldon, G. C. *Psychology of the Stock Market*. Wells, Vermont: Fraser Publishing Co., 1965.

Schabacker, R. W. *Stock Market Theory and Practice*. New York: B.C. Forbes Publishing Co., 1930.

Schultz, Harry. *A Treasure of Wall Street Wisdom*. Palisades Park, New Jersey: Investors' Press Inc., 1966.

Schwager, Jack D. *Market Wizards*. New York: New York Institute of Finance, a division of Simon & Schuster, 1989.

Wyckoff, Peter. *Wall Street and the Stock Market*. Philadelphia Chilton Book Co., 1972.

Von Mises, Ludwig. *Human Action*. Chicago: Contemporary Books, 1966.

—. *The Theory of Money and Credit*. Indianapolis: Liberty Classics, 1981.

Index